Harriette Brower
PIANO MASTERY

Harriette Brower

PIANO MASTERY

Talks with Paderewski, Hofmann,
Bauer, Godowsky, Grainger,
Rachmaninoff, and others

The Harriette Brower Interviews
1915-1926

Edited with an Introduction by
Jeffrey Johnson
Associate Professor
University of Bridgeport

DOVER PUBLICATIONS, INC.
Mineola, New York

Bibliographical Note

This Dover edition, first published in 2003, is a new selection of material from the following books by Harriette Brower, published by Frederick A. Stokes Company, New York: *Piano Mastery: Talks with Master Pianists and Teachers,* (1915); *Piano Mastery, Second Series: Talks with Master Pianists and Teachers,* (1917); and *Modern Masters of the Keyboard,* (1926). A new Introduction by Jeffrey Johnson has been specially prepared for this edition.

Library of Congress Cataloging-in-Publication Data

Brower, Harriette, 1869–1928.
    Piano mastery : talks with Paderewski, Hofmann, Bauer, Godowsky, Grainger, Rachmaninoff, and others : the Harriette Brower interviews 1915–1926 / edited and with introduction by Jeffrey Johnson.
        p. cm.
    "This Dover edition consists of selected chapters from Harriette Brower's Piano mastery (1915), Piano mastery, second series (1917), and Modern masters of the keyboard (1926). Chapters take the form of interviews, and all interviews included are essentially complete. Editorial insertions are in square brackets."
    Includes index.
    ISBN 0-486-42781-1(pbk.)
    1. Piano—Instruction and study. 2. Pianists—Interviews. I. Johnson, Jeffrey, 1964– II. Title.

MT220.B896 2003
786.2—dc21

                                                                    2003048529

Manufactured in the United States of America
Dover Publications, Inc., 31 East 2nd Street, Mineola, N.Y. 11501

Publisher's Note

This Dover Edition consists of selected chapters from Harriette Brower's *Piano Mastery* (1915), *Piano Mastery, Second Series* (1917), and *Modern Masters of the Keyboard* (1926). Chapters take the form of interviews, and all interviews included are essentially complete. Editorial insertions are in square brackets. Spelling has not been modernized. Brief contemporary introductions have been appended to the Bauer, Hofmann, and Sieveking interviews in order to set contexts of interest to the proceedings. The "Prelude" (page 1) is selected from texts originally appearing in both the "Prelude" and "Postlude" of *Piano Mastery*. With the exception of the Paderewski chapter that opens the set—following Brower's sequence in her 1915 edition—the contents are now reorganized alphabetically by the artist's last name. The index was created for this edition.

Contents

viii

Interviews from *Modern Masters of the Keyboard* [1926]:

Harriette Moore Brower
[1854-1928]

" I feel as though I know you very well indeed, although we have never spoken together,' was Mme. Carreras' greeting when I called at her beautiful home overlooking the Hudson, one August afternoon. 'How do I know you so well? From your writings—your intimate glimpses of keyboard artists. Such intimate, personal glimpses seem to me much more interesting than a mere interview without them.'" So exclaimed Maria Carreras in 1925 when Harriette Brower arrived to collect material for her final published book of interviews.

Brower was ambassador of an age fascinated by the mechanics of technic. But the grand style was not simply a way of playing the piano—it was an attitude. Harriette captured and wove it into the technical focus that originally motivated her. Like a camera, in an age when cameras were rare, she revealed personalities with unexpected clarity.

Known as a columnist and contributor to *Musical America* and for her "Page for Pianists" in *The Musician,* Brower developed a warm style of pedagogical prose intended for self-instruction. She authored ten books: *The Art of the Pianist, Home Help in Music Study, Self-Help in Piano Study,* and *What to Play What to Teach;* the acclaimed interview series *Piano Mastery [1915], Piano Mastery [1917], Vocal Mastery,* and *Modern Masters of the Keyboard;* biographical sketches of famous musicians with young readers in mind, *Story-Lives of Master Musicians,* and a book that remained in print some thirty years after her death in 1928, *The World's Great Men of Music.*

A statement from the foreword of the latter volume characterized her working process: "As a honey-bee flutters from flower to flower, culling sweetness from many blossoms, so the compiler of such stories as these must gather facts from many sources." And in compiling the story of this compiler—whose personality itself lent a critical continuity binding otherwise separate and isolated portraits—we must follow her similarly, with glimpses from her own texts and other contemporary sources, to understand her perspectives.

Harriette was born in Albany New York, "within the shadow of the Capitol," at the Brower family home on 23 Chestnut Street, September 8, 1854[1]. The family moved to 304 Madison Avenue in 1872 and remained there until her father, Walter S. Brower, an affluent second generation silversmith, died in 1910.

She was educated at the historic Albany Girl's Academy, where city directory ads boasted "unusual facility in modern languages and music." Looking back upon herself in the chapter that closes *Home Help in Music Study*, written in 1918, Brower painted a verbal self-portrait from that time in her life, dressed in "gaiters and white stockings with pantalettes; ruffled organdie frock with a silk sash at the side; coral beads about her neck and coral pins clasping the short sleeves at her shoulders; hair in long curls, held back with a round comb." While attending the Albany Girl's Academy, she developed the linguistic facility so important to her future European fieldwork, but her musical training was of insufficient calibre:

> "I was in the same condition that many young players are in: I had not been taught the principles underlying technic, tone production, rhythm, or interpretation. I had no intelligent idea of phrasing nor of musical forms. I began to awake to the fact that my technical equipment was very defective. My hands were weak, and I must discover how to make them strong; the touch was uneven, and I must find the means to make it clear and brilliant. So I took myself in hand, studied everything I could get hold of,—made many experiments and many discoveries."
>
> [*The Art of the Pianist*, p.26-27]

These "experiments and discoveries" included work at the Sherwood Summer Music School, where she met William H. Sherwood [p.73-77].

In the middle 1880s the family saved enough money to send both Harriette and her younger sister May to Berlin. May studied art, and Harriette worked with Xaver Scharwenka, later transferring to the Klindworth conservatory when she discovered that Scharwenka was absent for long periods of time. She found herself part of the month-long master class taught by Hans von Bülow for Klindworth's students and a few invited guests [p.23-29]. This was an artistic experience of some import, and she reminisced more than

---

[1][U.S. Census records from 1860-1880 agree with her death certificate [Manhattan Death Record Index #6982] but conflict with the 1900 Census Albany NY [ED53 P174A Line 35] which gives her date of birth incorrectly as 1867, the 1920 census, and with her standard contemporary biographical paragraph which gives her year of birth incorrectly as 1869.

once about it in print. Yet, she was motivated to become conscious of, and informed by, still deeper foundational principles in her playing:

> "[D]id I find, in the instruction given by the artist teacher, a solution of the problems which had troubled me? By no means. They taught musical interpretation, not foundational principles, which no one expected them to concern themselves about. My investigations into the heart of things went on, however,—indeed, they have never stopped. The progressive teacher should never rest satisfied over past attainments, but constantly press onward and upward." [*The Art of the Pianist*, p.27]

After returning from Germany, Harriette began her professional career with the same restless and searching spirit. According to Kaiser, "her first position was that of musical director of a large girls' school in Minnesota. Later, she became the Musical Director at St. Mary's Hall, an Episcopal school, in Burlington, N. J." A sense of being consumed by the process is evident in Brower's own testimony: "[I] had returned to my own land to join its teaching and playing force. My time soon became so largely occupied with teaching that I feared my playing would be entirely pushed to the wall unless I were under the guidance of some master. With this thought in mind, I presented myself to Dr. Mason." Unusual in its highly personal nature, the Mason reminiscence [p.57-59] reveals Brower as a practising musician. Unlike the von Bülow and Sherwood master classes, in which we presume to hear mostly unidentified students (the exception being Ethelbert Nevin playing Raff p.27), her work with Mason was a private lesson. With a little imagination we can mentally "hear" the way Harriette herself played repertoire she was working at that time—increasingly so in the Schumann F minor sonata and the Grieg concerto, as the chapter develops.

In 1897 Harriette surfaces in Albany to create a Virgil Piano School at 91 North Pearl Street, where her father's silversmith store was located. She was director of this school through 1906, and lived at the family home on 304 Madison. The Virgil School [p.141-145] amplified underlying technical consideration to a level most would consider torturous today. It advocated extensive mechanical exercises "played" on tabletops prior to touching a sounding keyboard. It also employed the "Virgil Practise Piano," which was a portable piano keyboard producing only a percussive click, in order to hone rhythmic aspects of technical work without losing sensitivity to, or being distracted by, the beauty of actual piano tone. The seduction of the

Virgil School for Brower is manifest most clearly in the posthumous book, *How a Dependable Technic was Won; A Story by Harriette Brower* [Oliver Ditson Co., 1929], where a healthy abundance of table exercises are recounted in a series of letters written between two friends learning to play the piano.

Next to Harriette's name in the 1906 directory for Albany NY, instead of listing her local address, it indicates that she "moved to New York City." In 1911, she signed the introduction to *The Art of the Pianist* while living in the residential Hotel Walton, located at that time on 104 West 70th street.

By her own admission, she attended virtually every significant piano recital given in the city, and kept her programs in special bindings. Her daily life must have centered on giving lessons and on developing her piano studio, which had an independent reality as a social group. She also interacted closely with other piano teachers, like the group dedicated to planning musicales in commemoration of the Chopin Centenary. "We started it at first as a necessary means of keeping alive our ambitions, our capacity for work, our ideals, and we had found the contact with others in the same calling as we were, very helpful. Each spurred the other on to more effort." [*The Musician*, Mar. 1909, p.117].

On the edge of a new career as a writer, Brower published five articles in *The Musician* in 1909—prototypes that expose her interests instantly. Along with the Chopin centennial piece, they include the first telling of the von Bülow lessons in Berlin, and three technical essays. In 1910 her texts are found in *The Etude Music Magazine*. By 1911 papers surface regularly in diverse sources like *Women's Health* and the short-lived *Delineator* in which "Interpreting MacDowell" appears. The best of the early technical works were retouched, and lightly edited into her first book, *The Art of the Pianist*. [Carl Fischer, 1911]. Marguerite C. Kaiser, a former student of Brower's who wrote "A Pioneer in Establishing Foundational Principles; The Valuable Contribution to the Art of Piano Mastery Made by Harriette Brower," noted 16 years after its publication that "never before had a knowledge of the principles underlying modern technic been set down in so extremely simple, clear and plain a manner. Miss Brower succeeded in outlining technical problems and giving their solution with such conviction that serious students everywhere fell under her guiding influence." [*The Musician*, Dec. 1927, p.37].

Piano Mastery; *Piano Mastery, Second Series*; and *Modern Masters of the Keyboard*

Inspiration—a technical focus, interview format, and Brower's sense of personality and enthusiasm—led to 900 pages published in three books.

John C. Freund originally asked her for a series of interviews with influential modern pianists to be published serially in *Musical America*, a weekly publication that he edited.

Brower had planned a summertime excursion in Europe, and shortly before embarking on the long ocean voyage in June, began collecting these interviews from prominent pianists in New York—including Schelling, Stojowski, Ganz, Leginska, who was visiting the US at the time, and Tapper.

Her first interview was with Ernest Schelling in March 1913, and it set the mold for the endearing style used throughout. As the scene opens, Harriette is in a "luxurious salon" hearing music that "floats from a distant chamber." The room is sketched "with its heavily beamed ceiling of old silver." Silence. Then enters Schelling with his bull terrier, "with coat as white as snow." The terrier becomes "a quiet, profound observer of all that passed." Not surprising, the subject soon veers toward piano technic, and ends abruptly, without any rounding of the story, or atmosphere that was created to open the interview. Another irresistible sample: "In many little, unexpected ways, Ignaz Friedman is unique and individual." One of these ways was in living near Washington Square, instead of uptown, and she personifies the setting leading to his residence to illuminate his bohemianism: "As one approaches the spot through a couple of these old streets, one finds here and there fascinating little shops, filled with wares from many parts of the world. Rare porcelains and bronzes peep out at you from basement windows; quaint signs on doorways invite you to enter and purchase. Odd eating-places along the way tempt you to try them, just to see what they are like. Some other time we will come this way and explore, but not today. For just now we are bound for the hotel where is to be found Ignaz Friedman, the astonishing pianist [p.170]."

She arrived in London in late June of 1913 and interviewed Goodson, Hambourg and Matthay. She then travelled to Paris, Salzburg, and Berlin, all the while writing and sending essays that appeared in *Musical America*. The turnaround time between meeting and publication for the Harold Bauer interview was a mere 15 days! The writing style itself, serial appearances, and close correspondence rates allows one to follow Harriette in a way that must have created anticipation and a sense of "live from the scene" excitement from readers. A statement announcing her triumphant return to the United States [with a rare headshot] is printed in the October 11,1913 edition of *Musical America* [p.139].

She continued to interview pianists who lived in or passed through New York, and in 1915 the Frederick A. Stokes Company published the initial collection of these interviews under the title *Piano Mastery*. The original texts were sometimes elaborated with information collected later. For example, the original Raoul Pugno article, as published in *Musical America* [Nov. 22, 1913] concluded above the parenthesis on page 67 of this edition.

The interview format was supplemented with vignettes from lessons and master classes with pianists of older generations with whom Brower had had contact. This idea, consistent with the pedagogical theme, extends our affiliation back to von Bülow, Sherwood, and William Mason. Shifted slightly in the second series, we find reminiscences of Joseffy by some of his pupils, and of MacDowell by his wife.

As testament to his pervading influence and fame, Brower used the infamous advertising portrait of Paderewski on the cover of *Piano Mastery*, and placed his article first, and yet she never secured an interview with him. But, in "Some Causes for Paderewski's Leadership in Piano Music." [*The Musician*, Sept. 1926, p.11, 32] Harriette further detailed her impressions as a witness to the events of spectacular 1891 season when Paderewski lit the New York musical scene ablaze. For this edition, an excerpt from this article that reveals these impressions is edited into Brower's 1915 *Piano Mastery* essay on Paderewski [p.7-8].

In a bold, creative, but impractical move, Brower organized the contents of *Piano Mastery* autobiographically, with each interview appearing in the order in which it was obtained. There was no index, meaning that one began to process its information by continually flipping through 299 pages or thumbing large sections of the contents page to find the exact passage sought.

Nonetheless, the book was justly well received. Typical reaction was voiced in the American Library Association Booklist, where its contents were described as, "Interviews, unexpectedly interesting, and valuable to students and the musically inclined . . . Supplements the material in Cooke's *Great Pianists on Piano Playing* and perhaps is better for 1st purchase." [ALA 1915, 12:121].

"Encouraged by the success attending the appearance of *Piano Mastery*, a second series of talks with great pianists and teachers has been prepared, at the request of the publishers [in 1917]." This brief "Prelude" to the second series of *Piano Mastery* continued by expressing the intention to embrace members of the younger generation, "who have achieved recognition for special gifts." Thus, Novaes and Ornstein appear, and Percy Grainger's inscribed photograph was chosen to adorn the cover. Regarding the second series, the New York Times review mused that:

"It is . . . interesting to hear from Mr. Hofmann to the effect that he himself does not consider that he has a perfect technique, for he still has limitations. 'The artist, however, must allow the public to guess his limitations.' Or to learn that he does no technical work outside of the composition, for the reason that he finds plenty of technique to work on in the piece itself. Mr. Hutcheson on 'rubato' is suggestive. 'The idea that one takes a 'liberty' in adding inflection and rubato not directly prescribed by the author is absurd." Hardly less is the suggestion made that while rubato may appropriately be used in playing Chopin and Schumann, it is out of place in Bach and Beethoven."

[NYT 1918, Feb. 24, VI 77:2]

The final series of interviews with pianists followed nine years later, and though it was published by the same publisher, it was given a new title; *Modern Masters of the Keyboard*, and a new cover design with a rich burgundy cloth and gold lettering. Unlike the two prior volumes, a single pianist was not chosen to be featured on the cover. Nonetheless, Rachmaninoff held a position of honor—his portrait is placed opposite the title page, and his interview is placed first. In *Modern Masters*, the majority of pianists were of the younger generation, born in the 1880s.

Piano Mastery [1915], alone of the three volumes, was given what Brower called a "Postlude." The postlude was an attempt at organization by reprinting large quotations representing consensus viewpoints. Often she could not resist the temptation to spin these statements toward her own inclinations. Nonetheless, many important ideas were crystallized there—even the place of technic in relation to audience and art;

"When we listen to a piano recital by a world-famous artist, we think—if we are musicians—primarily of the interpretation of the compositions under consideration. That the pianist has a perfect technic almost goes without saying. He must have such a technic to win recognition as an artist . . . Let us use the word technic in its large sense, the sense which includes all that pertains to the executive side of piano playing. It is in this significance that Harold Bauer calls technic 'an art in itself.'"

[*Piano Mastery,* 1915 edition, p. 270]

She then organized categories of technical consideration—Hand Position, Finger Action ("The question of lifting the fingers"), Artistic Touch, The Art of Practise, and How to Memorize. In each of these categories, she explored the consensus. For example, regarding hand position, she found:

"Most of them agree that an arched position with rounded finger joints is the correct one. . . . furthermore there should be no weakness nor giving in at the nail joint." [*Piano Mastery,* 1915 edition, p.271-272]. Regarding memory, she subscribed to von Bülow's opinion that "no pianist could be considered an artist unless he or she could play at least two hundred pieces by heart [p.25]." She calculated that this was possible if the student has learned the underlying principles of memorization and practices at least five hours daily. The benchmark she gave was to memorize one page of music each day, which accumulates into fifty compositions per year.

> "In my work as teacher I constantly meet students, and teachers too, who do little or no memorizing. Some do not even approve of it, though it is difficult to conceive how anyone in his right mind can disapprove knowing a thing thoroughly. The only way to know it thoroughly is to know it by heart . . . To those who wish to become pianists, I would say: 'Keep your memory active through constant use. Be always learning by heart; do it systematically, a little at a time. So it will be daily progress. So your repertoire is built!' "
>
> [*Piano Mastery,* 1915 Edition, p. 291-292]

The wide spectrum of personalities and viewpoints represented can become somewhat overstimulating when one first attempts to sift and compare them. The New York Times review of *Piano Mastery* articulated this concern: "There is naturally great variety of opinion and method disclosed in these various interviews. Doubtless there is much that will be suggestive and useful. It might be questioned whether or not there will also be bewilderment resulting from so much diversity." [NYT 1916, Apr 23, VII 176:4].

Brower predicted this concern and used the "Postlude" to filter the diversity of responses, recognizing the existence of contrary views and/or exceptions that cannot be ignored. Wisely, she opted to favor the diversity of potential approaches by calling upon the judgement of the "thoughtful" player. As an example, while spinning in favor of practicing scales and technic outside repertoire, she observes that:

> "There are very few exceptions to the general verdict in favor of technic practise apart from pieces. Godowsky asserts he never practises scales. Bauer cares little for pure technic practise, believing the composition itself contains sufficient material of a technical nature.
> Whether or not these brilliant exceptions merely prove the rule,

the thoughtful student of the piano must decide for himself. He has already discovered that modern piano playing requires a perfect technic, together with the personal equation of vigorous health, serious purpose and many-sided mentality. "   [*Piano Mastery*, 1915 edition, p. 285]

Technical discussions and interviews were common to early 20th century musical periodicals. But the personalities, music-rooms, decorations and lifestyles recorded by Harriette place technic within a human context. "As a man's surroundings and environment are often reflections of his character, it is always a matter of deep interest to get in touch with the surroundings of the creative or executive musician [p.30]."

Happily, eccentricities appear regularly to color these pages. As, for instance, when we imagine "Teresa Carreño . . . sometimes, if carrying something in hand, . . . will inadvertently let it drop, without realizing it— from sheer force of the habit of relaxation [p.55]." Or, the scene in which Nadia Boulanger, "a pretty young woman" is unexplainedly present and very much on the mind of Raoul Pugno [p.66-67]. Cortot is met with indignation when he insists that anyone not having a natural sense of rhythm should simply quit playing [p.161-162]. A similar indignation is raised with Sieveking's assertions that he has "solved all technical problems of the keyboard," using a manner familiar to Brower for "over thirty years" as introduced by Mason. She later succumbs to his charm on a visit to his inland retreat on Long Island: "His tall figure looming dark against the lambent sunset sky, the whole made an 'impression' not to be forgotten [p.146]." And perhaps the most lovely image, Vladimir de Pachmann playing the D flat Nocturne of Chopin in his apartment wearing "a coat which had once belonged to Chopin. It was of mohair of a chocolate brown color, with large collar and long skirt."

Brower had the knack for capturing the suspense of a concert opening, as in the wonderful first-person anticipation of hearing Prokofieff in his American debut: "What will he look like, this new light, and how will he play? Like a composer or a virtuoso? Will his music have the flavor, the qualities, of the Russian music with which we are already familiar? Will it be anything like the music of Rachmaninoff, who is in the audience today? For we have grown somewhat accustomed to his idiom by now. Or will it be strange, weird, cacophonous? We shall know what it will be like in a few moments [p.201-202]."

150 West 80th Street, where Harriette lived with her sister May, is a nine-story brick building with massive concrete ornaments symmetrically

arranged above the entrance. It still stands today, located mid-block on the south side of 80th street. The entrance is tiled with the original mosaic tiles common to the age when the subway was built. Harriette often captured the feel of her interviewee's lifestyle, yet glimpses of her own are rare. We can imagine her though, walking leisurely on 80th street, passing brownstones with cascading multilevel stairs, across Columbus Ave to Theodore Roosevelt Park, where the American Museum of Natural History is now located. We can almost see her passing along the tree-lined street looking over at the impressive high-rises on the North side of 81st. She would have entered Central Park through the 81st street entrance across Central Park West. Then we lose sight of her among curved trails, stark rock outcroppings, and the Winterdale Arch.

It was on 80th street that Harriette centered her writing and teaching activities until her death. Neither Harriette nor May was ever married. On Tuesday, March 6, 1928, Harriette developed a bronchial pneumonia, and was visited by her doctor, H. G. Guile, from East 61st Street. She was attended to by May, and her best friend, next-door-neighbor Bertha Firgau. As was the custom for any illness in the Christian Science faith, she would have been read scriptures.

Friday March 9 brought to the city a significant and unexpected snowstorm. *The Daily News* reported that "Madcap March threw a wet blanket of snow on New York's hope for an early spring yesterday, and left New Yorkers swimming about like nuts in a chocolate chop suey sundae." It reminded everyone of the infamous blizzard of 1888, and broke close to the eve of its fortieth anniversary. Both storms approached New York from the South.

Harriette died "suddenly" from a cerebral embolism at 7 A.M. at home on Saturday March 10, 1928. "Private services were held Tuesday March 13 at 12 o'clock." [NYT 1928, Mar. 11, II 7:4].

Harriette Brower was a pianist and teacher. One whose energy reflected others more than herself. But her personality was strong, her dedication and intensity immense. She said:

> "I have been through so much for the sake of music,—both as student, teacher and player,—that it has awakened in me the deepest sympathy with the struggles, the aims and aspirations of other workers along the same lines. And it will give me the keenest satisfaction and delight to help my fellow teachers and students." [*Art of the Pianist, ix*]

Jeffrey Johnson
Bridgeport, CT

PRELUDE

[By Harriette Brower]

To American Piano Teachers and Students

How things are done, how others do them, and the reasons for the doing of them in one way and not in another, used to occupy my thoughts back as far as I can remember. As a child I was fond of watching any one doing fine needlework or beautiful embroidery, and tried to imitate what I saw, going into minutest details. This fondness for exactness and detail, when applied to piano study, led me to question many things; to wonder why I was told to do thus and so, when other people seemed to do other ways; in fact I began to discover that every one who played the piano played it in a different fashion. Why was there not one way?

One memorable night I was taken to hear Anton Rubinstein. What a marvelous instrument the piano was, to be sure, when its keys were moved by a touch that was at one moment all fire and flame, and the next smooth as velvet or soft and light as thistle-down. What had my home piano in common with this wonder? Why did all the efforts at piano playing I had hitherto listened to sink into oblivion when I heard this master? What was the reason of it all?

More artists of the piano came within my vision, Mehlig, Joseffy, Mason, and others. As I listened to their performances it was brought to me more clearly than ever that each master played the piano in the manner which best suited himself, at the same time each and every player made the instrument utter tones and effects little dreamed of by the ordinary learner. What was the secret? Was it the manner of moving the keys, the size of hand, the length of finger, or the great strength possessed by the player? I had always been taught to play slowly and carefully, so that I should make no mistakes; these great pianists had wonderful fearlessness; Rubinstein at least did not seem to care whether or not he hit a few wrong notes here and there, if he could only secure the speed and effect desired. Whence came his fearless velocity, his tremendous power?

Essentials of Pianism

Little by little I began to realize the essentials of effective piano playing were these: clear touch, intelligent phrasing, all varieties of tone, all the force the piano would stand, together with the greatest delicacy and the utmost speed. These things the artists possessed as a matter of course, but the ordinary student or teacher failed utterly to make like effects, or to play with sufficient clearness and force. What was the reason?

In due course I came under the supervision of various piano pedagogues. To the first I gave implicit obedience, endeavoring to do exactly as I was told. The next teacher said I must begin all over again, as I had been taught "all wrong." I had never learned hand position nor independence of fingers— these must now be established. The following master told me finger independence must be secured in quite a different fashion from the manner in which I had been taught, which was "all wrong." The next professor said I must bend the finger squarely from the second joint, and not round all three joints, as I had been doing. This so-called fault took several months to correct.

To the next I am indebted for good orthodox (if somewhat pedantic) ideas of fingering and phrasing, for which he was noted. The hobby of the next master was slow motions with soft touch. This course was calculated to take all the vim out of one's fingers and all the brilliancy out of one's playing in less than six months. To the next I owe a comprehension of the elastic touch, with devitalized muscles. This touch I practised so assiduously that my poor piano was ruined inside of a year, and had to be sent to the factory for a new keyboard. The next master insisted on great exactness of finger movements, on working up velocity with metronome, on fine tone shading and memorizing.

The Desire for Real Knowledge

Such, in brief, has been my experience with pedagogues and teachers of the piano. Having passed through it (and in passing having tried various so-called and unnamed methods) I feel I have reached a vantage ground upon which I can stand and look back over the course. The desire to know the experience of the great artists of the keyboard is as strong within me as ever. What did they not have to go through to master their instrument? And having mastered it, what do they consider the vital essentials of piano technic and piano playing? Surely they must know these things if any one can know them. They can tell, if they will, what to do and what to avoid, what to exclude as unnecessary or unessential and what to concentrate upon.

The night Rubinstein's marvelous tones fell upon my childish ears I longed to go to him, clasp his wonderful hands in my small ones and beg him to tell me how he did it all. I now know he could not have explained how, for the greater the genius—the more spontaneous its expression—the less able is such an one to put into words the manner of its manifestation. In later years the same impulse has come when listening to Paderewski, Hofmann and others. If they could only tell us exactly what is to be done to master the piano, what a boon it would be to those who are awake enough to profit by and follow the directions and experiences of such masters.

In recognition of the strength of this desire, months after a half-forgotten wish had been expressed by me, came a request by *Musical America* to prepare a series of interviews with the world famed pianists who were visiting our shores, and also with prominent teachers who were making good among us, and who were proving by results attained that they were safe and efficient guides.

Searching for Truth

Never was an interesting and congenial labor undertaken with more zest. The artists were plied with questions which to them may have seemed prosaic, but which to the interrogator were the very essence of the principles of piano technic and piano mastery. It is not a light task for an artist to sit down and analyze his own methods. Some found it almost impossible to put into language their ideas on these subjects. They had so long been concerned with the highest themes of interpretation that they hardly knew how the technical effects were produced, nor could they put the manner of making them into words. They could only say, with Rubinstein, "I do it this way," leaving the questioner to divine how and then to give an account of it. However, with questions leading up to the points I was anxious to secure light upon, much information was elicited.

One principle was ever before me, namely the Truth. I desired to find out the truth about each subject and then endeavored to set down what was said, expressed in the way I felt would convey the most exact meaning.

In short the pianist draws from many sources the experience, the feeling and emotion with which he strives to inspire the tones he evokes from his instrument. The keener his perceptions, the more he labors, suffers, and lives, the more he will be able to express through his chosen medium—the piano!

The summer of 1913 in Europe proved to be a veritable musical pilgrimage, the milestones of which were the homes of the famous artists, who generously gave of their time and were willing to discuss their methods of playing and teaching. The securing of the interviews has given the author satisfaction and delight. She wishes to share both with the fellow workers of her own land.

Interviews

from

Piano Mastery
1915

IGNACE JAN PADEREWSKI

[1860-1941]

One of the most consummate masters of the piano at the present time is Ignace Jan Paderewski. Those who were privileged to hear him during his first season in this country will never forget the experience. The Polish artist conquered the new world as he had conquered the old; his name became a household word, known from coast to coast; he travelled over our land, a Prince of Tones, everywhere welcomed and honored. Each succeeding visit deepened the admiration in which his wonderful art was held.

❧

The career of Paderewski in America[1] has been little short of marvelous. It is more than a quarter of a century ago—about thirty-five years, to be exact—that the Polish master set foot on American soil. As a forerunner, his picture—the familiar one with the mass of blond hair, was to be seen in old Steinway Hall and in a few of the music store windows, but otherwise no one knew much about him. His debut took place on the evening of November 17, 1891, in Carnegie Hall, with the assistance of the New York Symphony Orchestra, under Walter Damrosch. That was a memorable evening. A great audience had assembled, among which were many notables in the world of music and art. After the opening overture—[Karl] Goldmark's "In Spring-time," a hush fell, almost painful in its intensity. What would he be like, this new genius? Would he be really great or only *near* great? The conductor's stand had been moved to the side of the piano and he stood awaiting the entrance of the new artist. Ah, there he came, threading his way between the orchestra, until he reached the piano and could acknowledge the storm of welcome that greeted him. How slender and slight he looked as he sat at the piano, his blond head turned toward the conductor, waiting to begin the concerto—[the] Saint-Saëns in G Minor. Paderewski always used a special piano chair of low height, so he looked particularly small at the instrument.

Not many minutes after those wonderful hands had begun their work it was realized that here was a true master of piano playing. Here was one who could create beautiful soulful tone, warm, vibrant, and in all degrees of

---

[1]This insertion, not part of the original article, was part of an article written by Brower for *The Musician,* September 1926. Brower's original essay, which appears in its entirety, continues after the mark on page 8.

quality, from the most airy *pianissimo* to thundering *fortissimo*, yet without harshness. People listened almost breathlessly—as they do only when a great master performs. And the interest seemed to grow as moments passed. After the concerto came a group of soli—all Chopin. Could anything have been more appropriate? Polish music made to live again by the art of the Polish master. The effect was thrilling, electrical. Such romantic spirit— such tonal effects had not been heard before, although in the late 80's and early 90's, a number of distinguished artists had visited and performed in New York. But the newcomer had conquered. His own Concerto, Op. 17, completed the conquest. The house rose to him and would not be quieted until he had played again. In my recollection his choice was Liszt's Second Hungarian Rhapsodie, not then quite as hackneyed as now, and never before heard. I venture to say, with such fiery virtuosity, such massive power, such delicacy such bravura. No wonder everything fell before him!

Next day the papers were glowing in their accounts of his victory. Critics wrote columns about the pianism of the new artist, his power, his beauty of touch and tone, his unusual interpretations. Henry T. Finck, in the *Post* perhaps exceeded all the rest in his praise. For he always looked for something deeper than technical virtuosity, and now had found it in the throbbing tones of the Polish pianist.

A series of programs now lie before me. The paper is yellowing slightly, but what of that! These bits of paper tell the story of Paderewski's recitals in New York, and as such they are simply priceless. I cherish them with the jealous care that a book collector treasures his rare possessions.

The question has often been raised as to the reason of Paderewski's remarkable hold on an audience; wherein lay his power over the musical and unmusical alike. Whenever he played there was always the same intense hush over the listeners, the same absorbed attention, the same spell. The superficial attributed these largely to his appearance and manner; the more thoughtful looked deeper. Here was a player who was a thoroughly trained master in technic and interpretation; one who knew his Bach, Beethoven, Chopin, Schumann and Liszt. These things of themselves would not hold an audience spellbound, for there were other artists equally well equipped. In a final analysis it was doubtless Paderewski's wonderful *piano tone*, so full of variety and color, so vital with numberless gradations of light and shade, that charmed and enthralled his listeners. It mattered to no one— save the critics—that he frequently repeated the same works. What if we heard the Chromatic Fantaisie a score of times? In his hands it became a veritable Soliloquy on Life and Destiny, which each repetition invested with new meaning and beauty. What player has ever surpassed his poetic conception of Schumann's Papillons, or the Chopin Nocturnes, which he made veritable dream poems of love and ecstasy. What listener has ever forgotten the tremendous power and titanic effect of the Liszt Rhapsodies, especially No. 2? When Paderewski first came to us, in the flush of his young manhood, he taught us what a noble instrument the piano really is in the hands of a consummate master. He showed us that he could make the piano speak with the delicacy and power of a Rubinstein, but with more technical correctness; he proved that he could pierce our very soul with the intensity of his emotion, the poignant, heart-searching quality of his tones, the poetry and beauty of his interpretation.

Paderewski is known as composer and pianist, only rarely does he find time to give instruction on his instrument. Mme. Antoinette Szumowska [1868-1938], the Polish pianist and lecturer was at one time termed his "only pupil." Mr. Sigismond Stojowski [1869-1946], the Polish composer, pianist and teacher has also studied with him. Both can testify as to his value as an instructor.

Mme. Szumowska says:

"Paderewski lays great stress on legato playing, and desires everything to be studied slowly, with deep touch and with full, clear tone. For developing strength he uses an exercise for which the hand is pressed against the keyboard while the wrist remains very low and motionless and each finger presses on a key, bringing, or drawing out as much tone as possible.

"Paderewski advises studying scales and arpeggios with accents, for instance, accenting every third note, thus enabling each finger in turn to make the accent impulse: this will secure evenness of touch. Double passages, such as double thirds and sixths, should be divided and each half practised separately, with legato touch. Octaves should be practised with loose wrists and staccato touch. As a preparatory study practise with thumb alone. The thumb must always be kept curved, with joints well rounded out; it should touch the keys with its tip, so as to keep it on a level with the other fingers. Paderewski is very particular about this point.

"It is difficult to speak of Paderewski's manner of teaching expression, for here the ideas differ with each composer and with every composition. As to tonal color, he requires all possible variety in tone production. He likes strong contrasts, which are brought out, not only by variety of touch but by skilful use of the pedals.

"My lessons with Paderewski were somewhat irregular. We worked together whenever he came to Paris. Sometimes I did not see him for several months, and then he would be in Paris for a number of weeks; at such seasons we worked together very often. Frequently these lessons, which were given in my cousin's house, began very late in the evening —around ten o'clock— and lasted till midnight, or even till one in the morning.

"Paderewski the teacher is as remarkable as Paderewski the pianist. He is very painstaking; his remarks are clear and incisive: he often illustrates by playing the passage in question, or the whole composition. He takes infinite trouble to work out each detail and bring it to perfection. He is very patient and sweet tempered, though he can occasionally be a little sarcastic. He often grows very enthusiastic over his teaching, and quite forgets the lapse of time. In general, however, he does not care to teach, and naturally has little time for it."

Mr. Stojowski, when questioned in regard to his work with the Polish pianist, said:

"Paderewski is a very remarkable teacher. There are teachers who attempt to instruct pupils about what they do not understand, or cannot do themselves: there are others who are able to do the thing, but are not able to explain how they do it. Paderewski can both do it and explain how it is done. He knows perfectly what effects he wishes to produce, how they are to be produced, the causes which underlie and bring them about; he can explain and demonstrate these to the pupil with the greatest exactness and detail.

"As you justly remark the quality of tone and the variety of tonal gradations are special qualities of Paderewski's playing. These must be acquired by aid of the ear, which tests and judges each shade and quality of tone. He counsels the student to listen to each tone he produces, for quality and variety.

Clearness a First Principle
"The player, as he sits at the piano, his mind and heart filled with the beauty of the music his fingers are striving to produce, vainly imagines he is making the necessary effects. Paderewski will say to him: 'No doubt you feel the beauty of this composition, but I hear none of the effects you fancy you are making; you must deliver everything much more clearly: distinctness of utterance is of prime importance.' Then he shows how clearness and distinctness may be acquired. The fingers must be rendered firm, with no giving in at the nail joint. A technical exercise which he gives, and which I also use in my teaching, trains the fingers in up and down movements, while

the wrist is held very low and pressed against the keyboard. At first simple five-finger forms are used; when the hand has become accustomed to this tonic, some of the Czerny Op. 740 can be played, with the hand in this position. Great care should be taken when using this principle, or lameness will result. A low seat at the piano is a necessity for this practise; sitting low is an aid to weight playing: we all know how low Paderewski himself sits at the instrument.

"You ask what technical material is employed. Czerny, Op. 740; not necessarily the entire opus; three books are considered sufficient. Also Clementi's *Gradus*. Of course scales must be carefully studied, with various accents, rhythms and tonal dynamics; arpeggios also. Many arpeggio forms of value may be culled from compositions.

"There are, as we all know, certain fundamental principles that underlie all correct piano study, though various masters may employ different ways and means to exemplify these fundamentals. Paderewski studied with Leschetizky and inculcates the principles taught by that master, with this difference, that he adapts his instruction to the physique and mentality of the student; whereas the Vorbereiters of Leschetizky prepare all pupils along the same lines, making them go through a similar routine, which may not in every instance be necessary.

Fingering

"One point Paderewski is very particular about, and that is fingering. He often carefully marks the fingering for a whole piece; once this is decided upon it must be kept to. He believes in employing a fingering which is most comfortable to the hand, as well as one which, in the long run, will render the passage most effective. He is most sensitive to the choice of fingering the player makes, and believes that each finger can produce a different quality of tone. Once, when I was playing a Nocturne, he called to me from the other end of the room: 'Why do you always play that note with the fourth finger? I can *hear* you do it; the effect is bad.' He has a keen power of observation; he notices little details which pass unheeded by most people; nothing escapes him. This power, directed to music, makes him the most careful and painstaking of teachers. At the same time, in the matter of fingering, he endeavors to choose the one which can be most easily accomplished by the player. The von Bülow editions, while very erudite, are apt to be laborious and pedantic; they show the German tendency to over-elaboration, which, when carried too far becomes a positive fault.

Correct Motion

"Another principle Paderewski considers very important is that of appropriate motion. He believes in the elimination of every unnecessary movement, yet he wishes the whole body free and supple. Motions should be as carefully studied as other technical points. It is true he often makes large movements of arm, but they are all thought out and have a dramatic significance. He may lift the finger off a vehement staccato note by quick up-arm motion, in a flash of vigorous enthusiasm; but the next instant his hand is in quiet position for the following phrase.

Studying Effects

"The intent listening I spoke of just now must be of vital assistance to the player in his search for tonal variety and effect. Tone production naturally varies according to the space which is to be filled. Greater effort must be put forth in a large hall, to make the tone carry over the footlights, to render the touch clear, the accents decisive and contrasts pronounced. In order to become accustomed to these conditions, the studio piano can be kept closed, and touch must necessarily be made stronger to produce the desired power.

Interpretation

"A great artist's performance of a noble work ought to sound like a spontaneous improvisation; the greater the artist the more completely will this result be attained. In order to arrive at this result, however, the composition must be dissected in minutest detail. Inspiration comes with the first conception of the interpretation of the piece. Afterward all details are painstakingly worked out, until the ideal blossoms into the perfectly executed performance. Paderewski endeavors uniformly to render a piece in the manner and spirit in which he has conceived it. He relates that after one of his recitals, a lady said to him:

" 'Why, Mr. Paderewski, you did not play this piece the same as you did when I heard you before.'

" 'I assure you I intended to,' was the reply.

" 'Oh, it isn't necessary to play it always the same way; you are not a machine,' said the lady.

"This reply aroused his artist-nature.

" 'It is just because I am an artist that I ought at all times to play in the same way. I have thought out the conception of that piece, and am in duty bound to express my ideal as nearly as possible each time I perform it.'

"Paderewski instructs, as he does everything else, with magnificent generosity.

He takes no account of time. I would come to him for a stipulated half-hour, but the lesson would continue indefinitely, until we were both forced to stop from sheer exhaustion. I have studied with him at various times. One summer especially stands out in my memory, when I had a lesson almost every day."

Speaking of the rarely beautiful character of Paderewski's piano compositions, Mr. Stojowski said:

"I feel that the ignorance of this music among piano teachers and students is a crying shame. What modern piano sonata have we to-day, to compare with his? I know of none. And the songs—are they not wonderful! I love the man and his music so much that I am doing what lies in my power to make these compositions better known. There is need of pioneer work in this matter, and I am glad to do some of it."

WILHELM BACHAUS[1]
[1884-1969]

TECHNICAL PROBLEMS DISCUSSED

How do I produce the effects which I obtain from the piano?" The young German artist, Wilhelm Bachaus, was comfortably seated in his spacious apartments at the Ritz, New York, when this question was asked. A grand piano stood close at hand, and the pianist ran his fingers lightly over its keys from time to time, or illustrated some technical point as he talked.

"In answer I would say I produce them by listening, criticizing, judging—working over the point, until I get it as I want it. Then I can reproduce it at will, if I want to make just the same effect; but sometimes I want to change and try another.

"I am particular about the seat I use at the piano, as I sit lower than most amateurs, who in general are apt to sit too high. My piano stool has just been taken out for a few repairs, or I could show you how low it is.

Then I am old-fashioned enough to still believe in scales and arpeggios. Some of the players of the present day seem to have no use for such things, but I find them of great importance. This does not necessarily mean that I go through the whole set of keys when I practise the scales; but I select a few at a time, and work at those. I start with ridiculously simple forms—just the hand over the thumb, and the thumb under the hand—a few movements each way, especially for arpeggios. The principle I have referred to is the difficult point; a few doses of this remedy, however, bring the hand up into order again."

The pianist turned to the keyboard and illustrated the point very clearly.

"As you see, I slant the hand considerably across the keys," he said, "but this oblique position is more comfortable, and the hand can accommodate itself to the intervals of the arpeggio, or to the passing of the thumb in scales. Some may think I stick out the elbow too much, but I didn't care for that, if by this means the scale becomes smooth and even.

Overhauling One's Technic

"I have to overhaul my technic once or twice a week, to see that everything is all right—and of course the scales and arpeggios come in for their share of

---

[1] The text-contemporary spelling of this last name is maintained throughout the volume. Modern sources concur on the spelling "Backhaus."

criticism. I practise them in legato, staccato and in other touches, but mostly in legato, as that is somewhat more difficult and more beautiful than the others.

"Perhaps I have what might be called a natural technic; that is I have a natural aptitude for it, so that I could acquire it easily, and it stays with me. Hofmann has that kind of natural technic; so has d'Albert. Of course I have to practise technic; I would not allow it to lapse; I love the piano too much to neglect any part of the work. An artist owes it to himself and the public to keep himself up in perfect condition—for he must never offer the public anything but the best. I only mean to say I do not have to work at it as laboriously as some others have to do. However, I practise technic daily, and will add that I find I can do a great deal in a short time. When on tour I try to give one hour a day to it, not more."

Speaking of the action of fingers, Mr. Bachaus continued:

"Why, yes, I raise my fingers whenever and wherever necessary—no more. Do you know [Rudolf] Breithaupt? Well, he does not approve of such technical exercises as these (illustrating); holding down some fingers and lifting others, for technical practise, but I do. As for the metronome, I approve of it to cultivate the sense of rhythm in those who are lacking in this particular sense. I sometimes use it myself, just to see the difference between the mechanical rhythm and the musical rhythm—for they are not always the same by any means.

"Do you know these Technical Exercises of Brahms? I think a great deal of them, and, as you see, carry them around with me; they are excellent.

"You ask me about octaves. It is true they are easy for me now, but I can remember the time when they were difficult. The only alternative is to work constantly at them. Of course they are more difficult for small hands; so care must be taken not to strain nor overtire the hand. A little at a time, in frequent doses, ought in six months to work wonders. Rowing a boat is good to develop wrists for octave playing.

"You ask if I can tell how I obtain power. That is a very difficult question. Why does one child learn to swim almost immediately, while another cannot master it for a long time? To the first it comes naturally—he has the *knack*, so to speak. And it is just so with the quality of power at the piano. It certainly is not due to physique, nor to brute strength, else only the athlete would have sufficient power. No, it is the 'knack,' or rather it is the result of relaxation, as you suggest.

"Take the subject of velocity. I never work for that special thing as some do. I seldom practise with great velocity, for it interferes with clearness. I prefer to play more slowly, giving the greatest attention to clearness and good tone. By pursuing this course I find that when I need velocity I have it.

"I am no pedagogue and have no desire to be one. I have no time for teaching;

my own studies and concert work fill all my days. I do not think that one can both teach and play successfully. If I were teaching I should no doubt acquire the habit of analyzing and criticizing the work of others; of explaining and showing just how a thing should be done. But I am not a critic nor a teacher, so I do not always know how I produce effects. I play 'as the bird sings,' to quote an old German song.

Modern Piano Music

"Your MacDowell has written some nice music, some pretty music; I am familiar with his Concerto in D minor, some of the short pieces and the Sonatas. As for modern piano concertos there are not many, it is quite true. There is the Rachmaninoff, the MacDowell I mentioned, the D minor of Rubinstein, and the Saint-Saëns in G minor. There is also a Concerto by Neitzel, which is a most interesting work; I do not recall that it has been played in America. I have played it on the other side, and I may bring it out here during my present tour. This Concerto is a fine work, into which the author has put his best thought, feeling and power."

A Brahms Concerto

As I listened to the eloquent reading of the Brahms second Concerto, which Mr. Bachaus gave soon afterward with the New York Symphony, I was reminded of a memorable event which occurred during my student days in Berlin. It was a special concert, at which the honored guest and soloist was the great Brahms himself. Von Bülow conducted the orchestra, and Brahms played his second Concerto. The Hamburg master was not a virtuoso, in the present acceptance of the term: his touch on the piano was somewhat hard and dry; but he played the work with commendable dexterity, and made an imposing figure as he sat at the piano, with his grand head and his long beard. Of course his performance aroused immense enthusiasm; there was no end of applause and cheering, and then came a huge laurel wreath. I mentioned this episode to Mr. Bachaus a few days later.

"I first played the Brahms Concerto in Vienna under Hans Richter; he had counseled me to study the work. The Americans are beginning to admire and appreciate Brahms; he ought to have a great vogue here.

"In studying such a work, for piano and orchestra, I must not only know my own part but all the other parts—what each instrument is doing. I always study a concerto with the orchestral score, so that I can see it all before me."

HAROLD BAUER

[1873-1951]

THE QUESTION OF PIANO TONE

*[Mr. **Harold Bauer**, who is now making his sixth tour of America, is one of the most interesting personalities of the musical world. In the ordinary understanding of the word, his training has been singularly paradoxical, since it has differed radically from the paths in which most of the celebrated pianists have gone. As a boy Mr. Bauer studied privately with the celebrated violin teacher Pollitzer. At the age of ten he became so proficient that he made his debut as a violinist in London. Thereafter he made many tours of England as a violinist, meeting everywhere with flattering success. In the artistic circles of London he had the good fortune to meet a musician named Graham Moore who gave him some ideas of the details of the technic of pianoforte playing, which Mr. Bauer had studied, or rather "picked up" by himself, without any thought of ever abandoning his career as a violinist. As requests for his service as a pianist followed, he gradually gave more and more attention to the instrument and through great concentration and the most careful mental analysis of the playing of other virtuosos, as well as a deep consideration of the musical aesthetical problems underlying the best in the art of pianoforte interpretation, he has risen to a unique position in the tone world.]*

[THE ETUDE MUSIC MAGAZINE, March 1912]

B URIED deep in the heart of old Paris, in one of the narrow, busy thoroughfares of the city, stands the ancient house in which the master pianist, Harold Bauer, has made a home.

One who is unfamiliar with Paris would never imagine that behind those rows of uninviting buildings lining the noisy, commercial street, there lived people of refined and artistic tastes. All the entrances to the buildings look very much alike—they seem to be mere slits in the walls. I stopped before one of the openings, entered and crossed a paved courtyard, climbed a winding stone stairway, rang at a plain wooden doorway, and was ushered into the artist's abode. Once within, I hardly dared to speak, lest what I saw might vanish away, as with the wave of a fairy's wand. Was I not a moment before down in that dusty, squalid street, and here I am now in a beautiful room whose appointments are all of quiet elegance—costly but in exquisite taste, and where absolute peace and quiet reign. The wide windows open upon a lovely green garden, which adds the final touch of restful repose to the whole picture.

Mr. Bauer was giving a lesson in the music salon beyond, from which issued, now and again, echoes of well-beloved themes from a Chopin sonata. When the lesson was over he came out to me.

"Yes, this is one of the old houses, of the sort that are fast passing away in Paris," he said, answering my remark; "there are comparatively few of them left. This building is doubtless at least three hundred years old. In this quarter of the city—in the rue de Bac, for instance—you may find old, forbidding looking buildings, that within are magnificent—perfect palaces; at the back of them, perhaps, will be a splendid garden; but the whole thing is so hidden away that even the very existence of such grandeur and beauty would never be suspected from without."

He then led the way to the music-room, where we had an hour's talk.

"I was thinking as I drove down here," I began, "what the trend of our talk might be, for you have already spoken on so many subjects for publication. It occurred to me to ask how you yourself secure a beautiful tone on the piano, and how you teach others to make it?"

Mr. Bauer thought an instant.

"I am not sure that I do make it; in fact I do not believe in a single beautiful tone on the piano. Tone on the piano can only be beautiful in the right place—that is, in relation to other tones. You or I, or the man in the street, who knows nothing about music, may each touch a piano key, and that key will sound the same, whoever moves it, from the nature of the instrument. A beautiful tone may result when two or more notes are played successively, through their *difference of intensity,* which gives variety. A straight, even tone is monotonous—a dead tone. Variety is life. We see this fact exemplified even in the speaking voice; if one speaks or reads in an even tone it is deadly monotonous.

Variety of Tone

"Now the singer or the violinist can make a single tone on his instrument beautiful through variety; for it is impossible for him to make even *one* tone which does not have shades of variation in it, however slight they may be, which render it expressive. But you cannot do this on the piano: you cannot color a single tone; but you can do this with a succession of tones, through their difference, through their relation to each other. On the other hand you may say any tone is beautiful if in the right place, no matter how harsh it may be. The singer's voice may break from emotion, or simulated emotion, in an impassioned phrase. The exact note on which it breaks may not be a beautiful one, it may even be very discordant, but we do not think of that, for we are moved by the meaning back of the tones. So on the piano there may be one note in a phrase which, if heard alone, would sound harsh and unpleasant, but in its relation to other tones it sounds beautiful, for it gives the right meaning and effect. Thus it is the *relation of tones* which results in a 'beautiful tone' on the piano.

"The frequent trouble is that piano teachers and players generally do not understand their instrument. A singer understands his, a violinist, flutist or drummer knows his, but not a pianist. As he only has keys to put down and they are right under his hand, he does not bother himself further. To obviate this difficulty, for those who come to me, I have had this complete model of piano-key mechanism made. You see I can touch the key in a variety of ways, and the results will be different each time. It is necessary for the pianist to look into his instrument, learn its construction, and know what happens inside when he touches a key.

"As you say, there are a great many methods of teaching the piano, but to my mind they are apt to be long, laborious, and do not reach the vital points. The pianist may arrive at these after long years of study and experimenting, but much of his time will be wasted in useless labor.

"In my own case, I was forced by necessity to make headway quickly. I came to Paris years ago as a violinist, but there seemed no opening for me then in that direction. There was opportunity, however, for ensemble work with a good violinist and cellist. So I set to work to acquire facility on the piano as quickly as possible. I consulted all the pianists I knew—and I knew quite a number—as to what to do. They told me I must spend many months on technic alone before I could hope to play respectably, but I told them I had no time for that. So I went to work to study out the effects I needed. It didn't matter to me *how* my hand looked on the keyboard; whether my fingers were curved, flat, or stood on end. I was soon able to get my effects and to convince others that they were the effects I wanted. Later on, when I had more leisure, I took more thought about the position of hand and fingers. But I am convinced that much time is spent uselessly on externals, which do not reach the heart of the matter.

"For instance, players struggle for years to acquire a perfectly even scale. Now I don't believe in that at all. I don't believe a scale ever should be even, either in tone or in rhythm. The beginner's untrained efforts at a scale sound like this"—the speaker illustrated at the piano with a scale in which all the tones were blurred and run into each other; then he continued, "After a year's so-called 'correct training,' his scale sounds like this"—again he illustrated, playing a succession of notes with one finger, each tone standing out by itself. "To my thinking such teaching is not only erroneous, it is positively poisonous—yes, *poisonous!*"

"Is it to be inferred that you do not approve of scale practise?"

"Oh, I advise scale playing surely, for facility in passing the thumb under and the hand over is very necessary. I do not, however, desire the even, monotonous scale, but one that is full of variety and life.

"In regard to interpretation, it should be full of tonal and rhythmic modifications. Briefly it may be said that expression may be exemplified in four ways: loud, soft, fast, and slow. But within these crude divisions what infinite shades and gradations may be made! Then the personal equation also comes in. Variety and differentiation are of supreme importance—they are life!

"I go to America next season, and after that to Australia; this will keep me away from my Paris home for a long time to come. I should like to give you a picture to illustrate this little talk. Here is a new one which was taken right here in this room, as I sat at the piano, with the strong sunlight pouring in at the big window at my left."

On a subsequent occasion, Mr. Bauer spoke further on some phases of his art.

"As you already know I do not believe in so-called 'piano technic,' which must be practised laboriously outside of pieces. I do not believe in spending a lot of time in such practise, for I feel it is time wasted and leads nowhere. I do not believe, for instance, in the struggle to play a perfectly even scale. A scale should never be 'even,' for it must be full of variety and life. A perfectly even scale is on a dead level; it has no life; it is machine-made. The only sense in which the word 'even' may be applied to a scale is for its rhythmic quality; but even in this sense a beautiful scale has slight variations, so that it is never absolutely regular, either in tone or rhythm.

"Then I do not believe in taking up a new composition and working at the technical side of it first. I study it in the first place from the musical side. I see what may be the meaning of the music, what ideas it seeks to convey, what was in the composer's mind when he wrote it. In other words, I get a good general idea of the composition as a whole; when I have this I can begin to work out the details.

"In this connection I was interested in reading a statement made by Ruskin in his *Modern Painters*. The statement, which, I think, has never been refuted, is that while the great Italian painters, Raphael, Coreggio, and the rest have left many immature and imperfect pictures and studies in color, their drawings are mature and finished, showing that they made many experiments and studies in color before they thought of making the finished black and white

drawing. It seems they put the art thought first before the technical detail.
This is the way I feel and the way I work.

Avoid Restricting Rules

"Because our ancestors were brought up to study the piano a certain way,
and we—some of us—have been trained along the same rigid lines, does
not mean there are no better, broader, less limited ways of reaching the goal
we seek. We do not want to limit ourselves or our powers. We do not need to
say: 'Now I have thought out the conception of this composition to my
present satisfaction; I shall always play it the same way.' How can we feel
thus? It binds us at once with iron shackles. How can I play the piece twice
exactly alike? I am a different man today from what I was yesterday, and
shall be different tomorrow from what I am today. Each day is a new world,
a new life. Don't you see how impossible it is to give two performances of
the piece which shall be identical in every particular? *It is* possible for a
machine to make any number of repetitions which are alike, but a human,
with active thought and emotion, has a broader outlook.

"The question as to whether the performer must have experienced every
emotion he interprets is as old as antiquity. You remember in the Dialogues
of Plato, Socrates was discussing with another sage the point as to whether
an actor must have felt every emotion he portrayed in order to be a true
artist. The discussion waxed warm on both sides. Socrates' final argument
was, If the true artist must have lived through every experience in order to
portray it faithfully, then, if he had to act a death scene he would have to die
first in order to picture it with adequate fidelity!'"

The Question of Velocity

In speaking of velocity in piano playing and how it is to be acquired, Mr.
Bauer continued:

"I believe the quality of velocity is inherent—an integral part of one's
thought. Even a child, if he has this inherent quality, can play a simple
figure of five notes as fast as they need to be played. People of the South—
not on this side of the water—but of Spain and Italy, are accustomed to
move quickly; they gesticulate with their hands and are full of life and energy.
It is no trouble for them to think with velocity. Two people will set out to
walk to a given point; they may both walk fast, according to their idea of
that word, but one will cover the ground much more quickly than the other.
I think this idea of a time unit is again a limiting idea. There can be *no* fixed
and fast rule as to the tempo of a composition; we cannot be bound by such

rules. The main thing is: Do I understand the meaning and spirit of the composition, and can I make these clear to others? Can I so project this piece that the picture is alive? If so, the fact as to whether it is a few shades slower or faster does not enter into the question at all.

Obtaining Power

"Many players totally mistake in what power consists. They think they must exert great strength in order to acquire sufficient power. Many women students have this idea; they do not realize that power comes from contrast. This is the secret of the effect of power. I do not mean to say that we must not play with all the force we have at times; we even have to pound and bang occasionally to produce the needed effects. This only proves again that a tone may be beautiful, though in itself harsh, if this harshness comes in the right time and place.

"As with velocity so with power; there is *no* fixed and infallible rule in regard to it, for that would only be another limitation to the feeling, the poetry, the emotion of the executant's thought. The quality and degree of power are due to contrast, and the choice of the degree to be used lies with the player's understanding of the content of the piece and his ability to bring out this content and place it in all its perfection and beauty before the listener. This is his opportunity to bring out the higher, the spiritual meaning."

HANS VON BÜLOW

[1830-1894]

AS TEACHER AND INTERPRETER

Those who heard Hans von Bülow in recital during his American tour, in 1876, listened to piano playing that was at once learned and convincing. A few years before, in 1872, Rubinstein had come and conquered. The torrential splendor of his pianism, his mighty crescendos and whispering diminuendos, his marvelous variety of tone—all were in the nature of a revelation; his personal magnetism carried everything before it. American audiences were at his feet.

In von Bülow was found a player of quite a different caliber. Clarity of touch, careful exactness down to the minutest detail caused the critics to call him cold. He was a deep thinker and analyzer; as he played one saw, as though reflected in a mirror, each note, phrase and dynamic mark of expression to be found in the work. From a Rubinstein recital the listener came away subdued, awed, inspired, uplifted, but disinclined to open the piano or touch the keys that had been made to burn and scintillate under those wonderful hands. After hearing von Bülow, on the other hand, the impulse was to hasten to the instrument and reproduce what had just seemed so clear and logical, so simple and attainable. It did not seem to be such a difficult thing to play the piano—like *that*! It was as though he had said: "Any of you can do what I am doing, if you will give the same amount of time and study to it that I have done. Listen and I will teach you!"

Von Bülow was a profound student of the works of Beethoven; his edition of the sonatas is noted for recondite learning, clearness and exactness in the smallest details. Through his recitals in America he did much to make these works better known and understood. Nor did he neglect Chopin, and though his readings of the music of the great Pole may have lacked in sensuous beauty of touch and tone, their interpretation was always sane, healthy, and beautiful.

Toward the end of a season during the eighties, it was announced that von Bülow would come to Berlin and teach an artist class in the Klindworth Conservatory. This was an unusual opportunity to obtain lessons from so famous a musician and pedagogue, and about twenty pianists were enrolled for the class. A few of these came with the master from Frankfort, where he was then located.

Carl Klindworth, pianist, teacher, critic, editor of Chopin and Beethoven, was then the Director of the school. The two men were close friends, which is proved by the fact that von Bülow was willing to recommend the Klindworth Edition of Beethoven, in spite of the fact that he himself had edited many of the sonatas. Another proof is that he was ready to leave his work in Frankfort, and come to Berlin, in order to shed the luster of his name and fame upon the Klindworth school—the youngest of the many musical institutions of that music-ridden, music-saturated capital.

It was a bright May morning when the Director entered the music-room with his guest, and presented him to the class. They saw in him a man rather below medium height, with large intellectual head, beneath whose high, wide forehead shone piercing dark eyes, hidden behind glasses.

He bowed to the class, saying he was pleased to see so many industrious students. His movements, as he looked around the room, were quick and alert; he seemed to see everything at once, and the students saw that nothing could escape that active mentality.

The class met four days in each week, and the lessons continued from nine in the morning until well on toward one o'clock. It was announced that only the works of Brahms, Raff, Mendelssohn and Liszt would be taught and played, so nothing else need be brought to the class; indeed Brahms was to have the place of honor.

While many interesting compositions were discussed and played, perhaps the most helpful thing about these hours spent with the great pedagogue was the running fire of comment and suggestion regarding technic, interpretation, and music and musicians in general. Von Bülow spoke in rapid, nervous fashion, with a mixture of German and English, often repeating in the latter tongue what he had said in the former, out of consideration for the Americans and English present.

In teaching, von Bülow required the same qualities which were so patent in his playing. Clearness of touch, exactness in phrasing and fingering were the first requirements; the delivery of the composer's idea must be just as he had indicated it—no liberties with the text were ever permitted. He was so honest, so upright in his attitude toward the makers of good music, that it was a sin in his eyes to alter anything in the score, though he believed in adding any marks of phrasing or expression which would elucidate the intentions of the composer. Everything he said or did showed his intellectual grasp of the subject; and he looked for some of the same sort of intelligence on the part of the student. A failure in this respect, an inability to apprehend at once the ideas he endeavored to convey, would annoy the sensitive and nervous little Doctor; he would become impatient, sarcastic and begin to pace the floor with hasty strides. When in this state he could see little that was worthy in the student's performance, for a small error would be so magnified as to dwarf everything that was excellent. When the lion began to roar, it behooved the players to be circumspect and meek. At other times, when the weather was fair in the class-room, things went with tolerable smoothness. He did not trouble himself much about technic, as of course a pupil coming to him was expected to be well equipped on the technical side; his chief concern was to make clear the content and interpretation of the composition. In the lessons he often played detached phrases and passages for and with the student, but never played an entire composition.

One of the most remarkable things about this eccentric man was his prodigious memory. Nearly every work for piano which could be mentioned he knew and could play from memory. He often expressed the opinion that no pianist could be considered an artist unless he or she could play at least two hundred pieces by heart. He, of course, more than fulfilled this requirement, not only for piano but for orchestral music. As conductor of the famous Meiningen orchestra, he directed every work given without a note of score before him—considered a great feat in those days. He was a ceaseless worker, and his eminence in the world of music was more largely due to unremitting labor than to genius.

From the many suggestions to the Berlin class, the following have been culled.

"To play correctly is of the first importance; to play beautifully is the second requirement. A healthy touch is the main thing. Some people play the piano as if their fingers had *migran*e and their wrists were rheumatic. Do not play on the sides of the finger nor with a sideways stroke, for then the touch will be weak and uncertain.

"Clearness we must first have; every line and measure, every note must be analyzed for touch, tone, content and expression.

"You are always your first hearer; to be one's own critic is the most difficult of all.

"When a new theme enters you must make it plain to the listener; all the features of the new theme, the new figure, must be plastically brought out.

"Brilliancy does not depend on velocity but on clarity. What is not clear cannot scintillate nor sparkle. Make use of your strongest fingers in brilliant passages, leaving out the fourth when possible. A scale to be brilliant and powerful must not be too rapid. Every note must be round and full and not too legato—rather a mezzo legato—so that single tones, played hands together, shall sound like octaves. One of the most difficult things in rhythm, is to play passages where two notes alternate with triplets. Scales may be practised in this way alternating three notes with two.

"We must make things sound well—agreeably, in a way to be admired. A seemingly discordant passage can be made to sound well by ingeniously seeking out the best that is in it and holding that up in the most favorable light. Practise dissonant chords until they please the ear in spite of their sharpness. Think of the instruments of the orchestra and their different qualities of tone, and try to imitate them on the piano. Think of every octave on the piano as having a different color; then shade and color your playing. (*Also bitte coloriren!*)"

If Bülow's musical trinity, Bach, Beethoven, and Brahms, had a fourth divinity added, it would surely have been Liszt. The first day's program contained chiefly works by the Hungarian master; among them Au bord d'une Source, Scherzo and March, and the Ballades. The player who rendered the Scherzo was advised to practise octaves with light, flexible wrist; the Kullak Octave School was recommended, especially the third book; the other books could be read through, practising whatever seemed difficult and passing over what was easy. Of the Ballades the first was termed more popular, the second finer and more earnest—though neither makes very much noise.

The Années de Pèlerinage received much attention. Among the pieces played were, Les cloches, Chasse neige, Eglogue, Cloches de Genèva, Eroica, Feux follets and Mazeppa. Also the big Polonaise in E, the two Etudes, Waldesrauschen and Gnomenreigen; the Mazourka, Valse Impromptu, and the first Etude, of which last he remarked: "You can all play this; thirty years have passed since it was composed and people are only just finding out how fine it is. Such is the case with many of Liszt's works. We wonder how they ever could have been considered unmusical. Yet the way some people play Liszt the hearer is forced to exclaim, 'What an unmusical fellow Liszt was, to be sure, to write like that!'

"Exactness in everything is of the greatest importance," he was fond of saying. "We must make the piano speak. As in speaking we use a separate movement of the lips for each word, so in certain kinds of melody playing, the hand is taken up after each note. Then, too, we cannot make the piano speak without very careful use of the pedals."

The Mazourka of Liszt was recommended as one of the most delightful of his lighter pieces. The Waldesrauschen also, was termed charming, an excellent concert number. "Begin the first figure somewhat louder and slightly slower, then increase the movement and subdue the tone. *Everything which is to be played softly should be practised forte.*"

Of Joachim Raff the Suite Op. 91 held the most important place. Each number received minute attention, the Giga being played by Ethelbert Nevin. The Metamorphosen received a hearing, also the Valse Caprice, Op. 116, of which the master was particular about the staccato left hand against the legato right. Then came the Scherzo Op. 74, the Valse Caprice and the Polka, from Suite Op. 71. Von Bülow described the little group of notes in left hand of middle section as a place where the dancers made an unexpected slip on the floor, and suggested it be somewhat emphasized. "We must make this little witticism," he said, as he illustrated the passage at the piano.

"Raff showed himself a pupil of Mendelssohn in his earlier compositions; his symphonies will find more appreciation in the coming century—which cannot be said of the Ocean Symphony, for instance."

Of Mendelssohn the Capriccios Op. 5 and 22 were played, also the Prelude and Fugue in E. Von Bülow deplored the neglect which was overtaking the works of Mendelssohn, and spoke of the many beauties of his piano compositions. "There should be no sentimentality about the playing of Mendelssohn's music," he said; "the notes speak for themselves.

"The return to a theme, in every song or instrumental work of his is particularly to be noticed, for it is always interesting; this Fugue in E should begin as though with the softest register of the organ."

The subject of Brahms has been deferred only that it may be spoken of as a whole. His music was the theme of the second, and a number of the following lessons. Bülow was a close friend of the Hamburg master, and kept in touch with him while in Berlin. One morning he came in with a beaming face, holding up a sheet of music paper in Beethoven's handwriting, which Brahms had discovered and forwarded to him. It seemed that nothing could have given Bülow greater pleasure than to receive this relic.

The first work taken up in class was Brahms' Variations on a Handel theme. Von Bülow was in perfect sympathy with this noble work of Brahms and illumined many passages with clear explanations. He was very exact about the phrasing. "What can not be sung in one breath cannot be played in one breath," he said; "many composers have their own terms for expression and interpretation; Brahms is very exact in these points—next to him comes Mendelssohn. Beethoven not at all careful about markings and Schumann extremely careless. Brahms, Beethoven, and Wagner have the right to use their own terms. Brahms frequently uses the word *sostenuto* where others would use *ritardando*."

Of the Clavier stücke, Op. 76, von Bülow said: "The Capriccio, No. 1 must not be taken too fast. First page is merely a prelude, the story begins at the second page. How wonderfully is this melody formed, so original yet so regular. Compare it with a Bach gigue. Remember, andante does not mean dragging (*schleppando*), it means going (*gehend*)." To the player who gave the Capriccio, No. 5 he said: "You play that as if it were a Tarantelle of Stephan Heller's. Agitation in piano playing must be carefully thought out; the natural sort will not do at all. We do not want *blind* agitation, but *seeing* agitation (*aufregung*). A diminuendo of several measures should be divided into stations, one each for *f*, *mf*, *m*, *p*, and *pp*. Visit the Zoological Gardens, where you can learn much about legato and staccato from the kangaroos."

The Ballades were taken up in these lessons, and the light thrown upon their poetical content was often a revelation. The gloomy character of the Edward Ballade, Op. 10, No. 1, the source of the Scottish poem, the poetic story, were dwelt upon. The opening of this first Ballade is sad, sinister and mysterious, like the old Scotch story. The master insisted on great smoothness in playing it—the chords to sound like muffled but throbbing heartbeats. A strong climax is worked up on the second page, which dies away on the third to a *pianissimo* of utter despair. From the middle of this page on to the end, the descending chords and octaves were likened to ghostly footsteps, while the broken triplets in the left hand accompaniment seem to indicate drops of blood.

The third Ballade also received an illumination from Von Bülow. This is a vivid tone picture, though without motto or verse. Starting with those fateful fifths in the bass, it moves over two pages fitfully gloomy and gay, till at the end of the second page a descending passage leads to three chords so full of grim despair as to impart the atmosphere of a dungeon. The player was hastily turning the leaf. "Stop!" cried the excited voice of the master, who had been pacing restlessly up and down, and now hurried from the end of the salon. "Wait! We have been in prison—but now a ray of sunshine pierces the darkness. You must always pause here to make the contrast more impressive. There is more music in this little piece than in whole symphonies by some of the modern composers."

Both Rhapsodies Op. 79 were played; the second, he said, has parts as passionate as anything in the Götterdammerung. Both are fine and interesting works.

Again and again the players were counseled to make everything sound well. Some intervals, fourths for instance, are harsh; make them as mild as possible. For one can play correctly, but horribly! Some staccatos should be shaken out of the sleeve as it were.

The first time a great work is heard there is so much to occupy the attention that only a small amount of pleasure can be derived from it. At the second hearing things are easier and by the twelfth time one's pleasure is complete. The pianist must consider the listener in a first rendering, and endeavor to soften the sharp discords.

With a group of five notes, play two and then three it sounds more distinguished. Remember that unlearning gives much more trouble than learning.

In this brief resume of the von Bülow lessons, the desire has been to convey some of the hints and remarks concerning the music and its interpretation. The master's fleeting sentences were hurriedly jotted down during the lessons, with no thought of their ever being seen except by the owner. But as Bülow's fame as a teacher became so great, these brief notes may now be of some value to both teacher and student.

If it were only possible to create a picture of that Berlin music-room, with its long windows opening out to a green garden—the May sunshine streaming in; the two grand pianos in the center, a row of anxious, absorbed students about the edge of the room—and the short figure of the little Doctor, pacing up and down the polished floor, or seating himself at one piano now and then, to illustrate his instruction. This mental picture is the lifelong possession of each of those players who were so fortunate as to be present at the sessions. It can safely be affirmed, I think, that the principles of artistic rectitude, of exactness and thorough musicianship which were there inculcated, ever remained with the members of that class, as a constant incentive and inspiration.

FERRUCCIO BUSONI

[1866-1924]

AN ARTIST AT HOME

As a man's surroundings and environment are often reflections of his character, it is always a matter of deep interest to get in touch with the surroundings of the creative or executive musician. To meet him away from the glare of the footlights, in the privacy and seclusion of the home, gives one a far more intimate knowledge of the artist as a man. Knowing how difficult it often is to obtain such an opportunity, I can be the more thankful that this privilege has been granted me many times, even with those artists who hold themselves most aloof. I was told Busoni was exceedingly difficult to approach, and the only way I could see him was to call at his house quite unannounced, when I might have the good fortune to find him at home and willing to see me. Not wishing to take him by storm in this way, I quietly waited, until I received the following note: "While I am not fond of interviews, if you will come to tea on Thursday afternoon, you will be welcome."

Busoni is located in a stately *Wohnung* overlooking the handsome Victoria Luise Platz, in the newer western section of Berlin. Mme. Busoni met us as we arrived, and conducted us to the master, who rose from a cozy nook in a corner of the library to greet us. Tea was soon brought in and our little party, which included a couple of other guests, was soon chatting gaily in a mixture of French, German and English.

During the sprightly chat I could not help glancing from time to time around the great library in which we sat, noting its artistic furnishings, and the rows upon rows of volumes in their costly bindings, which lined the walls. One appreciates what Dr. Johnson meant when he said that whenever he saw shelves filled with books he always wanted to get near enough to them to read their titles, as the choice of books indicates character.

Presently Busoni turned to me: "I am composing a rhapsodie on American Indian themes."

"And where did you capture the themes?" he was asked.

"From a very charming lady, a country woman of yours, Miss Natalie Curtis. She has taken great interest in the idea and has been most helpful to me."

"One of the German music papers announced that you are about to leave Berlin, and have accepted an offer elsewhere was it in Spain?"

"I intend leaving Berlin for a time," he admitted, "and will go to Bologna—perhaps you thought that was in Spain," with a sly side glance and a humorous twinkle in his eyes. "My offer from Bologna appears most flattering. I am appointed head of the great conservatory, but I am not obliged to live in the city, nor even to give lessons. I shall, however, go there for a time, and shall probably teach. I am to conduct six large orchestral concerts during the season, but aside from this I can be absent as much as I wish. We shall probably close up our house here and go to Italy in the autumn. Living is very cheap in Bologna; one can rent a real palace for about $250 a year."

Mme. Busoni now invited us to inspect other parts of the house. We passed to the adjoining room, which contains many rare old prints and paintings and quaint old furniture—"everything old," as Mme. Busoni said, with a smile. In this room stands a harpsichord, with its double keyboard and brilliant red case. It is not an antique but an excellent copy made by Chickering.

Farther on is a veritable musician's den, with upright piano, and with a large desk crowded with pictures and mementoes. On the walls hang rare portraits chiefly of Chopin and Liszt. Beyond this room came the salon, with its two grand pianos side by side. This is the master's teaching and recital room, and here are various massive pieces of richly carved furniture. Mme. Busoni called our attention to the elaborate chandelier in old silver, of exquisite workmanship, which, she said, had cost her a long search to find. There are several portraits here of the composer-pianist in his youth—one as a boy of twelve, a handsome lad—*bildschön*, with his curls, his soulful eyes and his big white collar.

Busoni soon joined us in the salon and the conversation was turned to his activities in the new field.

"When you have finished the new rhapsodie you will come and play it to us in America—and in London also," he was urged.

"Ah, London! I am almost homesick for London; it is beautiful there. I am fond of America, too. You know I lived there for some years; my son was born there; he is an American citizen. Yes, I will return, though just when I do not yet know, and then I will assuredly play the rhapsodie."

TERESA CARREÑO
[1853-1917]

EARLY TECHNICAL TRAINING

As was recently remarked in *Musical America* [Nov. 8, 1913], "That ever youthful and fascinating pianist, Teresa Carreño is with us again."

I well remember how fascinated I was, as a young girl, with her playing the first time I heard it—it was so full of fire, enthusiasm, brilliancy and charm. How I longed and labored to imitate it—to be able to play like that! I not only loved her playing but her whole appearance, her gracious manner as she walked across the stage, her air of buoyancy and conscious mastery as she sat at the piano; her round white arms and wrists, and—the red sash she wore!

During a recent talk with Mme. Carreño, I recalled the above incident, which amused her, especially the memory of the sash.

"I assure you that at heart I feel no older now than in the days when I wore it," she said. The conversation then turned to questions of mastering the piano, with particular reference to the remarkable technic of the artist herself. "The fact that I began my studies at a very early age was a great advantage to me," she said. "I loved the sound of the piano, and began to pick out bits of tunes when I was little more than three. At six and a half I began to study seriously, so that when I was nine I was playing such pieces as Chopin's Ballade in A flat. Another fact which was of the utmost advantage to me was that I had an ideal teacher in my father. He saw that I loved the piano, and decided I must be properly taught. He was passionately fond of music, and if he had not been a statesman, laboring for the good of his country, he would undoubtedly have been a great musician. He developed a wonderful system for teaching the piano, and the work he did with me I now do with my pupils. For one thing he invented a series of stretching and gymnastic exercises which are splendid; they did wonders for me, and I use them constantly in my teaching. But, like everything else, they must be done in the right way, or they are not beneficial.

580 Technical Exercises

"My father wrote out for me a great many technical exercises; to be exact, there were 580 of them! Some consisted of difficult passages from the great composers—perhaps originally written for one hand—which he would arrange for two hands, so that each hand had the same amount of work to do. Thus both my hands had equal training, and I find no difference between them. These 580 exercises took just three days to go through. Everything must be played in all keys, and with every possible variety of touch—legato, staccato, half-staccato, and so on; also, with all kinds of shading."

(Think of such a drill in pure technic, O ye teachers and students, who give little or no time to such matters outside of etudes and pieces!)

"Part of my training consisted in being shown how to criticize myself. I learned to listen, to be critical, to judge my own work; for if it was not up to the mark I must see what was the matter and correct it myself. The earlier this can be learned the better. I attribute much of my subsequent success to this ability. I still carry out this plan, for there on the piano you will find all the notes for my coming recitals, which I work over and take with me everywhere. This method of study I always try to instill into my pupils.

I tell them any one can make a lot of *noise* on the piano, but I want them to make the piano *speak*! I can do only a certain amount for them; the rest they must do for themselves.

Value of Transposing

"Another item my zealous teacher insisted upon was transposing. I absorbed this idea almost unconsciously, and hardly know when I learned to transpose, so natural did it seem to me. My father was a tactful teacher; he never commanded, but would merely say, 'You can play this in the key of C, but I doubt if you can play it in the key of D.' This doubt was the spur to fire my ambition and pride: I would show him I could play it in the key of D, or in any other key; and I did!

"With all the technic exercises, I had many etudes also; a great deal of Czerny. Each etude must also be transposed, for it would never do to play an etude twice in the same key for my father. So I may say that whatever I could perform at all, I was able to play in any key.

"For one year I did nothing but technic, and then I had my first piece, which was nothing less than the Capriccio of Mendelssohn, Op. 22. So you see I had been well grounded; indeed I have been grateful all my life for the thorough foundation which was laid for me. In these days we hear of so many 'short cuts,' so many new methods, mechanical and otherwise, of studying the piano; but I fail to see that they arrive at the goal any quicker, or make any more thorough musicians than those who come by the royal road of intelligent, well-directed hard work."

Asked how she obtained great power with the least expenditure of physical strength, Mme. Carreño continued:

"The secret of power lies in relaxation; or I might say, power *is* relaxation. This word, however, is apt to be misunderstood. You tell pupils to relax, and if they do not understand how and when they get nowhere. Relaxation does not mean to flop all over the piano; it means, rather, to loosen just where it is needed and nowhere else. For the heavy chords in the Tchaikowsky Concerto my arms are absolutely limp from the shoulder; in fact, I am not conscious I have arms. That is why I can play for hours without the slightest fatigue. It is really mental relaxation, for one has to think it; it must be in the mind first before it can be worked out in arms and hands. We have to think it and then act it.

"This quality of my playing must have impressed Breithaupt, for, as you perhaps know, it was after he heard me play that he wrote his famous book on 'Weight Touch,' which is dedicated to me. A second and revised edition of this work, by the way, is an improvement on the first. Many artists and musicians have told me I have a special quality of tone; if this is true I am convinced this quality is the result of controlled relaxation."

I referred to the artist's hand as being of exceptional adaptability for the piano.

"Yes," she answered, "and it resembles closely the hand of Rubinstein. This brings to mind a little incident. As a small child, I was taken to London, and on one occasion played in the presence of Rubinstein; he was delighted, took me under his wing, and introduced me all about as his musical daughter. Years afterward we came to New York, and located at the old Clarendon Hotel, which has housed so many men of note. The first day at lunch, my aunt and I were seated at a table mostly occupied by elderly ladies, who stared at us curiously. I was a shy slip of a girl, and hardly ventured to raise my eyes after the first look around the room. Beside me sat a gentleman. I glanced at his hand as it rested on the table—then I looked more closely; how much it reminded me of Rubinstein's hand! My eyes traveled slowly up to the gentleman's face—it was Rubinstein! He was looking at me; then he turned and embraced me, before all those observing ladies!"

We spoke of Berlin, the home of the pianist, and of its musical life, mentioning von Bülow and Klindworth. "Both good friends of mine," she commented. "What a wonderful work Klindworth has accomplished in his editions of Beethoven and Chopin! As Goethe said of himself, we can say of Klindworth—he has carved his own monument in this work. We should revere him for the great service he has done the pianistic world.

"I always love to play in America, and each time I come I discover how much you have grown. The musical development here is wonderful. This country is very far from being filled with a mercenary and commercial spirit. If Europeans think so it is because they do not know the American at home. Your progress in music is a marvel! There is a great deal of idealism here, and idealism is the very heart and soul of music.

"I feel the artist has such a beautiful calling—a glorious message—to educate a people to see the beauty and grandeur of his art—of the ideal!"

OSSIP GABRILOWITSCH
[1878-1936]

CHARACTERISTIC TOUCH ON THE PIANO

A rthur Hochman, Russian pianist and composer, once remarked to me, in reference to the quality of tone and variety of tonal effects produced by the various artists now before the public:

"For me there is one pianist who stands above them all—his name is Gabrilowitsch."

The quality of tone which this rare artist draws from his instrument, is unforgettable. I asked him one morning, when he was kind enough to give me the opportunity for a quiet chat, how he produced this luscious singing quality of tone.

"A beautiful tone? Ah, that is difficult to describe, whether in one hour or in many hours. It is first a matter of experiment, of individuality, then of experience and memory. We listen and create the tone, modify it until it expresses our ideal, then we try to remember how we did it.

"I cannot say that I always produce a beautiful tone; I try to produce a characteristic tone, but sometimes it may not be beautiful: there are many times when it may be anything but that. I do not think there can be any fixed rule or method in tone production, because people and hands are so different. What does for one will not do for another. Some players find it easier to play with high wrist, some with low. Some can curve their fingers, while others straighten them out. There are of course a few foundation principles, and one is that arms and wrists must be relaxed. Fingers must often be loose also, but not at the nail joint; that must always be firm. I advise adopting the position of hand which is most comfortable and convenient. In fact all forms of hand position can be used, if for a right purpose, so long as the condition is never cramped or stiff. I permit either a high or low position of the wrist, so long as the tone is good. As I said, the nail joint must remain firm, and never be crushed under by the weight of powerful chords, as is apt to be the case with young players whose hands are weak and delicate.

Technical Study
"Yes, I am certainly in favor of technical practise outside of pieces. There

must be scale and arpeggio study, in which the metronome can be used. But I believe in striving to make even technical exercises of musical value. If scales are played they should be performed with a beautiful quality and variety of tone; if one attempts a Czerny etude, it should be played with as much care and finish as a Beethoven sonata. Bring out all the musical qualities of the etude. Do not say, 'I'll play this measure sixteen times, and then I'm done with it.' Do nothing for mechanical ends merely, but everything from a musical standpoint. Yes, I give some Czerny to my students; not many etudes however. I prefer Chopin and Rubinstein. There is a set of six Rubinstein Studies which I use, including the Staccato etude.

"In regard to technical forms and material, each player may need a different tonic. I have found many useful things in a work by your own Dr. William Mason, *Touch and Technic*. I have used this to a considerable extent. To my knowledge he was the first to illustrate the principle of weight, which is now pretty generally accepted here as well as in Europe.

"An ancient and famous philosopher, Seneca, is said to have remarked that by the time a man reaches the age of twenty-five, he should know enough to be his own physician, or he is a fool. We might apply this idea to the pianist. After studying the piano for a number of years he should be able to discover what sort of technical exercises are most beneficial; if he cannot do so he must be a fool. Why should he always depend on the exercises made by others? There is no end to the list of method books and technical forms; their name is legion. They are usually made by persons who invent exercises to fit their own hands; this does not necessarily mean that they will fit the hands of others. I encourage my pupils to invent their own technical exercises. They have often done so with considerable success, and find much more pleasure in them than in those made by others.

"Two of the most important principles in piano playing are: full, round, exact tone; distinct phrasing. The most common fault is indistinctness— slurring over or leaving out notes. Clearness in piano playing is absolutely essential. If an actor essays the role of Hamlet, he must first of all speak distinctly and make himself clearly understood; otherwise all his study and characterization are in vain. The pianist must likewise make himself understood; he therefore must enunciate clearly.

Velocity
"You speak of velocity as difficult for some players to acquire. I have found there is a general tendency to play everything too fast, to rush headlong through the piece, without taking time to make it clear and intelligible. When

the piece is quite clear in tone and phrasing, it will not sound as fast as it really is, because all the parts are in just relation to each other. As an illustration of this fact, there is a little Gavotte of mine, which I had occasion to play several times in Paris. A lady, a very good pianist, got the piece, learned it, then came and asked me to hear her play it. She sat down to the piano, and rushed through the piece in a way that so distorted it I could hardly recognize it. When she finished I remonstrated, but she assured me that her tempo was exactly like mine as she had heard me play the piece three times. I knew my own tempo exactly and showed her that while it did not differ so greatly from hers, yet my playing sounded slower because notes and phrasing were all clear, and everything rightly balanced.

Power

"How do I gain power? Power does not depend on the size of the hand or arm; for persons of quite small physique have enough of it to play with the necessary effect. Power is a nervous force, and of course demands that arms and wrists be relaxed. The fingers must be so trained as to be strong enough to stand up under this weight of arms and hands, and not give way. I repeat, the nail joint must remain firm under all circumstances. It is so easy to forget this; one must be looking after it all the time.

Memorizing

"In regard to memorizing, I have no special rule or method. Committing to memory seems to come of its own accord. Some pieces are comparatively easy to learn by heart; others, like a Bach fugue, require hard work and close analysis. The surest way to learn a difficult composition, is to write it out from memory. There is a great deal of benefit in that. If you want to remember the name of a person or a place, you write it down. When the eye sees it, the mind retains a much more vivid impression. This is visual memory. When I play with orchestra, I of course know every note the orchestra has to play as well as my own part. It is a much greater task to write out a score from memory than a piano solo, yet it is the surest way to fix the composition in mind. I find that compositions I learned in early days are never forgotten, they are always with me, while the later pieces have to be constantly looked after. This is doubtless a general experience, as early impressions are most enduring.

"An orchestral conductor should know the works he conducts so thoroughly that he need not have the score before him. I have done considerable conducting the past few years. Last season I gave a series of historical recitals, tracing the growth of the piano concerto, from Mozart down to the present. I played nineteen works in all, finishing with the Rachmaninoff Concerto."

Mr. Gabrilowitsch has entirely given up teaching, and devotes his time to recital and concert, conducting, and composing.

RUDOLPH GANZ
[1877-1972]

CONSERVING ENERGY IN PIANO PRACTISE

One of the most necessary things is the conserving of vital energy in piano practise," said the pianist Rudolph Ganz to me one day. "The wrong way is to continually practise the piece as though you were playing it in public—that is to say, with all possible energy and emotion. Some of the pianists now before the public do this, and it always makes me sorry for them, for I know what a needless waste of energy and vital force it is. An actor, studying his lines, does not need to continually shout them in order to learn how they should be interpreted. Neither does the lyric actress practise her roles with full tones, for she is well used to saving her voice. Why then should the pianist exhaust himself and give out his whole strength merely in the daily routine of practise? I grant this principle of saving one's self may not be easy to learn, but it should be acquired by all players, great and small. I think a pianist should be able to practise five or six hours daily without fatigue. If the player is accustomed to husband his vital force during the daily routine of practise, he can play a long, exacting program in public without weariness. In every day practise one often does not need to play *forte* nor use the pedals; a tone of medium power is sufficient. Suppose, for instance, you are studying the Chopin Etude Op. 10, No. 12, with the left hand arpeggio work. Every note and finger must be in place, every mark of phrasing obeyed; but during practise hours you need not give the piece all its dashing vigor and bravura at every repetition. Such a course would soon exhaust the player. Yet every effect you wish to make must be thoroughly studied, must be in mind, and used at intervals whenever a complete performance of the piece is desired.

"As I said before, it is often difficult to control the impulse to 'let loose,' if the work is an exciting one. At a recent rehearsal with the Symphony Orchestra, I told the men I would quietly run through the concerto I was to play, merely indicating the effects I wanted. We began, but in five minutes I found myself playing with full force and vigor.

"In regard to methods in piano study there seems to be a diversity of opinion, resulting, I think, from the various ways of touching the keys—

some players using the tip and others the ball of the finger. Busoni may be cited as one who employs the end of the finger—Pauer also; while the Frenchman, Cortot, who has an exquisite tone, plays with the hand almost flat on the keys, a method which certainly insures weight of hand and arm. Of course players generally, and teachers also, agree on the employment of arm weight in playing. The principles of piano technic are surely but few. Was it not Liszt who said: 'Play the right key with the right finger, the right tone and the right intention—that is all!' It seems to me piano technic has been pushed to its limit, and there must be a reversal; we may return to some of the older methods of touch and technic.

"The vital thing in piano playing is to bring out the composer's meaning, plus your own inspiration and feeling. You must study deeply into the composer's idea, but you must also put your own feeling, intensity and emotion into the piece. And not only must you feel the meaning yourself, but you must play it in a way to touch others. There are many pianists who are not cultured musicians; who think they know their Beethoven because they can play a few sonatas. In music 'knowledge is power.' We need all possible knowledge, but we also need to feel the inspiration. One of the greatest teachers of our time holds that personal inspiration is not necessary; for the feeling is all in the music itself. All we have to do is to play with such and such a dynamic quality of tone. Like a country doctor measuring out his drugs, this master apportions so many grains of power for *forte*, for *mezzo*, for *piano*, and so on. This plan puts a damper on individuality and enthusiasm, for it means that everything must be coldly calculated. Such playing does not really warm the heart.

"I believe in teaching tonal contrasts and tone color even to a beginner. Why should not the child form a concept of *forte* and *piano*, and so get away from the deadly monotony of *mezzo*? I have written some little descriptive piano pieces, and my small boy learned one of them to play for me. There is a closing phrase like this," and Mr. Ganz illustrated at the piano; "it is to be played *forte*, and is followed by a few notes to be touched very softly, like an echo. It was really beautiful to see how the little fellow reached out for the pedal to make the loud part more emphatic, and then played the echo very softly and neatly. He had grasped the first principle of tone color—namely tone contrast, and also a poetic idea.

"There are so many wonder children in these days, and many marvels are accomplished by infant prodigies. Very often, however, these wonder children develop no further; they fail to fulfil their early promise, or the expectations held of them.

"A youthful wonder in the field of composition is Eric Korngold, whose piano sonata I played in my New York recital. I have played this work eight times in all, during my present tour, often by request. To me it is most interesting. I cannot say it is logical in the development of its ideas; it often seems as though the boy threw in chords here and there with no particular reason. Thus the effort of memorizing is considerable, for I must always bear in mind that this C major chord has a C sharp in it, or that such and such a chord is changed into a most unusual one. One cannot predict whether the boy will develop further. As you say, Mozart was an infant prodigy, but if we judge from the first little compositions that have been preserved, he began very simply and worked up, whereas Korngold begins at Richard Strauss. His compositions are full of the influence of Strauss. The critics have much to say for and against these early works. I do not know the young composer personally, though he has written me. In a recent letter which I have here, he expresses the thought that, though the critics have found many things to disapprove of in the sonata, the fact that I have found it worth studying and bringing out more than compensates him for all adverse criticism. To make the work known in the great musical centers of America is surely giving it wide publicity."

On a later occasion, Mr. Ganz said:

"I thoroughly believe in preserving one's enthusiasm for modern music, even though, at first glance, it does not attract one, or indeed seems almost impossible. I enjoy studying new works, and learning what is the modern trend of thought in piano work; it keeps me young and buoyant.

"One of the novelties lately added to my repertoire is the Haydn sonata in D. On the same program I place the Korngold sonata. A hundred years and more divide the two works. While I revere the old, it interests me to keep abreast of the new thought in musical art and life."

KATHARINE GOODSON
[1872-1958]

AN ARTIST AT HOME

When one has frequently listened to a favorite pianist in the concert room, and has studied impersonally, so to speak, the effects of touch, tone and interpretation produced during a recital, it is a satisfaction and delight to come into personal touch with the artist in the inner circle of the home; to be able to speak face to face with one who has charmed thousands from the platform, and to discuss freely the points which impress one when listening to a public performance.

It has been my recent privilege thus to come into intimate touch with the artist pair, Mr. and Mrs. Arthur Hinton, the latter being known all over the world as Katharine Goodson. They have a quiet, beautiful home in London— a true artist's home. One feels at once on entering and enjoying its hospitality, that here at least is one instance where two musicians have perfect harmony in the home life. Mr. Hinton, as is widely known, is a composer and also a violinist and pianist. The beautiful music-room, which has been added to one side of the house and leads into the garden, contains two grand pianos on its raised platform. This music-room is Miss Goodson's own sanctum and workroom, and here piano concertos, with orchestral accompaniment supplied on the second piano, can be studied *ad infinitum.* Mr. Hinton has his own studio at the top of the house.

The garden music-room is lighted at one end by a great arched window, so placed that the trees of the garden are seen through its panes. It is easy to imagine one's self in some lovely sylvan retreat—which is indeed true! All the appointments of this room, and indeed of the whole house, every article of furniture and each touch of color, betoken the artistic sense for fitness and harmony. Miss Goodson has a keen and exquisite sense for harmony in colors as well as for color in the harmonies she brings from her instrument.

"My coming tour will be the fifth I have made in America," she said. "I enjoy playing in your country immensely; the cities of New York, Boston, Chicago, and Philadelphia are the most appreciative in the world. It is true we have masses of concerts in London, but few of them are really well attended and people are not so thoroughly acquainted with piano music as you are in America. And you are so appreciative of the best—even in the smaller cities.

"I can recall a recital which I gave in a city of not more than forty thousand, in the West. The recital was arranged by a musical club; they asked for the program some time in advance, studied it up and thus knew every piece I was to play. There was an enormous audience, for people came from all the country round. I remember three little elderly ladies who greeted me after the recital; in parting they said, 'You will see us tomorrow.' I thought it over afterward and wondered what they meant, for I was to play at a place many miles from there the next night. What was my surprise to be greeted by the same ladies the following evening. 'You see, we are here; we told you we would come.' Fancy taking a trip from London to Edinburgh just to hear a concert! For it was a journey like that. Such incidents show the enthusiasm in America for music—and for piano music.

"I hope to play both the Brahms and Paderewski concertos in America. To me the latter is a beautiful work—the slow movement is exquisite. I have as yet scarcely done any thing with the composition, for I have been on a long tour through Norway, Sweden, and Finland. It was most inspiring to play for these people; they want me to come back to them now, but I cannot do so, nor can I go next season, but after that I shall go. I returned home greatly in need of rest. I shall now begin work in earnest, however, as summer is really the only time I have for study throughout the year. I shall have six full weeks now before we take our usual holiday in the Grindelwald. On the way there we shall stop at Morges and visit Paderewski, and then I will go over the concerto with him and get his ideas as to interpretation.

Memorising by Analysis

"You ask how I memorize. First I go over the work several times to get a general idea of the whole. Then I analyze it, for I feel it absolutely necessary to know keys, chords, and construction. A work should be so well understood along these lines that it can be played in another key as well as in the one in which it is written. For the actual memorizing of the piece I generally do it phrase by phrase, not always 'each hand alone,' though occasionally I do this also. I remember learning the Bach A minor Prelude and Fugue in this way. If I were now asked to play any measure or passage in any part of it I could do so; it is mine forever, never to be forgotten."

Asked about the different ways of teaching the Leschetizky method by various teachers, Miss Goodson said:

"As we all know, people claim to understand and teach the Leschetizky principles who are not competent to do so. I do not recall, for instance, that the professor requires the tips of the fingers to form a straight line on the edge of the keys. I myself have never done this. I believe in a perfectly easy and natural position of hand at the keyboard. When this is the case the finger-tips form a curve, the middle fingers being placed a little farther in on the keys than is natural for the first and fifth. Of course the hand takes an arched position and the joints nearest the tip of the fingers must be firm; there should be no wavering nor giving in there. The whole arm, of course, is relaxed, and swings easily from the shoulder.

A Piano Hand

"I have, as you say, a good hand for the piano; much depends on that; I have always had a good deal of what is called a natural technic. Thus when I am obliged to forego practising I do not lose my facility; an hour's work puts the hand in condition again. What do I do to accomplish this? Different things. First some finger movements, perhaps with fingers in an extended chord position; then some scales and arpeggios; then a Chopin etude, and so on. When practising regularly, I do not generally work at the piano more than four hours a day; it seems to me that amount is sufficient, if used with absolute concentration."

Later we adjourned to the pretty garden back of the music-room, and here we were joined by a beautiful gray Angora cat, the pet and pride of his mistress, and a very important personage indeed. He has a trick of climbing to Miss Goodson's shoulder, from which point of vantage he surveys the world about him with all the complaisance of which an animal of such high degree is capable.

MARK HAMBOURG

[1879-1960]

FORM, TECHNIC, AND EXPRESSION

In one of the most quiet, secluded quarters of London can be found the home of the Russian pianist, Mark Hambourg. Mr. Hambourg lives on a terrace, "far from the madding crowd," and difficult enough of access to keep mere curiosity seekers at a distance. One can scarcely picture to one's self, without an actual sight of them, the quaint charm of these short passages or streets, usually termed "terraces," or "gardens." This particular terrace looks out on a restful green park, where luxuriant trees make long shadows on the sunlit turf. The house is large and comfortable—built over a hundred years ago; its rooms are spacious, and the drawing-room and library, which lead one into the other, form a fine music salon. Surely, amid such surroundings, with priceless pictures and *objets d'art* all about, with exquisite colors, with space and quiet, an artist must find an ideal spot for both work and play. I expressed this thought to Mr. Hambourg when he entered; then we soon fell to discussing the necessary equipment of the teacher and pianist.

"I agree with you," he said, "that it is the beginning of piano study which is the most difficult of all; this is where the teacher has such great responsibility and where so many teachers are so incompetent. Perhaps there are more poor teachers for the piano than for the voice. The organs of voice production cannot be seen, they can only be guessed at; so there may be a little more excuse for the vocal teacher; but for the piano we have the keys and the fingers. It should not therefore be such a very difficult thing to learn to play intelligently and correctly! Yet few seem to have got hold of the right principles or know how to impart them."

"I have heard a number of the young pianists here," I remarked, "and they all play with very little finger action—with fingers close to the keys. Do you advocate this?"

Low Hand Position

"Do not forget that for centuries England has been a country of organists; without doubt organ playing has had some effect on the piano touch. Some schools of piano playing advise lifting the fingers high above the keys, with a view to producing greater power; but I think the tone thus produced is often of a somewhat harsh and disagreeable quality. Then, too, high lifting interferes with smoothness and velocity. For myself I advocate keeping the fingers close to the keyboard, and pressing the keys, which gives the tone a warmer and more elastic quality."

"A point in hand position I should like to ask you about. Some teachers advise placing the finger-tips close to the edge of the keys, forming a straight line with them; it seems to me such a position is forced and unnatural."

Mr. Hambourg smiled assent.

"I do not advocate anything forced and unnatural," he answered. "So many people think that a beautiful touch is 'born, not made,' but I do not agree with them. One can acquire, I am sure, a fine piano touch with the proper study. The principal requirement is, first of all, a loose wrist. This point seems simple enough, but it is a point not sufficiently considered nor understood. No matter how much the player may *feel* the meaning of the music, he cannot express this meaning with stiff wrists and arms. Some people have a natural flexibility, and to such the securing of a musical tone presents far less difficulty; but with time, patience, and thought, I fully believe all can arrive at this goal.

Amount of Practise

"In regard to practise I do not think it wise for the aspiring pianist to spend such a great amount of time at the piano. Four hours of concentrated work daily seems to me sufficient. Of course it is the quality of practise that counts. The old saying, 'Practise makes perfect,' does not mean constant repetition merely, but constant thinking and listening. I advise students to stop after playing a passage several times, and think over what the notes mean. This pause will rest ears and hands; in a few moments work can be resumed with fresh vigor.

"I have been so frequently asked to write on the subject of technic that I have done so in a few articles which have been printed in a small booklet. From these you may see what my ideas are on these points. I do very little teaching myself—just a few talented pupils; they must be something out of the ordinary. You see, I do not live in London continuously; I am here only about four months of the year, the rest of the time is spent traveling all over the world. Only that small part of the year when I am stationary can I do any solid work. Here it is generally quiet enough: the Zoological Garden is not far away, however, and sometimes I have the roaring of the lions as an accompaniment to my piano.

"I am always increasing my repertoire, though I find the public does not care for new things; it prefers the old. It may listen to the new if forced to, but it will not attend a recital unless various familiar things are on the program.

"I have made several tours in America. The rush of travel from place to place over there, is fatiguing, but I feel that your people are very appreciative. You demand the best, and concert giving in America is so costly that a manager can afford to exploit only the highest artists. Here in London, where the expense is only about two hundred dollars, say, to get up a recital, almost any one can scrape together that sum and bring himself or herself before the public. In America the outlay is four or five times greater. No wonder that only a very good artist can take the risk."

On leaving, Mr. Hambourg took us to another room, where he showed us with much satisfaction a very valuable painting of the old Italian school, by Ghirlandajo, of which he is very fond.

EDWIN HUGHES

[1884-1965]

SOME ESSENTIALS OF PIANO PLAYING

When one has read with pleasure and profit the published ideas of a musical worker and thinker, it is always an interesting experience to meet one personally, and have the opportunity to discuss points of special import, particularly when the meeting can take place in some ideal spot in the old world. Such was my thought in visiting Mr. Edwin Hughes, an American who has made a name and place for himself among the pianists and teachers of Europe. After years of study in Vienna with Leschetizky, where he also acted as one of the Vorbereiters, he has established himself in Munich, where he feels he has found a true home of music and art. Here, amid beautiful and artistic surroundings, he lives and works, dividing his time between teaching and concert playing. As a pianist Mr. Hughes has met with gratifying success in the most important cities of Germany, while as a teacher he has been sought by students from almost every State in America, from Maine to Texas, and also from Canada. What has given him special satisfaction is that during the past year a number of pupils have come to him from the Conservatory here in Munich. They have been greatly pleased with their progress, only regretting they had not come to him before.

As to whether he uses the Leschetizky method in its entirety, Mr. Hughes testified in the affirmative.

"If you were to ask Leschetizky about the 'Leschetizky Method,' he would probably laugh and tell you he has no method, or he would tell you his 'method' consists of only two things—firm fingers and pliable wrist.

"These are the principles upon which I base the technical training of my pupils. I first establish an arched hand position, and then test the firmness of the fingers and knuckle joints by tapping them. At first the joints, particularly the nail joints, are very apt to sink in when tapped by a lead pencil; but by having the pupil continue the tapping process at home, it is not long before he acquires the feeling of conscious firmness in his fingers.

"Along with this exercise it is most important to begin at once with wrist exercises, as otherwise, from the effort to acquire firmness of finger, the wrist may become stiff and unwieldy. The wrist exercises consist in raising and lowering this joint, with the hand and arm supported first on each finger separately, then on two, three, four and five fingers. The wrist should not be so limp as to be incapable of resistance; but rather it should be like a fine steel spring—a 'spring-wrist,' I call it—capable of every degree of resistance or nonresistance the quality of tone demands.

"High finger action is not so necessary for beginners as most piano teachers imagine. It is much easier to teach pupils to raise their fingers high than it is to teach them the acquisition of the legato touch at the piano, which is only to be attained by playing close to the keys, without raising the fingers. It is difficult to get pupils to play a perfect legato who have had years of training with high finger action, something which should be taken up for non-legato and staccato finger work *after* the more difficult legato touch has been mastered.

Tone Production

"The subject of tone production is one which is much neglected by piano teachers. Viewed from this standpoint the piano is an instrument apart from every other, except in some respects the organ. A young violinist, cellist or flutist has to study for some time before he can produce a tone of good musical quality on his instrument. Think what the beginner on the violin has to go through before he can make a respectable middle C; but anybody, even a totally unmusical person, can play middle C on the piano without the least trouble. It is just this ease in tone production at the piano which leads to carelessness as to the *kind* of tone produced; and so piano teachers, above all others, complain they cannot get their pupils to listen to what they are playing. Pupils should be made to listen, by means of a special course in tone production, which should go hand in hand with the technical exercises used at the very beginning. Otherwise they imagine they are making music when they place the printed page on the rack, and set the correct keys in motion.

"There is no other instrument with which it is so easy to 'bluff' a large part of the audience; for the character of the piano is such that the general public often think it fine music if the player makes a big noise. Pianists of considerable reputation often take advantage of this lack of discrimination on the part of piano recital audiences, which, above all the other audiences, seem peculiarly incapable of judging correctly the musical value of a performance.

"Of the hundreds of piano recitals which take place yearly in the musical centers of Europe, only a comparatively small number are of real musical interest. In many cases it seems as though the players were merely repeating something learned by rote, in an unknown language; just as though I should repeat a poem in Italian. The words I might pronounce after a fashion, but the meaning of most of them would be a blank to me—so how could I make others understand them.

Rhythm in Piano Playing

"The subject of rhythm is an important one, and more attention should be given it. Leschetizky once said that tones and rhythm are the only things which can keep the piano alive as a solo instrument. I find in pupils who come to me so much deficiency in these two subjects, that I have organized classes in ear-training and rhythm.

"If pupils have naturally a poor sense of rhythm, there is no remedy equal to practising with a metronome, using this instrument of torture daily until results are evident, when, of course, there must be a judicious slowing down in its use. The mechanical sense of rhythm, the ability to count three or four to a measure, and to group the notes of a piece correctly, can be taught to any person, if one has the patience; but for those delicate rhythmic nuances required by a Chopin mazurka or a Viennese waltz, a specific rhythmic gift must be possessed by the pupil.

"Leschetizky says little to his pupils on the subject of technic; I cannot remember his having spoken a dozen words to me on the subject, during all the time I have known him. His interest, of course, lies wholly in the matter of interpretation, and technic comes into consideration only as a means and never as an end.

"Leschetizky likes to have the player talk to him, ask questions, do anything but sit still' and not speak. 'How do I know you comprehend my meaning,' he asks, 'that you understand what I am talking about, if you say nothing?' At first a student may be silent from nervousness, but if he is bright he will soon 'catch on,' and see what is expected of him. Leschetizky says sometimes: 'When the Lord made the ten commandments He omitted the eleventh, "Thou shalt not be stupid."

If one is not very quick, one may have a hard time with this master.

"As a high school in technic I use Joseffy's *School of Advanced Piano Playing* with my pupils. This work leads to the highest possible technical development at the keyboard, and I consider it the last word in piano technic. The hundreds of exercises have been devised with most wonderful ingenuity, and the musicianship of the author stands out on every page. The book is not a dry series of technics but has vital connection with all the big technical problems found in the literature of the piano.

"In teaching, I consider a second piano an absolute necessity. There are so many things in piano playing which cannot be put into words, and the teacher must constantly illustrate. How can one teach the interpretation of a Chopin nocturne, for instance, by merely talking about it. I can say, 'play loud here—soft there;' but how far do such directions go toward an artistic conception of the piece? One cannot indicate the swell of a melody, the tonal and rhythmic *nuance* of a *groupetto*—and a thousand other things in any other way than by the living example. Through imitation one learns rapidly and surely, until one reaches the point where the wings of one's own individuality begin to sprout.

About Memorizing

"On the subject of memorizing who can lay down rules for this inexplicable mental process, which will hold good for every one? For myself, I hear the notes mentally, and know their position on the keyboard. In actual performance much must be left to finger memory, but one must actually have the notes in his mind as well as in his fingers. Before a concert I go over all my program mentally, and find this an excellent method of practise when traveling from one city to another. To those who study with me I say, you must try various methods of memorizing; there is no universal way; each must find out by experiment which is most suited to his individual case.

"With some pianists visual memory of the printed page plays the principal role in memorizing; with others visual memory of the notes on the keyboard; with still others ear-memory, or memory of the harmonic progressions. I believe in making the pupil familiar with all these different ways, so that he may find out which one is most helpful to him.

"For pupils with weak hands and arms I recommend simple gymnastic exercises to be done morning and evening. Physical strength is a very necessary essential for a brilliant technic; the student who would accomplish big things must possess it in order to succeed.

Keeping Technic in Repair

"The only way to keep one's technic in repair is to be constantly working at it. Technic is the mechanical part of music-making; to keep it in good working order one must be constantly tinkering with it, just as the engine driver tinkers with his locomotive or the chauffeur with his automobile. In the course of his technical study every intelligent pupil will recognize certain exercises which are particularly important for the mechanical well-being of his playing; from these exercises he will plan his daily schedule of technical practise.

"In order to keep a large repertoire going at the same time, one must have a weekly practise plan, which will allow for a frequent repetition of the pieces. Those pieces which have been recently added to one's list will require more frequent repetition, while those which have been played for a longer period may be left for an occasional brushing up. Frequent playing before others, either publicly or privately, is above everything else to be recommended to the pianist, as the greatest incentive to keeping up his repertoire and toward growing in his art.

American versus European Conditions

"In America many people who have little talent study music, intending to make it their profession; whereas in Europe there is such a profusion of music and music-making that only those of more than average gifts think of making music their life work. In America we are still 'in the making,' from a musical standpoint, and although we have accomplished much there is still much to be done. It is the office of the piano teacher in America to make music study easy and interesting to pupils of moderate ability. Just these conditions have brought about very excellent methods of piano and music study for American children, which have no counterpart in Europe."

ETHEL LEGINSKA
[1886-1970]

RELAXATION THE KEYNOTE OF MODERN PIANO PLAYING

The brilliant young pianist, Ethel Leginska, who is located for a time in America, was seen in her Carnegie Hall studio, on her return from a concert tour. The young English girl is a petite brunette; her face is very expressive, her manner at once vivacious and serious. The firm muscles of her fine, shapely hands indicate that she must spend many hours daily at the keyboard.

"Yes, I have played a great deal in public—all my life, in fact ever since I was six. I began my musical studies at Hull, where we lived; my first teacher was a pupil of McFarren. Later I was taken to London, where some rich people did a great deal for me. Afterward I went to Leschetizky, and was with him several years, until I was sixteen; I also studied in Berlin. Then I began my career, and concertized all over Europe; now I am in America for a time. I like it here; I am fond of your country already.

"The piano is such a wonderful instrument to me; I feel we are only beginning to fathom its possibilities; not in a technical sense, but as a big avenue for expression. For me the piano is capable of reflecting every mood, every feeling; all pathos, joy, sorrow—the good and the evil too—all there is in life, all that one has lived." (This recalls a recently published remark of J. S. Van Cleve: "The piano can sing, march, dance, sparkle, thunder, weep, sneer, question, assert, complain, whisper, hint; in one word it is the most versatile and plastic of instruments.")

"As for the technic of the piano, I think of it only as the material—only as a means to an end. In fact I endeavor to get away from the thought of the technical material, in order that I may get at the meaning of the music I wish to interpret. I am convinced there is a great future for the piano and its music. Even now we are taking piano music very seriously, and are trying to interpret it in a far deeper and broader sense than the pianists of, say, fifty years ago ever thought of doing. I fancy if Clara Schumann, for instance, could return and play to us, or even Liszt himself, we should not find their playing suited to this age at all. Some of us yet remember the hand position Mme. Schumann had, the lack of freedom in fingers and arms. It was not the fashion of her time to play with the relaxed freedom, with the breadth and depth of style which we demand of artists today. In those days relaxation had not received the attention it deserved, therefore we should probably find the playing of the greatest artists of a former generation stiff and angular, in spite of all we have heard of their wonderful performances.

"Relaxation is a hobby with me; I believe in absolute freedom in every part of the arm anatomy, from the shoulder down to the fingertips. Stiffness seems to me the most reprehensible thing in piano playing, as well as the most common fault with all kinds of players. When people come to play for me, that is the thing I see first in them, the stiffness. While living in Berlin, I saw much of Mme. Teresa Carreño, and she feels the same as I do about relaxation, not only at the keyboard, but when sitting, moving about or walking. She has thought along this line so constantly, that sometimes, if carrying something in hand, she will inadvertently let it drop, without realizing it—from sheer force of the habit of relaxation.

"You ask how I would begin with a young pupil who never has had lessons. I use the principle of relaxation first of all, loosening arms and wrists. This principle can be taught to the youngest pupil. The wrist is elevated and lowered, as the hand is formed on the keys in its five finger position, with arched knuckles. It does not take long to acquire this relaxed condition; then come the finger movements. I do not believe in lifting the fingers high above the keys; this takes time and interferes with velocity and power. I lift my fingers but little above the keys, yet I have plenty of power, all the critics agree on that. In chords and octaves I get all the power I need by grasping the keys with weight and pressure. I do not even prepare the fingers in the air, before taking the chord; I do not find it necessary." Here the pianist played a succession of ringing chords, whose power and tonal quality bore out her words; the fingers seemed merely to press and cling; there was no striking nor percussion.

"To return to the beginning pupil. As for a book to start with, I often use the one by Damm, though any foundational work may be employed, so long as correct principles are taught. It is said by Leschetizky that he has no method. That may be understood to mean a book, for he certainly has what others would call a method. There are principles and various sets of exercises to be learned; but it is quite true that none of the Vorbereiters use a book.

"In teaching the piano, as you know, every pupil is different; each has his or her own peculiar hand, and a different degree of intelligence. So each pupil must be treated differently. This is really an advantage to the teacher; for it would be very monotonous if all pupils were alike.

"The piano is such a revealer of character; I need only to hear a person play to know what sort of character he has. If one is inclined to much careful detail in everything, it comes out in the playing. If one is indolent and indifferent, it is seen the moment one touches the keys; or if one is built on broad, generous lines, and sees the dramatic point in life and things, all this is revealed at the piano.

"To refer again to the subject of finger action. I do not believe in the so-called finger stroke; on the contrary I advocate fingers close to the keys, clinging to them whenever you can. This is also Arthur Schnabel's idea. You should hear Schnabel; all Berlin is wild over him, and whenever he gives a concert the house is sold out. He has quantities of pupils also, and is quite a remarkable teacher. One point I insist upon which he doesn't: I will not allow the joint of the finger next the tip to break or give in. I can not stand that, but Schnabel doesn't seem to care about it; his mind is filled with only the big, broad things of music.

"In regard to memorizing piano compositions. I do it phrase by phrase, and at the instrument, unless I am traveling or unable to get to a piano, in which case I think it out from the notes. If the piece is very difficult I take a short passage of two or three measures and play each hand separately and then together; but generally I play the passage complete—say half a dozen times with the notes, and then repeat it the same number of times from memory. Perhaps the next day I have forgotten it, so the work has to be done over again; the second time, however, it generally sticks.

"My great longing and ambition is to write music, to become a composer. With this end in view, I give whatever time I am able to the study of composition. I hope some day to create something that will be worthy the high aim I have before me."

DR. WILLIAM MASON

[1829-1908]

HINTS ON INTERPRETATION

I had the privilege of doing some work with the dean of all American piano masters, Dr. William Mason. I had spent several years in European study, with Scharwenka, Klindworth and von Bülow, and had returned to my own land to join its teaching and playing force. My time soon became so largely occupied with teaching that I feared my playing would be entirely pushed to the wall unless I were under the guidance of some master. With this thought in mind, I presented myself to Dr. Mason.

"You have studied with Sherwood," he began. "He has excellent ideas of touch and technic. Some of these ideas came from me, though I don't wish to claim too much in the matter. Sherwood has the true piano touch. Very few pianists have it; Klindworth did not have it, nor von Bülow, nor even Liszt, entirely, for he as well as the others, sought for a more orchestral manner of playing. Sherwood has this touch; Tausig had it, and de Pachmann and Rubinstein most of all. It is not taught in Germany as it should be. The best American teachers are far ahead in this respect; in a few years the Europeans will come to us to learn these things."

The first composition played to Dr. Mason was the G minor Rhapsodie of Brahms, with which, as it happened, he was unfamiliar. I played the entire piece through without interruption, and he seemed pleased.

"You have a beautiful tone—a really beautiful tone, and you play very artistically; much of this must be natural to you, you could not have acquired it. You also have an excellently trained hand. I may say that in my forty years of teaching I have never had any one come to me with a better position, or more natural and normal condition. Now, what do you think I can do for you?"

I explained that I needed some new ideas in my teaching, and wished to keep up my own practise.

"I will explain my theories to you, and we will then study some compositions together.

"There is everything in knowing how to practise, but it is something that cannot be taught. I played in public ten years before I found out the secret.

"Practise slowly and in sections. Not only must all the notes be there, they must be dwelt on. There must be a firm and rock-like basis for piano playing; such a foundation can only be laid by patient and persevering slow practise. If the player has not the control over his fingers to play a piece slowly, he certainly cannot play it fast. Slow practise—one difficulty at a time—one hand at a time; Napoleon's tactics, 'one division at a time,' applies to music study. Above all do not hurry in fugue playing, a universal fault. Bach needs a slower trill than modern music. Chords are not to be played with percussion but with pressure. The main things in piano playing are tone and sentiment. When you take up a new piece, practise a few measures slowly, till you know them, then play faster; take the next few measures in the same way; but at first do not practise the whole piece through at once.

"Just as in life every experience of great joy or great grief leaves one better or more callous, so every time you practise you have either advanced or gone back. Right playing, like good manners in a well-trained child, becomes habitual from always doing right. As we are influenced for good or evil by those we associate with, so are we influenced by the character and quality of the tones we make and hear. Be in earnest; put your heart, your whole soul, your whole self into your playing."

Among other pieces we studied together was the Schumann sonata in F minor, the *Eusebius* Sonata—a glorious work! In the opening movement the left hand should be very serious and ponderous, with the hand and fingers held close to the keys; using arm weight. The melody in octaves in right hand is beseeching, pleading, imploring. In many places the touch is very elastic. The second movement begins very softly, as though one heard something faintly in the distance, and did not quite know what it was, but thought it might be music. The accents in this movement are to be understood in a comparative degree, and are not as strong as the marks seem to indicate. The Scherzo is extremely pompous and is to be played with heavy accents and a great deal of vim and go; the chords with the utmost freedom and dash. One must use the "letting-go" principle, which Paderewski has to perfection.

We next took up the Grieg Concerto; the Peter's edition of this work has been corrected by the composer. At the first lesson, Dr. Mason accompanied on a second piano, and seemed pleased with the work I had done, making no corrections, except to suggest a somewhat quicker tempo. "Not that I would do anything to impair your carefulness and accuracy, but you must take a risk, and from the beginning, too. I am reminded of the young man who has been very carefully brought up. When the time comes for him to strike out and take his chance in life, he holds back and is afraid, while another with more courage, steps in and takes away his opportunity."

We discussed the slow movement at great length. "Note in this movement the slow, dreamy effect that can be made at the ending of the second solo, and the artistic use of the pedal in the following chords. The third movement must have great swing and 'go;' the octave passage cadenza should be practised in rhythmical groups, and the final Andante must be fast."

The third time we played the concerto I had it well in hand. Dr. Mason accompanied as only he could do, and at the close praised me on the way I had worked it up, and the poetry and fire I was able to put into it. Who could help playing with fire and enthusiasm when led by such a master!

Dr. Mason was a most inspiring teacher, quick to note and praise what was good, and equally vigilant in correcting what was blameworthy. His criticisms were of the utmost value, for he had such wide experience, and such a large acquaintance with music and musicians. Best of all he was a true artist, always ready to demonstrate his art for the benefit of the pupil, always encouraging, always inspiring.

TOBIAS MATTHAY
[1858-1945]

WATCHING THE ARTIST TEACHER AT WORK

One of the first things accomplished after my arrival in London was to seek out Tobias Matthay, the composer and teacher, for an echo of his fame had reached me across the water.

Matthay has done much to make the principles of piano technic so clear and simple that even a child can understand them. If he has stated facts in a way which seems to some revolutionary it is because these facts are seldom understood by the rank and file of piano teachers. The work he has done has compelled attention and admiration; his ideas are now accepted as undeniable truths by those who at first repudiated them. The writings of Mr. Matthay will doubtless be better known in America a little later on than they are at present. They consist in part of an exhaustive work on *The Act of Touch in all its Diversity; First Principles of Piano Playing; Relaxation Studies; The Child's First Steps in Piano Playing; The Principles of Fingering and Laws of Pedaling; Forearm Rotation Principle;* and, in press, *The Principles of Teaching Interpretation.* These very titles are inspiring and suggestive, and show Matthay to be a deep thinker along educational lines.

Matthay's activities are enormous. He is professor of advanced piano playing at the Royal Academy of Music; also founder and head of his own school of piano playing. So occupied early and late is he, that it is almost impossible to get a word with him. I was fortunate enough, however, to obtain an hour's audience, and also permission to attend various private classes at the Royal Academy, and hear a number of pupils in recital.

In appearance Matthay is a striking personality. His head and features recall pictures of Robert Louis Stevenson. His tall, muscular form has the stoop of the scholar; and little wonder when one remembers he must sit in his chair at work day in and day out. His somewhat brusk manner melts into kind amiability when discussing the topics in which he is vitally interested. In his intercourse with students he is ever kind, sympathetic and encouraging. They, on their part, treat him with profound respect.

Matthay believes, and rightly, that the beginning pupil should learn essentials of note values, rhythm, time, ear-training and so on, before attempting to play anything at the piano. When first taken to the instrument, its mechanism is carefully explained to the learner, and what he must do to make a really musical tone. He says (*Child's First Steps*): "Before you take the very first step in tone production, be sure to understand that you must never touch the piano without trying to make music. It is only too easy to sound notes without making music at all. To make music we must make all the sounds mean something, just as it is no use to pretend to speak unless the sounds we make with our lips mean something, that is unless they form reasoned phrases and sentences."

Here nothing is left vague. Matthay shows clearly how all musical Form and Shape imply Movement and Progression: the movement of a phrase toward its cadence; the movement of a group of notes toward a beat or pulse ahead, or the movement of a whole piece toward its climax, etc. This original view of his regarding form, which he has advocated for the last twenty years, is now being accepted generally by the more up-to-date of the English theorists and teachers.

In regard to key mechanism and what must be done to produce all varieties of touch and tone, Matthay has made exhaustive studies. He says (*First Principles of Piano Playing*): "The two chief rules of technic, as regards the key, are, therefore: Always feel how much the key resists you: feel how much the key *wants* for every note. Second, Always listen for the moment each sound begins, so that you may learn to direct your effort to the sound only, and not to the key bed. You must never hit a key down, nor hit *at* it. The finger-tip may fall on the key, and in gently reaching the key you may follow up such fall by acting against the key. This action against the key must be for the sole purpose of making it move—in one of the many ways which each give us quite a different kind of sound. And you must always direct such action to the point in key descent where the sound begins."

I quote also this little summary from the same work:

(a) It is only by making the hammer-end of the key move that you can make a sound.

(b) The swifter the movement the louder the sound.

(c) The more gradual this swiftness is obtained the more beautiful the quality of sound.

(d) For brilliant tone you may hit the string by means of the key, but do not, by mistake, hit the key instead.

(e) You must 'aim' the key to the *beginning* of each sound, because the hammer falls off the string as you hear that beginning, and it is too late then to influence the sound except its continuance.

(f) It is wrong to squeeze the key beds, because it prevents tone, impairs musical result, impedes agility, and is, besides, fatiguing.

(g) You must feel the 'giving way point' of the key, so that you may be able to tell how much force is required for each note. Never, therefore, really hit the keys."

Mr. Matthay as minutely gives directions as to the muscular problems of touch and technique. For instance, he explains how all varieties of tone, good and bad, are caused, all inflections of Duration, and the laws which govern the attainment of Agility and ease of Technique; and also explains the nature of incorrect muscular actions which prevent the attainment of all these things. He shows where the released arm weight should be applied, and again, where it should be eliminated; makes clear the two opposite forms of technic implied by "flat" and "bent" finger actions, and he goes exhaustively into the little-understood question of forearm rotary exertions, the correct application of which he proves to be necessary for every note we play.

In speaking of methods in piano teaching, Mr. Matthay said to me:

"I can say I have no method *of playing*, and moreover I have not much faith in people who have. My teachings merely show how all playing, good or bad, is accomplished. There are certain principles, however, which every player should know, but which, I am sorry to say, are as yet scarcely apprehended even by the best teachers. The great pianists have experimented till they have hit upon effects which they can repeat if all conditions are favorable, and they are in the mood. As a rule they do not know the laws underlying these effects. You may ask the greatest pianists, for example, how to play octaves. 'Oh, I play them thus'—illustrating. Just what to do to attain this result they cannot explain. In my own case I have done much experimenting, but always with the view to discovering *how* things are done—the facts and laws governing actual tone production and interpretation. I made a study of Rubinstein's playing, for I found he played a great deal better than I did. So I discovered many things in listening to him, which he perhaps could not have explained to me. These facts are incontrovertible and I have brought many of my colleagues to see the truth of them. More than this, I have brought many even of my older colleagues who had a lifetime of wrong mental habits to impede them, to realize the truth of my teachings.

"The work of a teacher should speak for itself. For my own part I never advertise, for I can point to hundreds of pupils—this is no exaggeration in the least!—who are constantly before the public, as concert pianists and successful teachers.

"If there is one thing that rouses me deeply, it is the incompetence of so many teachers of piano. They say to the pupil: 'You play badly, you must play better;' but they do not tell the pupil *how* to play better. They give doses of etudes, sonatas and pieces, yet never get at the heart of the matter at all. It is even worse than the fake singing teachers; I feel like saying it is damnable!"

It was my privilege to be present at some of Mr. Matthay's private lessons, given at the Royal Academy. Several young men were to try for one of the medals, and were playing the same piece, one of the Strauss-Tausig Valse Caprices.

Matthay listens to a complete performance of the work in hand, then turns back to the beginning and goes over it again for corrections and suggestions. He enters into it with absolute devotion, directing with movements of head and hands as a conductor might direct an orchestra; sometimes he dashes down a chord in the treble to urge more force; at other times lays a restraining hand on the player's arm, where the tone should be softer. His blue pencil is often busy adding phrasing marks. In the pauses he talks over with the pupil the character of the piece, and the effects he thinks should be made. In short his lessons are most helpful and illuminating.

I also had the opportunity to attend a pupils' "Practise Concert," and here the results attained were little short of marvelous. Small children, both boys and girls, played difficult pieces, like the Grieg Variations for two pianos, the Weber *Invitation to the Dance*, and works by Chopin and Liszt, with accuracy and fluency. Almost every selection was played from memory. The tone was always musical and often of much power, and the pupils seemed thoroughly to understand what they were doing and the meaning of the music. They certainly exemplified the professor's maxim:

"Never touch the piano without trying to make music."

Not long afterward I received a copy of the new book, which had just come from the press. Its comprehensive title is *Musical Interpretation, its Laws and Principles, and their Application in Teaching and Performing*. The material was first presented in the form of lectures; on repeated requests it has been issued in book form. The author at the outset claims no attempt to treat such a complex problem exhaustively; he has, however, selected the following seven points for elucidation:

1. The difference between Practise and Strumming.
2. The difference between Teaching and Cramming.
3. How one's mind can be brought to bear on one's work.
4. Correct ideas of Time and Shape.
5. Elements of Rubato and its application.
6. Elements of Duration and Pedaling and their application.
7. Some details as to the application of the Element of Tone-variety.

Such themes must cause the thoughtful reader to pause and think. They are treated with illuminating originality. The great aim of the teacher must ever be to awaken thought along correct lines; the pupil must be assisted to concentrate his thought on what he is doing: to constantly think and listen. Teaching does not consist merely in pointing out faults; the teacher must make clear the *cause* of each fault and the way to correct it. That section of the book devoted to the Element of Rubato, is illustrated with many examples from well-known compositions, by which the principle is explained. He shows how frequently this principle is misunderstood by the inexperienced, who seem to think that rubato means breaking the time; whereas true rubato is the *bending* of the time, but not *breaking* it. If we give extra time to certain notes, we must take some time from other notes, in order to even things up.

The subject of Pedaling is aptly explained by means of numerous illustrations. The author deplores the misuse of the damper pedal, which can be made to ruin all the care and effort bestowed on phrasing and tonal effects by the fingers. The fault can, in most cases, be traced to inattention to the sounds coming from the piano.

There are quotable paragraphs on every page, which in their sincerity and earnestness, their originality of expression, stamp themselves on the reader's imagination. Every teacher who is serious in his work and has the best interests of his pupils at heart, should read and ponder these pages.

A VISIT TO RAOUL PUGNO

[1852-1914]

An audience has been arranged for you today, with M. Raoul Pugno; he will await you at four o'clock, in his Paris studio." Thus wrote the courteous representative of *Musical America* in Paris.

It had been very difficult to make appointments with any of the famous French musicians, owing to their being otherwise engaged, or out of the city. I therefore welcomed this opportunity for meeting at least one of the great pianists of France.

At the appointed hour that afternoon, we drove through the busy rue de Clicy, and halted at the number which had been indicated. It proved to be one of those unpromising French apartment buildings, which present, to the passer-by, a stern façade of flat wall, broken by rows of shuttered windows, which give no hint of what may be hidden behind them. In this case we did not find the man we sought in the front portion of the building, but were directed to cross a large, square court. The house was built around this court, as was the custom in constructing the older sort of dwellings.

At last we discovered the right door, which was opened by a neat housekeeper.

"M. Pugno is not here, he lives in the country," she said, in answer to our inquiry. (How difficult these French musicians are to find; they seem to be one and all "in the country!")

"But, madame, we have an appointment with M. Pugno; will you not be good enough to see if he is not here after all?"

She left us standing, but returned almost immediately with the message that M. Pugno had only that moment entered his studio, to which she would conduct us.

In another moment we had crossed the tiny foyer and were standing within the artist's sanctuary. At first glance one felt as though in an Oriental chamber of some Eastern monarch. Heavy gold and silver Turkish embroideries hung over doors and windows. The walls were covered with many rare paintings; rich *objets d'art* were scattered about in profusion; an open door led out into a pretty garden, where flowers bloomed, and a fountain dripped into its marble basin. A raised dais at one side of the room held a divan, over which were draperies of Oriental stuffs. On this divan, as on a throne, sat the great pianist we had come to see. He made a stately and imposing figure as he sat there, with his long silvery beard and his dignified bearing. Near him sat a pretty young woman, whom we soon learned was Mlle. Nadia Boulanger, a composer and musician of brilliant attainments.

"I regret that I am unable to converse with you in English, as I speak no language but my own," began M. Pugno, with a courteous wave of the hand for us to be seated.

"You wish to know some of my ideas on piano playing—or rather on teaching. I believe a child can begin to study the piano at a very early age, if he show any aptitude for it; indeed the sooner he begins the better, for then he will get over some of the drudgery by the time he is old enough to understand a little about music.

Training the Child

"Great care must be taken with the health of the child who has some talent for music, so that he shall not overdo in his piano study. After all a robust physical condition is of the first importance, for without it one can do little.

"A child in good health can begin as early as five or six years. He must be most judiciously trained from the start. As the ear is of such prime importance in music, great attention should be paid to tone study—to listening to and distinguishing the various sounds, and to singing them if possible, in solfeggio.

"At the outset a good hand position must be secured, with correct finger movements. Then there must be a thorough drill in scales, arpeggios, chords, and a variety of finger exercises, before any kind of pieces are taken up. The young student in early years, is expected to play various etudes, as well as the technic studies I have mentioned—Czerny, Cramer, Clementi, and always Bach. In my position, as member of the faculty of the Conservatoire, a great many students pass before me. If I personally accept any pupils, they naturally must be talented and advanced, as I cannot give my time to the children. Still it is interesting to see the child-thought develop."

The conversation turned upon the charming studio with its lovely garden— where absolute quiet could be secured in spite of the noise and bustle of one of the busiest quarters of Paris. The studio itself, we were told, had formerly belonged to the painter Decamps, and some of the pictures and furnishings were once his. A fine portrait of Pugno, life size, filling the whole space above the piano, claimed our attention. He kindly rose, as we admired the painting, and sought a photograph copy. When it was found—the last one he possessed—he presented it with his compliments.

We spoke of Mlle. Boulanger's work in composition, a subject which seemed deeply to interest M. Pugno.

"Yes, she is writing an opera; in fact we are writing it together; the text is from a story of d'Annunzio. I will jot down the title for you."

Taking a paper which I held in my hand, he wrote,

"La Ville Morte, 4 Acts de d'Annuncio;
Musique de Nadia Boulanger et Raoul Pugno"

"You will certainly have it performed in America, when it is finished; I will tell them so," I said.

The great pianist smiled blandly and accepted the suggestion with evident satisfaction.

"Yes, we will come to America and see the work performed, when it is completed," he said.

With many expressions of appreciation we took our leave of the Oriental studio and its distinguished occupants; and, as we regained the busy, noisy rue de Clicy, we said to ourselves that we had just lived through one of the most unique experiences of our stay in Paris.

(The above is the last interview ever taken from this great French artist, who passed away a few months later.)

The following items concerning M. Pugno's manner of teaching and personal traits, were given me by Mme. Germaine Schnitzer, the accomplished French pianist and the master's most gifted pupil.

"Pugno had played the piano almost from infancy, and in early youth had taken several piano prizes. Later, however, he gave much more of his time to the organ, to the seeming neglect of the former instrument. How his serious attention was reverted to the piano happened in this wise. It was announced that Edward Grieg, the noted Norwegian, was coming to Paris. Pugno was one day looking over his piano Concerto which had recently appeared. 'Why don't you play the work for the composer when he comes?' asked a friend. 'I am no pianist,' objected Pugno. 'Why not?' said his friend; 'you know enough about the piano, and there are still four weeks in which to learn the Concerto.' Pugno took the advice, practised up the work, played it in the concert given by Grieg, and scored a success. He was then thirty-nine years of age. This appearance was the beginning; other engagements and successes followed, and thus he developed, into one of the great pianists of France.

"Pugno was a born pianist; he had a natural gift for technic, and therefore never troubled himself much about teaching technical exercises nor practising them. If the work of a pupil contained technical faults, he made no remarks nor explanations, but simply closed the music book and refused to listen any further. The pupil, of course, retired in discomfiture. He was fond of playing along with the pupil (generally with the left hand), or singing the melodies and themes, in order to give him ideas of the meaning and interpretation of the music. This gave independence to the pupils, though it often afforded them much amusement.

"With advanced students Pugno spoke much about music and what it could express; he translated themes and passages back into the feelings and emotions which had originated them; he showed how all emotions find their counterpart in tones. 'Above all let kindness and goodness control you,' he once wrote; 'if you are filled with kindness, your tone will be beautiful!'

"Pugno's instruction took the form of talks on the inner meaning of the composition, and the art of interpreting it, rather than any training on the technical side; about the latter he concerned himself very little. It goes with out saying that only talented pupils made progress under such a master; indeed those without talent interested him not at all. He was a wonderful teacher for those who had the insight to read between the lines, and were able to follow and absorb his artistic enthusiasms.

"I have said that Pugno did not concern himself about teaching the technical side of piano playing. Even with me, his best pupil, he rarely touched upon technical points. I must mention a notable exception. He gave me one technical principle, expressed in a few simple exercises, which I have never heard of from any one else. The use of this principle has helped me amazingly to conquer many knotty passages. I have never given these exercises to any one; I am willing however, to jot them down for you." (The following is a brief plan of the exercises, as sketched by Mme. Schnitzer)

"Pugno wished the thirty-seconds and sixty-fourths to be played with the utmost quickness. This idea is not alone applicable to all scales, but can be used with any difficult passage found in a composition.

"Pugno took a keen interest in my work, my progress and career. A few sentences culled here and there from the many letters of his which I have preserved, may serve to throw more light on the inner nature of the man:

"'I have endeavored to make clear to your young mind the thoughts expressed in music, so that your understanding and your emotions also might grow; all this has created a link of gratitude in you and an affection within me. I have opened the windows for you and have given you light, and I have reaped the satisfaction of my sowing.'

"'Hear all the music you can—do not miss any of the pianists either good or bad; there is always something to be learned, even from a poor player—if it is only what to avoid! Study great works, but even in those there are some figures and phrases which need not be brought into the foreground, lest they attain too much significance.'

"(After playing with Hans Richter's Orchestra): 'What intoxication of sound—what exhilaration and collaboration in music! What a force within us, which sways us and throbs through us, developing and expressing each sentiment and instinct! What art can be compared to music, which finds expression through this medium, called an orchestra. I feel myself greater amid the orchestra, for I have a giant to converse with. I keep pace with him, I lead him where I will—I calm him and I embrace him. We supplement each other; in a moment of authority I become his master and subdue him. The piano alone is too small for me; it does not tempt me to play it except under such conditions—with a grand orchestra!'"

ERNEST SCHELLING
[1876-1939]

THE HAND OF A PIANIST

A s I sat in the luxurious salon of the apartments near the Park, where Mr. and Mrs. Ernest Schelling were spending the winter, sounds of vigorous piano practise floated out to me from a distant chamber. It was unusual music, and seemed to harmonize with the somewhat Oriental atmosphere and coloring of the music-room, with its heavily beamed ceiling of old silver, its paintings and tapestries.

The playing ceased and soon the artist appeared, greeting the visitor with genial friendliness of manner. He was accompanied by the "lord of the manor," a beautiful white bull terrier, with coat as white as snow. This important personage at once curled himself up in the most comfortable arm-chair, a quiet, profound observer of all that passed. In the midst of some preliminary chat, the charming hostess entered and poured tea for us.

The talk soon turned upon the subject in which I was deeply interested— the technical training of a pianist.

"Technic is such an individual matter," began Mr. Schelling; "for it depends on so many personal things: the physique, the mentality, the amount of nervous energy one has, the hand and wrist. Perhaps the poorest kind of hand for the piano is the long narrow one, with long fingers. Far better to have a short, broad one with short fingers. Josef Hofmann has a wonderful hand for the piano; rather small, yes, but so thick and muscular. The wrist, too, is a most important factor. Some pianists have what I call a 'natural wrist,' that is they have a natural control of it; it is no trouble for them to play octaves, for instance. Mme. Carreño has that kind of wrist; she never had difficulty with octaves, they are perfect. Hofmann also has a marvelous wrist. I am sorry to say I have not that kind of wrist, and therefore have been much handicapped on that account. For I have had to work tremendously to develop not only the wrist but the whole technic. You see I was a wonder child, and played a great deal as a small boy [he played before the public at age four]. Then from fifteen to twenty I did not practise anything like what I ought to have done. That is the period when the bones grow, muscles develop—everything grows. Another thing against me is the length of my fingers. When the fingers are longer than the width of the hand across the knuckle joint, it is not an advantage but a detriment. The extra length of finger is only so much dead weight that the hand has to lift. This is another disadvantage I have had to work against. Yes, as you say, it is a rather remarkable hand in regard to size and suppleness. But I hardly agree that it is like Liszt's; more like Chopin's, judging from the casts I have seen of his hand.

"As for technical routine, of course I play scales a good deal and in various ways. When I 'go into training,' I find the best means to attain velocity is to work with the metronome. One can't jump at once into the necessary agility, and the metronome is a great help in bringing one up to the right pitch. You see by the firmness of these muscles at the back and thumb side of my hand, that I am in good trim now; but one soon loses this if one lets up on the routine.

"Then I practise trills of all kinds, and octaves. Yes, I agree that octaves are a most necessary and important factor in the player's technical equipment."

Going to the piano and illustrating as he talked, Mr. Schelling continued:

"Merely flopping the hand up and down, as many do, is of little use it does not lead to strength or velocity. As you see, I hold the hand arched and very firm, and the firmness is in the fingers as well; the hand makes up and down movements with loose wrist; the result is a full, bright, crisp tone. One can play these octaves slowly, using weight, or faster with crisp, staccato touch. I play diatonic or chromatic octave scales, with four repetitions or more, on each note using fourth finger for black keys.

"I sit low at the piano, as I get better results in this way; though it is somewhat more difficult to obtain them. I confess it is easier to sit high and bear down on the hands. Yes, I thoroughly approve of 'weight touch,' and it is the touch I generally use. Sometimes it is a certain pressure on the key after it is played, using arm weight.

"Ah, you are right. The young teacher or player, in listening to the artist, and noticing he does not lift his fingers to any extent, and that he always plays with weight, hastily concludes these are the principles with which he must begin to study or teach the piano. It is a mistake to begin in that way. Very exact finger movements must be learned in the beginning. As I said before, technic is such an individual matter, that after the first period of foundational training, one who has the desire to become an artist, must work out things for himself. There should be no straight-laced methods. Only a few general rules can be laid down, such as will fit most cases. The player who would rise to any distinction must work out his own salvation.

"In regard to memorizing piano music, it may be said this can be accomplished in three ways: namely, with the eye, with the ear, and with the hand. For example: I take the piece and read it through with the eye, just as I would read a book. I get familiar with the notes in this way, and see how they look in print. I learn to know them so well that I have a mental photograph of them, and if necessary could recall any special measure or phrase so exactly that I could write it. All this time my mental ear has been hearing those notes, and is familiar with them. Then the third stage arrives; I must put all this on the keyboard, my fingers must have their training; impressions must pass from the mind to the fingers; then all is complete."

WILLIAM H. SHERWOOD

[1854-1911]

HINTS ON INTERPRETATION

While a young student the opportunity came to attend a Summer Music School, founded by this eminent pianist and teacher. He had surrounded himself with others well known for their specialties in voice, violin and diction; but the director himself was the magnet who attracted pianists and teachers from the four corners of the land.

Perhaps the most intimate way to come in touch with a famous teacher, is to study with him during the summer months, in some quiet, retired spot. Here the stress of the metropolis, with its rush and drive, its exacting hours, its remorseless round of lesson giving, is exchanged for the freedom of rural life. Hours may still be exact, but a part of each day, or of each week, is given over to relaxation, to be spent in the open, with friends and pupils.

It was under such conditions that I first met Mr. Sherwood. I had never even heard him play, and was glad the session opened with a piano recital. His playing delighted me; he had both power and delicacy, and his tone impressed me as being especially mellow and fine. There was deep feeling as well as poetry in his reading of both the Chromatic Fantaisie of Bach, and the Chopin Fantaisie in F minor which were on the program. This opinion was strengthened at each subsequent hearing, for he gave frequent recitals and concerts during the season.

My summer study with Mr. Sherwood consisted mainly in gaining ideas on the interpretation of various pieces. Many of these ideas seem to me beautiful and inspiring, and I will set them down as fully as I can from the brief notes jotted down at the time. I trust I may be pardoned a few personal references, which are sometimes necessary to explain the situation.

With advanced students Mr. Sherwood gave great attention to tone study and interpretation, even from the first lesson. He laid much stress on the use of slow, gentle motions in practise and in playing; on the spiritualization of the tones, of getting behind the notes to find the composer's meaning. He had, perhaps, a more poetic conception of piano playing than any master I have known, and was able to impart these ideas in clear and simple language.

The first composition considered was Schumann's Nachtstück, the fourth of the set. He had a peculiar way of turning the hand on the middle finger, as on a pivot, for the extended chords, at the same time raising the whole outer side of the hand, so that the fifth finger should be able to play the upper melody notes round and full. In the middle section he desired great tenderness and sweetness of tone. "There are several dissonances in this part," he said, "and they ought to be somewhat accented—suspensions I might call them. In Bach and Handel's time, the rules of composition were very strict—no suspensions were allowed; so they were indicated where it was not permitted to write them."

Chopin's etude in sixths came up for analysis. "This study needs a very easy, quiet, limpid touch—the motions all gliding and sliding rather than pushing and forceful. I would advise playing it at first *pianissimo*; the wrist held rather low, the knuckles somewhat high, and the fingers straightened. In preparation for each pair of notes raise the fingers and let them down— not with a hard brittle touch, if I may use the word, but with a soft, velvety one. A composition like this needs to be idealized, spiritualized, taken out of everyday life. Take, for instance, the Impromptu Op. 36, Chopin; the first part of it is something like this etude, soft, undulating—smooth as oil. There is something very uncommon, spiritual, heavenly, about the first page of that Impromptu—very little of the earth, earthy. The second page is in sharp contrast to the first, it comes right down to the hard, everyday business of life—it is full of harsh, sharp tones. Well, the idea of that first page we get in this study in sixths. I don't want the bare tones that stand there on the printed page; I want them spiritualized—that is what reveals the artist. In the left hand the first note should have a clear, brittle accent, with firm fifth finger, and the double sixths played with the creeping, clinging movement I have indicated. If I should practise this etude for half an hour, you might be surprised at the effects I could produce. Perhaps it might take ten hours, but in the end I am confident I could produce this floating, undulating effect. I heard Liszt play nearly all these etudes at one time; I stood by and turned the pages. In this etude he doubled the number of sixths in each measure; the effect was wonderful and beautiful.

"The Chopin Octave study, number 22, needs firm, quiet touch, elevating the wrist for black keys (as Kullak explains) and depressing it for white keys. The hand must be well arched, the end fingers firm and strong, and the touch very pressing, clinging, and grasping. You always want to cling whenever there is any chance for clinging in piano playing. The second part of this etude should have a soft, flowing, poetic touch in the right hand, while the left hand part is well brought out. The thumb needs a special training to enable it to creep and slide from one key to another with snake-like movements.

"Rubinstein's Barcarolle in G major. The thirds on the first page are very soft and gentle. I make a good deal of extra motion with these thirds, raising the fingers quite high and letting them fall gently on the keys. The idea of the first page of this barcarolle is one of utter quietness, colorlessness; one is alone on the water; the evening is quiet and still; not a sound breaks the hushed silence. The delicate tracery of thirds should be very soft, thin—like an airy cloud. The left hand is soft too, but the first beat should be slightly accented, the second not; the first is positive, the second negative. Herein lies the idea of the barcarolle, the ebb and flow, the undulation of each measure.

"Begin the first measure very softly, the second measure a trifle louder, the third louder still, the fourth falling off again. As you stand on the shore and watch the great waves coming in, you see some that are higher and larger than others; so it is here. The concluding passage in sixths should diminish—like a little puff of vapor that ends in—nothing. On the second page we come upon something more positive; here is a tangible voice speaking to us. The melody should stand out clear, broad, beautiful; the accompanying chords should preserve the same ebb and flow, the advancing and receding wave-like movement. The exaggerated movement I spoke of a moment ago, I use in many ways. Any one can hit the piano, with a sharp, incisive touch; but what I refer to is the reaching out of the fingers for the notes, the passing of the hand in the air and the final gentle fall on the key, not in haste to get there, but with confidence of reaching the key in time. If you throw a stone up in the air it will presently fall back again with a sharp thud; a bird rising, hovers a moment and descends gently. This barcarolle is not at all easy; there is plenty of work in it for flexible hands; it is a study in *pianissimo*—in power controlled, held back, restrained."

Taking up the Toccatina of Rheinberger, Mr. Sherwood said: "I like this piece, there is good honest work in it; it is very effective, and most excellent practise. You ought to play this every day of the year. It is written in twelve-eighths, which give four beats to the measure, but I think that gives it too hard and square a character. I would divide each measure into two parts and slightly accent each. Though your temperament is more at home in the music of Chopin and Schumann, I recommend especially music of this sort, and also the music of Bach; these give solidity and strength to your conception of musical ideas."

We went through the Raff Suite, Op. 91. "The Preludio is very good," he said; "I like it. The Menuetto is, musically, the least strong of any of the numbers, but it has a certain elegance, and is the most popular of them all. The Romanza is a great favorite of mine, it is very graceful, flowing and melodious. The concluding Fugue is a fine number; you see how the theme is carried from one hand to the other, all twisted about, in a way old Bach and Handel never thought of doing. I consider this Raff fugue one of the best examples of modern fugue writing."

Mr. Sherwood was fond of giving students the Josef Wieniawski Valse, for brilliancy. "There are many fine effects which can be made in this piece; one can take liberties with it—the more imagination you have the better it will go. I might call it a *stylish* piece; take the Prelude as capriciously as you like; put all the effect you can into it. The Valse proper begins in a very pompous style, with right hand very staccato; all is exceedingly coquettish. On the fifth page you see it is marked *amoroso*, but after eight measures the young man gives the whole thing away to his father! The beginning of the sixth page is very piano and light—it is nothing more than a breath of smoke, an airy nothing. But at the *poco piu lento*, there is an undercurrent of reality; the two parts are going at the same time—the hard, earthly part, with accents, and the spiritual, thin as air. To realize these qualities in playing is the very idealization of technic."

The Chopin-Liszt Maiden's Wish, was next considered. "The theme here is often overlaid and encrusted with the delicate lace-like arabesques that seek to hide it; but it must be found and brought out. There is so much in being able to find what is hidden behind the notes. You must get an insight into the inner idea; must feel it. This is not technic, not method even; it is the spiritualization of playing. There are pieces that will sound well if the notes only are played, like the little F minor Moment Musicale of Schubert; yet even in this there is much behind the notes, which, if brought out, will make quite another thing of the piece.

"Schumann's Andante, for two pianos, should have a very tender, caressing touch for the theme. The place where the four-sixteenths occur, which make rather a square effect, can be softened down. On the second page, be sure and do not accent the grace notes; let the accent come on the fifth finger every time. For the variation containing chords, use the grasping touch, which might be described as a certain indrawing of force in the end of the finger, as though taking a long breath. The variation in triplets seems at first sight almost a caricature, a burlesque on the theme, but I don't think that Schumann had any such idea. On the contrary he meant it as a very sweet, gentle, loving thought. The last page has something ethereal, ideal about it; it should be breathed out, growing fainter and fainter to the end.

"The G minor Ballade, of Chopin, begins slowly, with much dignity. The opening melody is one of sadness, almost gloom. The *à tempo* on second page contains four parts going on at the same time. At the *piu forte*, care must be taken to have the outer side of the hand well raised, and moved from the wrist. The idea here is one of great agitation and unrest. The fifth page needs great power and the legato octaves well connected and sustained. The feeling of unrest is here augmented until it becomes almost painful, and not until the *animato* does a restful feeling come. This should be played lightly and delicately, the left hand giving the rhythm. The presto demands great power and dash. Let the wrist be low when beginning the chords, raise it after the first and let it fall after the second. Always accent the second chord. Begin the final double runs slowly and increase in speed and tone. So, too, with the octaves, begin slowly and increase in power and fire."

Numerous other compositions were analyzed, but the ones already quoted stand out in memory, and give some idea of Mr. Sherwood's manner of teaching.

SIGISMOND STOJOWSKI
[1869-1946]

MIND IN PIANO STUDY

M r. Sigismond Stojowski, the eminent Polish pianist and composer, was found one morning in his New York studio [at 249 West 74th Street], at work with a gifted pupil. He was willing to relax a little, however, and have a chat on such themes as might prove helpful to both teacher and student.

"You ask me to say something on the most salient points in piano technic; perhaps we should say, the points that are most important to each individual; for no two students are exactly alike, nor do any two see things in precisely the same light. This is really a psychological matter. I believe the subject of psychology is a very necessary study for both teacher and student. We all need to know more about mental processes than we do. I am often asked how to memorize, for instance—or the best means for doing this, another psychological process. I recommend students to read William James' *Talks on Psychology*; a very helpful book.

"The most vital thing in piano playing is to learn to think. Has it ever occurred to you what infinite pains people will take to avoid thinking? They will repeat a technical illustration hundreds of times it may be, but with little or no thought directed to the performance. Such work is absolutely useless. Perhaps that is a little too strong. With countless repetitions there may at last come to be a little improvement, but it will be very small.

"There is quite a variety of views as to what the essentials of piano technic are; this is a subject on which teachers, unluckily, do not agree. For instance, on the point of finger lifting there is great diversity of opinion. Some believe in raising the fingers very high, others do not. Lifting the fingers high is not good for the tone, though it may be used for velocity playing. I use quite the reverse where I wish beautiful, singing, tone quality. The young pupil, at the beginning, must of course learn to raise fingers and make precise movements; when greater proficiency is reached, many modifications of touch are used. That the best results are not more often obtained in piano teaching and study, is as much the fault of the teacher as the pupil. The latter is usually willing to be shown and anxious to learn. It is for the teacher to correctly diagnose the case and administer the most efficient remedy.

Natural Technic

"There is a certain amount of what I might call 'natural technic' possessed by every one—some one point which is easy for him. It is often the trill. It has frequently come under my notice that players with little facility in other ways, can make a good trill. Some singers have this gift; Mme. Melba is one who never had to study a trill, for she was born with a nightingale in her throat. I knew a young man in London who was evidently born with an aptitude for octaves. He had wonderful wrists, and could make countless repetitions of the octave without the least fatigue. He never had to practise octaves, they came to him naturally.

"The teacher's work is both corrective and constructive. He must see what is wrong and be able to correct it. Like a physician, he should find the weak and deficient parts and build them up. He should have some remedy at his command that will fit the needs of each pupil.

"I give very few etudes, and those I administer in homeopathic doses. It is not necessary to play through a mass of etudes to become a good pianist. Much of the necessary technic may be learned from the pieces themselves, though scales and arpeggios must form part of the daily routine.

Keeping up a Repertoire

"In keeping a large number of pieces in mind, I may say that the pianist who does much teaching is in a sense taught by his pupils. I have many advanced pupils, and in teaching their repertoire I keep up my own. Of course after a while one grows a little weary of hearing the same pieces rendered by students; the most beautiful no longer seem fresh. My own compositions are generally exceptions, as I do not often teach those. To the thoughtful teacher, the constant hearing of his repertoire by students shows him the difficulties that younger players have to encounter, and helps him devise means to aid them to conquer these obstacles. At the same time there is this disadvantage: the pianist cannot fail to remember the places at which such and such a student had trouble, forgot or stumbled. This has happened to me at various times. In my recitals I would be playing ahead, quite unconscious that anything untoward could occur—wholly absorbed in my work; when, at a certain point, the recollection would flash over me this is where such or such a pupil stumbled. The remembrance is sometimes so vivid that I am at some effort to keep my mental balance and proceed with smoothness and certainty.

"Yes, I go over my pieces mentally, especially if I am playing an entirely new program which I have never played before; otherwise I do not need to do so much of it.

Filling in a Passage

"You suggest that a composer may fill in or make up a passage, should he forget a portion of the piece when playing in public. True; but improvising on a well-known work is rather a dangerous thing to do in order to improve a bad case. Apropos of this, I am reminded of an incident which occurred at one of my European recitals. It was a wholly new program which I was to give at Vevay. I had been staying with Paderewski, and went from Morges to Vevay, to give the recital. In my room at the hotel I was mentally reviewing the program, when in a Mendelssohn Fugue, I found I had forgotten a small portion. I could remember what went before and what came after, but this particular passage had seemingly gone. I went down to the little parlor and tried the fugue on the piano, could not remember the portion in question. I hastened back to my room and constructed a bridge which should connect the two parts. When the time came to play the fugue at the recital, it all went smoothly till I was well over the weak spot, which, it seems, I really played as Mendelssohn wrote it. As I neared the last page, the question suddenly occurred to me, what had I done with that doubtful passage? What had really happened I could not remember; and the effort to recall whether I had played Mendelssohn or Stojowski nearly brought disaster to that last page.

"As soon as my season closes here I shall go to London and bring out my second piano concerto with the London Symphony Orchestra, under Nikisch. I shall also play various recitals."

It was my good fortune to be present at the orchestral concert at Queen's Hall, when Mr. Stojowski was the soloist. It was pleasant to see the enthusiasm aroused by the concerto itself, and the performance of it by the artist.

BERTHA FIERING TAPPER
[1859-1915]

MASTERING PIANISTIC PROBLEMS

I f environment and atmosphere are inspirational aids to piano teaching and playing, the students of Mrs. Thomas Tapper have the incentives of both in their lesson hours. Her apartments on the Drive have the glory of sunlight all the long afternoons [362 Riverside Drive]. Outside the Hudson shimmers in blue and gold; indoors all is harmonious and home-like. In the large music-room, facing the river, two grand pianos stand side by side; there are many portraits and mementoes of the great in music; fresh flowers, books—everything to uplift thought; while in the midst of it all is Mrs. Tapper herself, the serious, high-minded, inspiring teacher; the "mother confessor" to a large number of young artists and teachers.

"Music study means so much more than merely exercising the fingers," she said; "the student should have a good all-round education. When young people come to me for instruction, I ask what they are doing in school. If they say they have left school in order to devote their whole time to the piano, I say, 'Go back to your school, and come to me later, when you have finished your school course.' It is true that in rare cases it may be advisable for the student to leave school, but he should then pursue general or special studies at home. I often wish the music student's education in this country could be arranged as it is in at least one of the great music schools in Russia. There the mornings are given to music, while general studies are taken up later in the day. It is really a serious problem, here in America, this fitting in music with other studies. Both public and private schools try to cover so much ground that there is very little time left for music or anything else. The music pupil also needs to know musical literature, history and biography, to be familiar with the lives and writings of the great composers. Take the letters and literary articles of Robert Schumann, for instance. How interesting and inspiring they are!

"In regard to methods in piano study my principles are based wholly upon my observations of Leschetizky's work with me personally, or with others. What I know he has taught me; what I have achieved I owe to him. My first eight weeks in Vienna were spent in learning, first, to control position and condition of hands and arms according to the law of balance; secondly, to direct each motion with the utmost accuracy and speed. To accomplish this I began with the most elementary exercises in five-finger position, using one finger at a time. Then came the principles of the scale, arpeggios, chords and octaves. All these things were continued until every principle was mastered. I practised at first an hour a day, then increased the amount as my hands grew stronger and the number of exercises increased.

"Next came the study of tone production in various forms, a good quality invariably being the result of a free condition of the arm combined with strength of fingers and hands.

"The Leschetizky principles seem to me the most perfect and correct in every particular. Yes, there are several books of the method, by different authors, but I teach the principles without a book. The principles themselves are the essential things. I aim to build up the hand, to make it strong and dependable in every part, to fill out the weak places and equalize it. That this may be thoroughly and successfully accomplished, I require that nothing but technical exercises be used for the first nine, ten, or twelve weeks. We begin with the simplest exercises, one finger at a time, then two, three and so on through the hand. I believe in thus devoting all the practise time to technic, for a certain period, so that the mind is free to master the principles, undisturbed by piece playing. When the principles have been assimilated, the attention can then be directed to the study of music itself. If any weak places appear in the hand from time to time, they can be easily corrected.

"If a pupil comes to me who has played a great deal but with no idea of the principles of piano playing, who does not know how to handle herself or the keyboard, it is absolutely necessary to stop everything and get ready to play. If you attempt even a simple sonata with no legato touch, no idea of chord or scale playing, you can not make the piece sound like anything. It is like a painter trying to paint without brushes, or an artist attempting to make a pen and ink drawing with a blunt lead pencil; to do good work you must have the tools to work with.

"For application of all principles, the studies of Czerny, Op. 299, 740, and others, offer unequaled opportunity. They are simple, direct, and give the student a chance for undivided attention to every position taken and to every motion made.

"What happens afterward is altogether according to the individual characteristics of the student. How to recognize these and deal with them to the best advantage is the interesting task of my great master (and those who try to follow in his steps)—the man of keenest intelligence, of profound learning and experience. To learn this lesson from him has been my greatest aim, and to see him at work, as it has been my privilege to do for several summers, has been of the greatest influence and inspiration in my own work. "My chief endeavor is to create a desire for good musicianship. To this end I insist upon the study of theory, harmony, ear-training and analysis. In the piano lessons I do not have sufficient time to teach these things. I have assistant teachers who help me with these subjects and also with the technical training. Once a month during the season, my assistant teachers bring their pupils to play for me, and we have a class in piano teaching. There are sometimes eighteen or twenty students who come to a class, I can in this way supervise all the work done, and keep in touch with my teachers, their work, and with all the students.

"On the first Saturday of the month I have my own pupils here for a class; they play for me and for each other. Everything is played from memory, not a printed note is used. Students tell me it is very difficult to play here, where all listen so intently. Especially is it difficult the first time a student plays in class, to keep the mind wholly on what he is doing, with sufficient concentration. Later on, at the end of the season, it comes easier.

"This idea of separating the technical work at the outset from the study of music itself, secures, in my opinion, the most perfect foundation, and later on the best results. It is sometimes wonderful how, with proper training, the hand will improve and develop in a comparatively short time. I often marvel at it myself."

The writer had the privilege of being one of the guests at the last audition of the season. Eight or nine young artists played a long and difficult program. Among the numbers were a Beethoven sonata, entire; Chopin's Ballade in A flat major; Cesar Franck, Prelude, Fugue and Variations; a Mozart Fantaisie; Grieg Concerto, first movement; Weber's Concertstück, and Chopin's Scherzo in E. The recital was most instructive from an educational point of view. All the players had repose and concentration, and there were no noticeable slips, though every piece was played from memory. Hands were well arched at the knuckles, fingers curved—with adequate action at the knuckle joint; wrists in normal position, and extremely loose; the whole arm swung from the shoulder and poised over the keys, thus adjusting itself to every requirement of the composition. Every note had its amount of hand or arm weight. The tone quality was full and singing. These points were exemplified even in the playing of the youngest pupils. Furthermore they had an intelligent grasp of the meaning of the music they played, and brought it out with conviction, power, and brilliancy.

Interviews

from

Piano Mastery, Second Series
1917

MRS. H. H. A. [Amy Marcy Cheney] BEACH
[1867-1944]

HOW A COMPOSER WORKS

Our American-born artist, Mrs. H. H. A. Beach, is both a composer of high rank and a pianist of distinction.

As a player, one critic has said: "She has many of those rare elements that conspire to make the true pianist. We have seldom heard delicacy and force, a poetic interpretation and a prosaic vigor so well combined. Grace, intelligence and sympathy are chief characteristics of her playing."

After years of quiet study and home life in Boston, followed more recently by a lengthy sojourn in Europe, Mrs. Beach, again at home, has emerged somewhat from her seclusion, and is now bringing the message of her own music to the many who are eager to hear it. Thus she is becoming personally known through her interpretative recitals and her very characteristic rendering of her compositions.

As a composer Mrs. Beach is known and loved over the length and breadth of the land, for her many beautiful songs and piano pieces. Those who are familiar with such gems as *Ecstasy*, *The Year's at the Spring*, *June*, and many others may not know that the composer has written in the larger forms. Her Gaelic Symphony has been played a number of times by the Boston Symphony Orchestra, and also by the symphony orchestras of many other cities. It has lately met with an enthusiastic reception in Philadelphia, under the baton of Stokowski. Her piano Quintet, Mass in E-flat, Sonata for piano and violin, and her choral works attest the variety and scope of her creative activities.

Dr. Percy Goetschius says of Mrs. Beach, the composer:

"She writes both like a man and a woman. Her music manifests traits of a delicacy and tenderness scarcely attainable by a masculine nature, and masculine traits as genuine and virile as any man could exhibit." If a recital of her works could be given without her name being attached, "those accustomed to proclaim the superiority of the male composer would possibly, without exception, fail to suspect they were listening to the artistic creations of a woman."

It had long been my desire to come into personal touch with this rare individuality. My desire was realized when I was privileged to visit her apartments in the heart of old New York, which she has made her headquarters for the past two months. Who could help feeling at home in the presence of this cheery little lady, with her cordial handclasp, her genial manner, her clear blue eyes and sunny smile? The moments flew all too quickly as she spoke of her work as pianist and composer.

"Really, I cannot remember when I did not play the piano and compose. I know I was doing both at the age of four. I improvised little melodies then, but did not know how to write them down.

"My first piano teacher was my mother, with whom I studied for a number of years, until she felt I might be benefited by a change, when I was placed under well-known masters. I played with the Boston Symphony Orchestra, under Theodore Thomas, when I was still in short dresses, with my hair in a pigtail. I have kept up my piano work, and always expect to do so. When I am not playing I am composing, and vice versa. I do them both interchangeably and constantly, but not both at the same time. This keeps me fresh for each one.

I am a dual personality and lead a double musical life.

"I have naturally a very flexible hand, which does not become stiff if practice is relaxed for a bit. Then I am old-fashioned enough to believe in scales and exercises. I like to give an hour a day to these whenever possible. I do them on this little dumb keyboard, this small black case, which serves my purpose on trains and in hotels. At home in Boston I use the Virgil clavier, and thoroughly enjoy working on it. People are so fond of saying a soundless keyboard is mechanical; is it any less mechanical to do your technical work on a keyboard with tone? The exercises are the same. Should we not wish to save the wear and tear on our ears! My hearing is extremely sensitive, and I want to save it all I can. I often learn my pieces and all difficult passages on the clavier. It is a good idea to learn the Debussy Toccata on the clavier. Did you ever try to practice this piece slowly on the piano? The discords are so distressing they fairly hurt. The clavier came to my relief in this instance, I don't believe I ever could have learned the piece if I had done it all on the piano.

"As for practice material, I use the Rosenthal Technics. There are several books of these, and I have found them excellent. Then, of course, I invent a good many exercises of my own."

"Can you tell me something about your work in composition—how you do it; or is that too difficult a question?"

Mrs. Beach's eyes twinkled.

"It would be very difficult to tell *how* I do it, but I can tell you *where*; always in the open, if possible. I like to sit out of doors, I want to be in the midst of nature when I write. If it is cold or bad weather when I write I try to have a room with wide windows, or a balcony.

"I cannot write unless I am in the mood, or have the inspiration. I cannot say to myself, 'I will compose three hours a day.' That would reduce the work to mere mechanism, without the divine spark. A theme or subject often rests in my mind for months or a year before I put it on paper. I always compose away from the piano—unless it be an accompaniment that I want to try with the voice part, then I sometimes take it to the piano, to see what changes are needed.

"The subject for the Fugue which I played at my recent concert was in my thought for over a year before I ever jotted it down. I was in Switzerland at the time. We had gone to Meran. It was about this time last year. From my windows could be seen the whole range of snow-capped mountain peaks; the sight was truly enough to inspire one. I felt moved to put down the general plan of the Fugue on paper. A correct copy of the Fugue has not yet been made. This leaves me free to makes changes whenever I wish. Sometimes a new idea occurs to me when I am playing in public; I use it then and there. The Prelude to this Fugue was actually composed at the piano: I wanted to give it the character of an improvization, and think I have succeeded.

"The first draft of a composition is so fragmentary that it looks almost like shorthand. I can hardly write my thoughts down fast enough, and don't take time to make everything clear. For instance, if I have a chromatic run, I put the first note and the last, and draw a line between them, for I can't stop to write all those accidentals. I know what the signs mean, though others might not.

"Although I like to let an idea rest quietly in mind for a long time, so that I can live with it before I put it on paper, yet sometimes I write it down at once, while I am in the mood.

"Mr. Stoddard, the poet, once sent me, through a friend, a few verses, wondering if I could do anything with them. They arrived in the morning mail. I read them; they suggested a musical setting. I began to work; and by twelve the song lay finished on my desk.

"I have spent the last three years in Europe, mostly in Munich, and have done much writing, besides a good deal of concert work. When Miss Kitty Cheatham came to Munich and gave a recital, she asked me to do some things for her. I had so much work on hand that I could not think of it then, but told her when the right moment came I would see what I could do. Months afterward a little volume of verses was sent me. I glanced through them, and felt that here were just the things for Miss Cheatham. I wrote quite a set of these little songs, and it gave me such pleasure to do them.

Character of the Composition

"I do not sit down, as some imagine I do, and say: 'Now I will write a concerto, a fugue, or some large work.' The character of that composition depends entirely on how the subject works up, whether it becomes a small form or grows into a larger work. I love to work in the large forms, they are just as easy if not easier for me than the small ones.

"Do not imagine, because the large forms come easier to me now, that I have not studied very seriously. I worked very hard for years. At the start I had one season with Junius Hill, in Boston, but everything beyond that has been my own labor. I possess about every treatise that has ever been written on the subject of harmony, theory, counterpoint, double counterpoint, fugue and instrumentation. I have a large library of these books. I have a good knowledge of French and German, and have made exhaustive studies of works in these languages. I can repeat whole chapters from Berlioz' delightful book on instrumentation.

"In studying Bach I memorized a large number of fugues from the Well-Tempered Clavichord, not for the mere sake of committing them, but because I had made such a careful study of them. I wrote many of them out in score, in order to find exactly how they were constructed, and how the voices were led. I could write out the parts from memory, so thoroughly did I know them.

"In the study of instrumentation, the orchestra was my teacher; I was a close student of it. For obvious reasons it is difficult for a woman to become familiar with all instruments in use. Some of the largest she cannot play; in any event it is not practical to take lessons on them all. But the orchestral composer must know the various voices of the orchestra. Thus I made a deep study of the band in action. I always had the score with me, and learned to know each voice as intimately as I know the voices of my own family. I wrote out scores of Beethoven from memory, and then would take my work next day and compare it with the playing of the orchestra. In this way I learned whole movements from symphonies by heart. Thus I feel that the knowledge I have acquired has been by my own effort; and what I compose is a part of myself."

To quote another sentence from Dr. Goetchius:

"The development of her very uncommon talent for composition has been almost wholly achieved by her own effort—unaided but also unbiased. In consequence of this somewhat unique fact, she has succeeded in preserving her individuality to a rare degree. What she gives is peculiarly herself."

The Gaelic Symphony will probably be heard in New York next season and we also hope to become more familiar with other works of this composer in the larger forms.

LEOPOLD GODOWSKY

[1870-1938]

THE LAWS GOVERNING TECHNIC AND INTERPRETATION

Y EARS ago, when Leopold Godowsky was a resident of America—
or was it when he was making his first tour here?—I remember
vividly on one occasion studying his pianistic work from a position
of vantage almost directly over the piano, when he played with the orchestra
under Theodore Thomas. I noted many things about his playing then, besides
the ease, fluency and dynamic effects, which belong, of course, to every
pianist's equipment. One of the principal points which struck me was the
absolute precision with which everything was accomplished. Chords
especially were prepared through the fingers taking form—in the air—of
the arrangement of keys and intervals, and then descending on the group, or
gripping them, as the case demanded. That is to say, the fingers and hand
were prepared and made ready for the chord before it was played, so that
each tone had its place and value in the chord group. Single tones were also
prepared and fingers made ready to take the key before the arm descended;
arms and hands were slanted for scales and arpeggios; all was clean-cut,
exact and well articulated.

Technical Difficulties Unknown

Since those days the pianist has, through constant study and effort of thought,
risen to a more exalted height. Technical mastery and perfection, such as
few possess, have been won. Technical difficulties do not exist for him. All
gradations of tone, from powerful crescendi to fine-spun *pianissimi* of
gossamer delicacy, are alike delivered without trace of effort. There can be
no question about the consummate perfection which molds and permeates
everything he touches.

"The deep things of our art," says the master, "are little understood by
general students of the piano. The great artist is an autocrat, a monarch; his
work can only make appeal to the few; they alone can understand. That this
should be so lies in the character of the instrument and its music. The piano
is a marvel, perhaps the greatest instrument we have. It is so intimate, yet so
impersonal. The singer must be supplemented by an accompanist, and can
only sing one note at a time. The violinist can at best play but two notes at a

time and he also must be assisted. The pianist, on the other hand, comes unaided before his audience; he alone must speak, for he has the field to himself. He must make clear his meaning on a more or less responsive medium of wood and metal; he must revivify the signs and symbols which are to paint the mood or picture. He must translate thought and feeling into tones; he must express what is subtle and deep, yet too intangible to put into words. Where language ends music begins.

"Among those who play the piano, we have almost every variety of exposition. There are some whose deep learning leads them to be philosophers; others feel called to be preachers of their art. Then we have the refined poets, the dramatic players, the *causseurs*, the entertainers, or those who have such high animal spirits that they exemplify a wild pony galloping over the plains." The speaker mentioned examples of each of these varieties among the artists now before the public.

Variety of Treatment and Aims

"We need to consider what a man is aiming at before we judge him. A *causseur* cannot measure up to the standard of the philosopher, yet he may be most excellent in his line. It is seen that comparisons are not possible. It is futile to ask, 'Who is the greatest?' as is so often done. The public does not understand these distinctions; therefore, as I said, the truly great artist speaks to the few who can understand. This condition will doubtless exist for hundreds of years to come. And when, eventually, the masses do understand, the artist must also advance, so as to be always to the fore, always above the rest, to uplift others, for his calling is a very high one.

Piano Methods

"As to so-called piano methods I feel it necessary to look deeper than method in order to find the underlying principles. Perhaps the most important principle of all—one that I have been elucidating for many years—is relaxation. This is not the same as devitalization, which, if used indiscriminately and to excess, is very detrimental. Relaxed weight on the key differs from the old pressure touch, which tended to stiffen muscles and make the touch rigid. The finger rests with easy arm weight on the key. If more power is desired use more weight, if less hold back some of the weight.

Finger Action

"You ask if I approve of finger action, and finger lifting? We must have that; we cannot throw it away. Wide, free movements are necessary to develop the fingers, to stretch the skin and flesh between them, to render the hand and its playing members supple and flexible. So we must be able to raise the fingers and move them freely."

"You refer to the early stages of piano study?"

"Not only during the early stages, but at any time. I consider these large, free movements and decided action of fingers as a necessary kind of gymnastics. Just as one exercises the body with all sorts of gymnastics, so we need well-articulated finger movements. I make a distinction, however, between the mechanics of piano study and the art of piano technic. To the former belong all forms of hand culture, finger training and gymnastic exercises. To the latter all the finer qualities of touch, tone, fingering, phrasing, pedaling, agogics and nuance. Each one of these technical divisions is an art in itself.

"When these are thoughtfully considered, as being necessary for the equipment of the player, it is easily seen why there are so few really great artists among the many who come before the public as pianists. For it is a comparatively easy thing to learn how keys are manipulated, to attain speed, be able to make a crescendo here, a diminuendo there, to accent, to copy more or less perfectly the notes and marks in a composition. Almost any one can do these things with sufficient study. But these things do not make an artist—far from it. An artist worthy the name is only evolved after minute and exhaustive study added to musical gifts of high order.

"There have been musicians, like Liszt and Rubinstein, who were so gifted that the lack of exact knowledge did not prevent them from winning the world. Rubinstein was a child of impulse as well as genius; he never did things twice the same way; he relied on the inspiration of the moment, and one might say the same of Liszt. The art of piano playing has developed into a more exact science since their day.

Art of Phrasing

"Among the things I have mentioned as belonging to the art of technic, we will speak first of phrasing. The question of phrasing is of exceeding importance, for phrasing itself is a great art. At the present time we know so much more about these things than was known even fifty years ago. Formerly composers put few marks on their music; there was little or no punctuation. Look at Rubinstein's compositions, for instance. It may be said that von Bülow was one of the first to formulate the laws of phrasing. Christiani's book on this subject is an interesting study, also one by Mathais Lussy. Perhaps the best book on music itself and its performance, at least the best I have ever seen, is by Adolph Kullak, a brother of Theodore Kullak. This is a learned and exhaustive work. The earlier edition has been translated into English; the revised edition is still, I believe, in the original German.

"In the matter of phrasing, Beethoven was considered very particular, Chopin also, but neither knew as much about the subject as we do now; Von Bülow did a great work in editing and phrasing Beethoven. Yet Klindworth, who also edited the master, is perhaps subtler in his readings. You remember that von Bülow himself gave preference to Klindworth's over his own edition, by advising students to use that of his friend. Of Klindworth's work for Chopin I cannot speak so highly. He has changed so many things from the original that it is not always clear just what the composer really meant. What Klindworth should have done in many cases was to put the changes in footnotes and leave the music of the original as it was written.

Art of Fingering

"Another branch of piano technic is fingering, also a fine art. Before Bach's time, as we all know, the thumb was not used at all. When he advised its use, it was not to be employed on the black keys. Fingering, like everything else in piano playing, has been an evolution. Even the fingering of the C scale, which seems so natural, was not known until Dussek thought of it. Chopin made great use of thumb on black keys. Von Bülow believed in much changing of fingers in order to make use of all. So did Klindworth. They evidently desired to make things difficult instead of easy. It can readily be seen that the use of thumb on black keys must throw the hand out of position, tend to make the movement jerky, and force the hand nearer the nameboard, where leverage is heavier. I believe in avoiding the use of thumb on black keys when possible, in order to keep the hand in a more natural position; this idea seems to me easier and more logical.

Subjective and Objective

"We hear much talk of subjective and objective in musical interpretation. These terms are apt to be misleading. Pianists look at the subject from different viewpoints, according to their temperaments and aims. The impulsive nature takes the composition as it first appears to him, without further analysis, and strives to preserve that conception. He trusts to the present moment to furnish inspiration. Under extremely favorable circumstances he may be able to give a really inspired performance. Without these conditions his utterances may lack all glow and power. Rubinstein was an illustration of this style.

"On the other hand, the careful analytical player, who does not trust to first impressions, who studies every point and determines beforehand exactly how he will render the composition may lack true inspiration and leave us cold. Von Bülow might be cited as a player of this type. The ideal interpreter is one who, keeping before him the first ideal, has thought out every effect and nuance he wishes to make, yet leaves himself mentally untrammeled, to be moved by the inspiration which may come to him during performance.

Tone Color and Agogics

"These subjects are vitally important in piano playing. What dynamics are to the tone, agogics are to time and rhythm; this is the new term for the old one of *tempo rubato*. Rubato means "robbed," which is again misleading, for it says nothing about *giving*. If we take away, we must return, to even things up; the new term expresses this better than the old.

"In order to have every note, every phrase clear, we must not run them all together, as the Germans sometimes make a long combined word extend across the page. If you open an English book you see each work separated from its neighbor by a slight space. Just so we learn to make the musical thought or phrase clear by the way we make it stand in relation to other phrases; the right distance between them; it is the flexibility of rhythm, one might say, where everything is in artistic relation and balance."

Legato Melody Playing

"Do you consider a legato melody is just as successfully connected with the pedal as with the fingers?" he was asked.

"By no means," was the quick reply; "though it can be used for special effects. The relaxed weight of hand on the key, the transference of weight from finger to finger, the condition of the hand in connecting a legato melody is very different from that of the hand lifted between each note; the tone has a different quality also. If a passage is marked legato, I insist on its being played with that touch. If chords are written in quarter, half or whole notes, I want them held in full time. One thing is unendurable—to hear the left hand before the right, constantly appoggiating. For real appoggiated chords, if the waved line only extends the length of each chord, both hands are played simultaneously. If one long waved line connects the two chords, the left hand plays first, followed by the right.

The Progressive Series

"*The Progressive Series of Piano Lessons*, with which I have been occupied for a number of years, in conjunction with a number of well-known artists, provides an eight-year course for teachers. Besides this there are, in conclusion, a resume of the entire subject, the pith of the whole matter.

Although the courses are nominally finished, I have about six years more work on compositions to be used with them."

On a subsequent occasion Mr. Godowsky was seen just before leaving for a Pacific Coast tour. We were soon in animated discussion, which lasted for an hour and would have extended much longer had not time pressed. Mr. Godowsky is a thorough master of English and expressed himself with fluency and exactness.

As we had discussed the technical problems of piano playing during a previous conference, I requested the pianist to go further and give his ideas on interpretation.

"One of the means, or perhaps it should be said the backbone, of interpretation is technic. I place technic on a higher plane than mechanism. Others combine the two; I differentiate between them. Technic is the means of expression, the medium through which we give out the music. I believe that each pianist presents a certain mental type, which is revealed through his performance; one is a poet, another a philosopher, a third an orator or even a stump orator, and so on. For some it is possible to express what they feel; others are more reticent, and not given to showing emotion; they rather repress it and seem to stand aloof. Some are ready to reveal everything; they are the ones who are popular with the public. We do not say of these players that they 'descend to the public,' for they merely work out their natural temperament; they are *one with the public,* therefore they never fail to please. Those who have the highest ideals move in a realm apart; they never become popular in the above sense. Men who have made the greatest scientific discoveries are generally unknown to the world.

Factors of Interpretation

"The two great factors in interpretation are Logic and Proportion. If you examine a Greek statue you find it perfect in classic form and line. Its proportions are faultless. Among the composers the most perfect examples of proportion are Beethoven and Brahms. They are the Greeks of musical art.

"These two qualities—logic and proportion —must dominate the thought of the interpreter also—he must express them in his work. In just the degree that he lacks them will his performance fall short of beauty and expressiveness.

"Some players might be called pianists of the piano. The instrument itself is paramount with them rather than the music. The piano itself stands first with them. They will make all possible effects that are legitimate within the scope of the instrument, but never strive to make it something it is not. De Pachmann, Grunfeld and Sauer are of this type. Busoni, on the other hand, does not entertain this view. He is so great, such a deep, profound thinker, such a philosopher; he is a class by himself. For him the piano often represents the organ. See his transcriptions of the Bach organ compositions. He interprets them in this style, with much pedal and great tonal sonority. As organ tones in a cathedral resound and reverberate, owing to the vast spaces, so are the effects Busoni makes on the piano—of continuous tone-vibrations."

"The piano is a wonder; there is so much to think of and study about it and its marvelous literature. I have found pianists generally are much deeper thinkers than singers, for example," I remarked.

"Singers do not analyze their work as pianists do. If one has a beautiful voice, the mere quality of tone will enthrall the listener, outside of the song to be interpreted. If the singer merely vocalize a scale, it is still beautiful and appealing. But the pianist must do so many things besides merely playing the notes before he can make an appeal. He must consider tone quality, dynamics, pedaling, power and the whole concept of the piece.

"You speak of the word pianism. The word as used now includes, I take it, the entire subject of touch, technic, tone and performance. How odd that a word affects society like a new disease! All hasten to acquire it. The word pianism is the only one that can be applied to an instrument outside of the human voice. You can say vocalism, but not violinism.

The Pianist a Conductor

"The pianist is virtually a conductor, and his ten fingers are the instruments over which he holds sway. They are to do his bidding. He has a whole orchestra under his hands. The orchestral conductor merely directs his men; the pianist must both direct his whole orchestra and play all his various instruments, the fingers. His task is a more strenuous one than that of any other soloist.

"Then the literature of the piano. When you think of it, no other instrument has the literature of the piano. Has there ever been a composer like Chopin for any instrument? The greatest composers for violin were Vieuxtemps and Wieniawski; but their work cannot compare in value to what Chopin has done for the piano. He wrote solely for that one medium; he is the poet of the piano. Look at Beethoven; he did more for the piano than for any other instrument. He composed nine symphonies for orchestra and thirty-two sonatas for piano. A sonata, as you know, is a symphony for one instrument. His last five sonatas are greater than anything he ever wrote for orchestra. The Opus 57, Appassionata, is a superb symphony. His last symphonies, outside of the Ninth, the greatest, are not equal to the last five piano sonatas in value. Berlioz wrote principally for orchestra; he may be called the first romanticist for that medium. I call him the apostle of ugliness. His works for orchestra cannot compare in value to what either Beethoven or Chopin has given to the literature of the piano.

Principles of Interpretation

"To come down to more explicit terms in regard to ideas of interpretation, I feel that, after a certain period of study, the pianist should trust more to his intuitions in the interpretation of a composition. Intuition first, backed up by logical reasoning. Some put it the other way round; they put reason first, and as a result their performance is dry and soulless. For instance, I play a passage and make it sound pleasant, expressive; it pleases my ear. I then analyze the effects I have made and see if they are logical and correct. For I must prove each point according to laws of interpretation.

"There are laws of interpretation. One of them is never to lay stress on a concord, but rather on a dissonance. The stronger the dissonance the heavier the stress put upon it.

That is a fundamental law. Another principle is, not to fill rest places with sound. How many players sin in this way; either by not observing rests or by filling up the place of silence by tones prolonged by pedal. Silence plays a very important role in music. Silence should not be interfered with, filled up or obstructed. Many times it is necessary to hold pedal, if one has to jump from the bottom to the top of the keyboard. But one must know whether to bridge over the skip with pedal or to let there be silence between the two.

Traditions

"We speak of traditions of interpretation. This should not mean dry, academic formulas—it should not mean the traditions of the schools and conservatories. They conserve the old ideas, for that is the meaning of the word. Real tradition in piano playing originates with great artists who have discovered and evolved certain effects through intuition. When these intuitions stand the test, and measure up to the highest standards of art, they become traditions.

"The subject of interpretation is a very broad as well as a deeply interesting one. It is one upon which I have bestowed a great deal of thought and made many discoveries. I repeat, I feel we should trust more to our intuitions than we do. It is claimed by one learned man [Nietzsche, *The Birth of Tragedy from the Spirit of Music*] that, if the world had followed this course, we should now be on a higher plane of civilization than we are; present events seem to bear out his theory."

PERCY GRAINGER

[1882-1961]

FREEDOM OF THOUGHT IN PIANO STUDY

W hen Percy Grainger, the Australian pianist and composer, arrived in America he was not known as a player and but little as a composer, although a couple of his works for orchestra had been performed during a former season. When he gave his first recital, he proved to be a pianist of solid attainments and also of unusual freshness and charm. His playing, his compositions, his personality, went straight to the hearts of his hearers; he soon found himself the lion of the hour; success attended each subsequent appearance.

It has been aptly said that a musician can do little or nothing without enthusiasm. In Percy Grainger, the quality of enthusiasm is a potent force in his character and career. According to his own testimony, he loves to play, to compose, to teach, to visit new lands, to become familiar with new people. He has the youthful buoyancy that welcomes with eagerness each new event and experience.

To come into personal touch with Percy Grainger, to hear him in recital and with orchestra, is to be conscious of an entirely new series of experiences. Personally you feel here is a particular kind of mentality, one which is carefree, untrammeled; of most gentle spirit, yet bold and heaven-storming when bent on carrying out a purpose. Perhaps the words original and unconventional would apply, though no words can aptly describe so unique and complex a nature. At one moment he speaks of the homely matters of everyday living, with the utmost simplicity; at the next his remarks bespeak wide knowledge of men and affairs, of various countries and peoples. Whether he thoughtfully fixes a serious, searching gaze on you, or whether his face is sunny with smiles, you have the same impression of the utter sincerity and single-heartedness of the man, of the radiant vitality of his individuality.

It is the same when he plays. Sincerity shines through everything he does, and the buoyancy of a fresh, earnest, healthful spirit carries you along with it. There is no flagging of energy, no moment of languor, all is vital and alive. At times his playing is electrifying. To hear him deliver the opening of the Tchaikowsky B minor Concerto is the most exciting experience;

something that carries you off your feet like a whirlwind. As a pianist remarked to me recently, "A recital by Percy Grainger always makes one feel happy, inspired and ready to meet everything."

Although it has been my privilege to confer with Mr. Grainger at various times, it is pleasant to recall the memory of our first conversation. We were seated in the sitting room of their apartment in the hotel, and Mrs. Grainger had just poured tea for us. She might easily be taken for an elder sister of the young artist, instead of his mother. The same sunbright hair, clear blue eyes and fresh ruddy color. She is his devoted and constant companion, accompanying him everywhere. You feel they must both have lived much in the open, have tramped "o'er moor and fen," have been steeped in fresh air and sunshine.

"I had not expected to come to America at this time," began Mr. Grainger; "but we came primarily on account of my mother's frail health, which I am happy to say she has regained in this country. My European tour, embracing many concerts, had of course to be relinquished on account of the war. We sailed at three days' notice, and our intention was to stay two or three months at the most. It looks now as though we would remain in America for a long time.

"My mother, who is an excellent musician, was my first teacher. She began with me when I was five, and worked with me constantly, two hours daily, for five years. This was in Melbourne, Australia, where I was born. We left there when I was twelve. At about the age of ten I appeared in public and my career as pianist began. My teacher at that time was Professor Pabst, who subsequently became connected with the Moscow Conservatory. When we came to Germany, I went to Professor Kwast, at Frankfort, with whom I remained six years. Later I studied with Busoni, whom as pianist and teacher I most deeply revere.

"Together with playing and composing, I have found some time for teaching, though this work suffered frequent interruption on account of my tours as a pianist. But I enjoy teaching immensely; it is such individual work; it is like conducting in its effort to bring out the meaning of the composer by means of another medium or mentality. It is showing others how to express the idea. This is where the true teacher can so greatly assist the student, by being able to show him exactly how various effects are to be made, provided, of course, the pupil is anxious to learn how. As for methods of teaching technic, I do not in general care for them; I avoid them. They are often only an excuse for laziness, as they prevent the pupil from thinking for himself. As for technical training, he can get it—after the foundation is laid—in the pieces he studies. I do not believe in set rules for technic; if the player wants to turn his hand upside down and play with the palm uppermost, I dare say he could do it, if he worked at it with the same zeal that he does with the accepted position. In other words, I believe we should inculcate principles of technical freedom and individuality in every player.

"Pupils often come to study with me from the various countries where I have played. I have appeared frequently in Scandinavia and Holland, and have had numerous pupils from both those lands, as well as from England and the Colonies. The Dutch are a very musical people. I might say English and American pupils are perhaps the most talented, but their talent takes the form of doing things easily. There is talent that acquires all with hard work, and another sort that achieves without great labor.

The Sense of Rhythm
"You ask if I approve of the metronome. I certainly do; and it is amusing sometimes to see how different the mechanical idea of rhythm is from the true sense and feeling for it. We can also use the metronome for working up velocity.

"In regard to the natural feeling for rhythm, I don't find people in general so deficient in this quality as is so often imagined. The common peasant, with no cultivation whatever, has an innate sense of rhythm. It will not harmonize, I grant you, with the beat of the metronome, but it is a very forceful and individual thing. He will put a swing and 'go' into a popular air which can never be found in mechanical rhythm. Mechanical means may be necessary in the student's early stages, especially if the learner has not a just conception of the various note values.

Mental Processes during Performance
"About mental processes during actual performance of the piece in public, it is difficult to speak, as so many subtle influences are brought to bear. It is to be regretted that the custom prevails of playing everything without notes. I think many a fine pianist is greatly worried over the fear of failure of memory. This may affect his playing; it may prevent the freedom of utterance he might have, were he relieved of the fear of forgetting. All pianists agree that it is a great mental strain to perform a long and exacting program from memory; it is no wonder that even the greatest artists occasionally forget. It is no crime to have a lapse of memory, though it is annoying, especially if one is playing with orchestra. This has never happened to me; if it ever should I think I would treat the situation quite calmly; perhaps I would go

and get the notes—I always have them with me or I would look over the conductor's shoulder, assure myself of the place and then go on. The great thing is to have presence of mind in such an emergency. If one is not very strong physically, or if a great deal depends on the result of one's performance, the strain of performing an exacting program in public, from memory, is greater. Of course it is not artistic to play badly, so it were much better to have the notes in front of one than to produce poor results. Most artists would play more naturally with notes before them—if accustomed to use them. Fear often destroys the perfection of what might be a fine rendition. The comfortable, the ideal way, I suppose would be to really know the piece from memory and yet play from the notes.

Art is Natural

"Art is the expression of natural impulses; therefore I do not believe in being fettered by many rules. Rather I believe in being as natural and free as possible in the working out of artistic ideals at the instrument. For instance, I do not believe in people striving to acquire a certain pianistic style they are not fitted for. If the hand is small and the physique delicate, why not keep the dynamic scale small? Why not play with delicacy and fineness, instead of striving to become heroic? Pachmann, for instance, is a pianist whose limitations are to a certain extent responsible for his greatness. It is said he never makes a real *fortissimo*; but we admire his delicacy and finesse and do not wish him to strive for great power.

Technic grows out of Habit

"The technic of an art is, to a certain extent, mainly habit. I do believe in habit. We get used to measuring skips, for instance, with eye and hand, until we can locate them automatically, from habit. It is the same with all sorts of technical figures; we acquire the habit of doing them through constant repetition. When the mechanical part has become automatic, we can give the mind fully to the emotion to be expressed. For I do not believe you can feel the structure of the piece and its emotional message at the same time. For my own part I am not much concerned about how the piece is put together; I think of it as music, as the expression of natural impulses, desires or aspirations.

Pedal and Melody Effects

"When teaching piano, I make a great study of pedal effects with my pupils. Many fine effects of diminuendo can be made with quick half pedaling. The subject of pedaling is none too well understood; most wonderful tonal colors can be produced by an artistic use of the pedals." Mr. Grainger seated himself at the piano and played a brilliant passage ending with sustained chords, for which latter he used shifting, vibrating pedals with charming effect.

"Another point I make is the bringing out of a melody note above the other tones of a chord; that is to say, making one tone in a chord louder than the rest. This is not new, of course, but students forget to study it. The ability to bring out a desired tone comes with practice, for it is not easy to accomplish at first. Most learners think they must play such chords *forte*, whereas the best way to study them is *piano*.

Pieces that Improve touch
"Many of the modern French compositions are very useful in developing sensitiveness of finger, and I make much use of them with pupils. From Debussy *Reflets dans l'eau*, and *Pagodes* may be chosen; also the *Ondine* and other pieces by Ravel. From Cyril Scott take the *Lotus Land* and *Sphinx*, also the set of five *Poems*; all are valuable as touch developers. I find little attention is given to the study of *pianissimo* effects; these pieces give one much opportunity to acquire delicacy.

Delights of Study
"Do not imagine I want less study because I seek to avoid many formalities. Study is the only thing I care about in life, but I love the study of nature as well as art. No one can study too much; but let us have the heart of everything, not only the formal side. I like to study the language of a people, but rather the phonetics than the grammar.

"To me art is joy. The more intensely studious the artist, the more joyous will he be in his art. To my mind everything connected with art and the study of art, should be easy, natural, individualistic, untrammeled and instinctive. Above all instinctive; 'Von innen heraus.'

"In art there is no escaping from one's true inner nature; neither for beginner nor for finished artist. It seems to me the teacher should not strive to teach any one pupil the entire gamut of pianistic technic, but concentrate rather upon those phases of it to which the pupil seems physically addicted, or emotionally attracted.

"One hour spent in practicing a phase of music for which a pupil has a natural physical or imaginative ability, will generally prove more fruitful than many hours devoted to problems towards which the pupil is less instinctively impelled.

"Let each student and subsequently each artist choose those compositions that contain in abundance the particular pianistic styles for which his emotional and physical nature equips him. This course will make for individuality in the artist's repertory, and tend to banish samishness from concert programs.

Beginning Music Study

"Beginners at the piano need to learn so many things at the start. There is the training of eye, ear and hand, the learning of notes and note-values, together with all sorts of movements. If students could have thorough drill in these things before they come to us, how much greater progress they would make in the real business of playing the piano!

"As to instructing beginners, I find naturally no necessity for doing this on the piano; but I have taught beginners on the mandolin and guitar. I am fond of the combination of these instruments with strings and have written a number of compositions for a small body of string players. I play the guitar myself, and so does my mother; I have a special method of performing on it. I prefer to take an out-and-out beginner on this instrument than to take some one who has played it a good deal, and be obliged to show him all over again."

New Instruments

Mr. Grainger had-much to say about composing for a small orchestra.

"Very interesting to a modern composer," he remarked, "are the several newly invented or perfected instruments, such as the Mustel organ, the various Saxophones, the Haeckelphone; also the percussion instruments, such as the Marimbaphone, Bass-xylophones, Resonaphone, and the like. The tone of most of these new instruments is fairly delicate and sensitive, and would be swamped or lost in a modern mammoth orchestra. My own feeling is that it is in combinations of chamber music that these smaller, subtle, but highly characteristic instruments come into their own, and are heard at their full value. The latter-day tendencies are not toward noise and tonal effects on a gigantic scale, but rather toward delicacy, sensitiveness and, above all, transparency of color. Personally, I enjoy best of all writing for combinations of—let us say—six to twenty instruments, such as four strings, celesta, English horn, two guitars and resonaphone. Or such a combination as this: five men's voices, Mustel organ, four woodwind instruments and six strings."

Some of Mr. Grainger's compositions already published embody the folk tunes of various countries in new and original forms. Those for piano include Shepherd's Hey, Green Bushes, Country Tune, and Colonial Song; these are also scored for full orchestra. They can be obtained for a smaller company of players, even as small a number as twelve.

Percy Grainger has been called by Runciman "the one cheerful, sunny composer living." Finck says of his music: "One really feels tempted to say that these are the best things that have ever come to us from England." Other critics have written much in praise of his compositions. "He catches us up and whirls us away in the spirit of the country dance." "His music sounds like the dawning of a new era." "Such genuine humor and wit, such enthusiasm, such virility and masterly musicianship as Mr. Grainger shows are met with only on the rarest occasions in a musician of any country. Indeed it is doubtful if all these qualities are combined in any other composer now before the public."

These are words of high praise, from well-known authorities. We should rejoice to find a composer who can write in a healthy, sane and buoyant spirit. We do not want to be forever in the depths, racked by violent unhealthy emotions; we want to be on the heights, in the sunlight, whenever we can reach such altitudes.

Mr. Grainger's compositions are popular in England and on the Continent, and bid fair to become equally so in America. Like most true artists, he feels strongly that "wars or rumors of wars" should not be allowed to upset the internationality of art. The young Australian is deeply touched by the true spirit of artistic neutrality he has met on all sides in New York, amongst musicians of every nationality, and he points with pride to the fact that some of the best criticisms he has received in America have appeared in the German newspapers. He is no less proud of the high spirit of neutrality which permeates English musical life at present. Not long ago two large festivals of German music, one devoted to Brahms, the other to Wagner, were held there. Another "Festival of German Music" is shortly to be held in London, side by side with a "Festival of British Music," in which the works of Cyril Scott, Frederick Delius, Stanford, Elgar and Percy Grainger figure largely. At present Frederick Delius, the great Anglo-German composer, and Percy Grainger run one another very close in popularity. Mr. Grainger is boundlessly enthusiastic over his "rival," who, in his judgment, is the greatest of living composers.

"It is inspiring to live in an age in which such noble and altruistic interpretations of the universality of art are displayed," said Mr. Grainger. "In Frederick Delius," continued his Australian admirer, "German and British qualities are most fortunately blended and have contrived to produce a unique genius, whose work recalls at once such creative types as Bach, Walt

Whitman, Keats and Grieg."

Mr. Grainger is gifted as a linguist and is enthusiastic over the various tongues and dialects of the different countries through which he has traveled. He speaks German, Danish, Dutch and Norwegian, and has some knowledge of Icelandic, Jutish, Frisian, Faroese and the peasant dialects of Norway. This acquaintance with the languages has greatly assisted in the study of folk melodies. He is considered one of the greatest authorities on folk songs and primitive music, having himself collected and carefully noted down nearly five hundred examples of traditional singing and playing in Great Britain, Scandinavia, New Zealand and the South Seas.

As a pianist Percy Grainger plays with clarity of touch, variety of tone color and splendid sweep and virility. He is able to set the composition before the listener in well-balanced proportions, and direct simplicity of thought. One feels the composer of the work under consideration would wish it played in just this way, with just this directness of utterance. At the same time the pianist lends to everything he touches the glow of his own buoyancy and enthusiasm, by means of which well-known themes take on a new meaning and make a new and unusual appeal.

JOSEF HOFMANN

[1876-1957]

INSPIRATION IN PIANO PLAYING

Josef Hofmann has been before the public from his early childhood, for he was exploited as a prodigy, and created a sensation wherever he appeared. Born at Cracow, he was the son of a professor of the conservatory and director of the opera at Warsaw. His mother was a distinguished singer, and his sister, two and a half years his senior, showed a strong predilection for music. So readily were the rudiments of pianoforte playing mastered that Josef appeared in public at a concert given for charity when he was not yet six years old, and when he was eight he played the Beethoven Concerto in C minor, on which occasion Rubinstein heard him for the first time, and declared that he was a boy such as the world of music had never before produced.

During [his] tour in 1887 the boy was overworked, and a good deal of indignation was aroused over the way in which he was treated. The Society for the Prevention of Cruelty to Children took up the matter, and the child was vigilantly watched by medical men, who took his temperature, felt his pulse, and made examinations of him at all times and in all places. Eventually the tour was abandoned, Hofmann's health having given way under the constant strain. He gave fifty-two concerts in two months and a half.

Fortunately for him he was no longer exhibited as a prodigy, but settled down to continue his education, and in the course of some ten years he reappeared, stronger, more mature and more musical than ever. His early prestige remains with him, and he is undoubtedly one of the finest pianists of his day, though hardly yet more than a boy."

[Lahee, Henry C., *Famous Pianists*, 1906. p.265]

AMERICANS naturally feel a peculiar interest in the art of Josef Hofmann, for they have seen it grow and develop from the wonder child of ten to the matured artist, who stands today on the mountain height of his profession. There must be thousands in this country who remember the marvelous exhibition of piano playing offered by the little Polish boy during the season of 1888, when, as a wonderful child prodigy, he was brought over to make his first tour of America.

He was such a little fellow, with such a serious face, as he came upon the stage in his simple sailor suit and climbed on to the piano stool. But we soon forgot all else, after the orchestral prelude, when he began to play. Ah, then it was no longer a tiny child, in a blue sailor suit; it was a man, who grappled with those handfuls of notes and flung them out into space with such sureness and freedom. That powerful, singing tone did not belong to the puny strength of a child of ten. Neither did that sympathetic reading of the score, that understanding of the meaning of the music. No human power could have taught him these things; it was inborn genius.

No wonder people went wild with excitement and split their gloves in vociferous applause. It was almost beyond belief. The climax came when this mite of a boy began to improvise on a theme handed up to him by chance from any one in the audience. Then his powers were tested and not found wanting.

People shook their heads and said such precocity could not mature; that the lad would probably never be heard from in the future. In this they were vastly mistaken. The child prodigy retired from the footlights and spent seven or eight years in close study. Then he emerged into the light and returned to us a full-fledged artist. But that was not the end. Josef Hofmann was never content to stand still; it was only a milestone in his upward flight. He has always been at work, always progressing, never content with present attainments. Each year we have watched his growth, have felt his art become finer, more expressive, more subtle, until at the present moment it seems wellnigh perfect. Yet the artist does not take this view.

"There are still difficulties I have not yet overcome, limitations beyond which I have not passed. I have not yet all the power I desire, nor always the ability to express every shade of emotion I wish to portray. There is still much I hope to accomplish in the expression of emotion and inspiration in piano playing." Admissions like these, coming from the lips of such a musician, are further proofs of the humility of the truly great artist.

Mr. Hofmann, in spite of pressing concert engagements, permitted me to come and talk over with him some of the phases of pianistic art.

I found him in his apartments overlooking the park. A fluffy white poodle took great interest in the entrance of the visitor, but was cautioned by his master, who held up a warning fore finger, "not to be a bore."

"You will meet my family by degrees," remarked the artist, smiling: "first my dog, then Mrs. Hofmann (who entered later) and my little daughter, Josepha." This little girl of nine has marked ability along artistic lines, and is already doing creditable sketches in water color.

We spoke first of the little Polish boy, who aroused such a furore in America at the age of ten.

"That was in '88," said Mr. Hofmann. "At that time I played the Mendelssohn Concerto in G minor, also his Capriccio, and the Beethoven

Concertos in C major and C minor."
"Do not forget the improvising, which seemed so marvelous to us then."
"Oh, yes, I improvised, of course."
"Surely one who has such a perfect technic, who has solved every technical problem, can accomplish all one desires in interpretation."
"It goes without saying that an artist in these days must have a great technic: that is where piano playing really begins. But I do not consider that I yet possess a perfect technic, for I still have limitations. The artist, however, must allow the public to guess his limitations. There is as much art in choosing the right kind of compositions as in playing them. There are still some pieces I would not attempt; some that require more power, for instance, than I now have. The player should never urge his force to the limit; he must always keep something in reserve. If the tone is at its utmost capacity of production, it will sound hard; there must always be some reserve power back of it. Rubinstein was capable of immense power, for he had a very heavy hand and arm. His fifth finger was as thick as my thumb—think of it! Then his fingers were square on the ends, with cushions on them. It was a wonderful hand, and very large besides. Yet with all his power, one felt he had more in reserve.

Technic Study
"I do no technical work outside of the composition, for the reason that I find plenty of technic to work on in the piece itself. Every passage that presents the least difficulty is studied in minute detail, with well raised fingers, clear distinct touch, always taking care to put the finger down exactly in the middle of each key, not on the side of it. The piece is studied with every kind of touch, tempo and dynamics studied till the player has command of every possible variety of tone, touch and degree of power or delicacy. When all these things are under control, he is ready to interpret the composition.

Ideal Interpretation
"I repeat that only when the player has control of the means, has he the true freedom to clearly and adequately express himself. Then his interpretation takes on the nature of an improvisation.
"There are many circumstances which influence the artist's interpretation. His prevailing mood at the moment, the piano, the mental quality of the audience, the acoustics of the space he has to fill, and so on. I play very differently in the concert hall from what I do at home in my study. When before an audience, I must take into account all the things I have mentioned. If I am to fill Carnegie Hall, my scale of dynamics is quite different from

the one I use in a smaller space. There must likewise be corresponding differences in touch and tone color.

"You speak of the spiritual side of piano interpretation. To bring out that side surely depends on the absolute freedom and untrammeled condition, both mentally and physically, which one is in.

"I can affirm, therefore, that I do not know, beforehand, how I shall be able to play the piece, until I have tried the space, the piano, the hearers and myself. I may be able to control every point, and to express myself with perfect freedom, and then I may not. There are times when it seems I have nothing to say. The notes of the piece are there, an inanimate skeleton. It is like a dinner table, daintily laid out, where the viands are wanting, and the listener goes away unfed.

Two Kinds of Pianists

"As I see it, there are two kinds of pianists. The more numerous sort may master every note, finger mark and sign of expression with commendable exactness; everything is thought out in the privacy of the studio. When they come before an audience they merely transfer this conception to the larger space, playing just as they would at home. They always try to play the piece in precisely the same way.

"I cannot believe this is the only way. I cannot do it myself and my master Rubinstein never did so. He never played a piece just as he had played it before; I cannot do this either.

"The other kind of artist, and their number is small, I admit, never play the piece twice in just the same way. They strive for the control which gives absolute freedom of expression. They realize how many forces react on the artist upon the platform—even the temperature! If I am playing the Appassionata Sonata on a sultry day, the passion may be somewhat milder than it would be if the temperature were more bracing.

"It is of course necessary to plan a model in the studio, though the performance in public may differ from it, as it admits certain elements of improvisation. This results in a higher artistic mastery, because it is—within certain limits—free, spontaneous, and personal.

"This freedom of interpretation presupposes the artist's mind and taste to be so well trained as to warrant him in relying on the inspiration of the moment. But back of it all must be his logical plan of action. I think I can say I belong to this small class of pianists who yield to the inspiration of the moment and improvise the composition at the piano.

Taking Risks

"If one is to play with freedom and inspiration, one must strike out boldly and not hold back in timidity or bashfulness; these are bad faults. We sometimes see people in society who fear to make a *faux pas* here or there; so they hold back stiffly and bore everybody, besides being very uncomfortable themselves. The player must cast fear to the winds and risk everything. He should be an absolutely free and open avenue for the expression of the emotional and spiritual meaning of the music. When one can thus improvise the composition, it seems that the piano no longer sounds like a piano. It has been said that when Rubinstein played, the instrument did not sound like a piano. As you have heard Rubinstein, you remember how different his piano sounded from the ordinary kind; like another sort of medium, or like a whole orchestra—in spite of the many wrong notes. When playing himself he often struck wrong notes, yet in teaching he was very exact; he could not endure wrong notes or slips of any kind, in his pupils or in himself. But in public he took the risk! He was not troubled about the false notes if only he could present the emotional content of the music in the most compelling light.

"I heard Rubinstein play in Berlin, at his last concert there. Moszkowski sat beside me. Rubinstein, in playing his Valse Caprice, missed all but one of those treacherous high skips. When he hit that solitary one correctly, Moszkowski turned to me and whispered, humorously, 'We must excuse him, for he can't see any more.' "

The Metronome

"I notice, Mr. Hofmann, that you have a metronome standing here. In one of your answers to questions in the *Ladies' Home Journal*, I believe you disapproved of it."

"That was a misunderstanding. We cannot do without the metronome. It is the policeman! I may have said not to play with metronome, as a true sense of rhythm cannot be acquired in this way. But I never said not to use one. On the contrary the metronome is a necessity, for it gives us the correct idea of tempo; in that capacity I use it frequently.

Modern Music

"What do I think of modern music? Some of it is only contortion, Stravinsky and Schoenberg, for instance. Yet it is much sought after as a fad, nowadays, from curiosity, if for no other reason. If one falls in a fit on the street people run together, curious to see what has happened. What do they see?

Contortion! The Stravinsky ballet, recently given at the Century, was fascinating in color, movement and ensemble, but the music was again— contortion.

The Piano as a Means of Expression
"Absolute control of all means in the performer's power does not belong alone to the pianist, it may belong to the flute player, the violinist or cellist. It should always be possessed by the player who would improvise his interpretations.

"The piano is the universal instrument, the one independent medium. All other instruments either require or are improved by an accompaniment, even the voice. But the pianist stands alone, and controls everything. He can express every emotion, even despotism, by means of his instrument. We often say the piano expresses all these, when we really know it can say nothing at all without the pianist. If he have many emotions and the ability to express them, the piano will do his bidding."

Playing with Orchestra
"We regret you elect to give but one recital in New York during the season."

"But I play a number of times with orchestra here. You have good ones in America.

"In assisting the artist the orchestra should take the part of an accompaniment, and although the conductor directs it, he should, for the time being, efface himself. This the conductor of the New York Symphony is able to do. After we have played together five or six times, we come to be in perfect accord. A soloist ought to play with his orchestra in smaller places before appearing in the large cities if he wishes his ensemble to be at its best.

"Yes, I am a co-worker with Godowsky on the *Progressive Series of Piano Lessons*. It is slow and tedious business, this editing of the various pieces required. Every finger mark and sign of phrasing must be absolutely correct. It takes me several hours to edit a short piece. It is work fit for a schoolmaster.

"After my touring season, we shall spend the summer in Maine. Ah, how beautiful it is there, by the sea! I love it. Of course wherever I am, my time is fully taken up. In summer I exchange the rush of travel, the catching of trains, for the repose and quiet of a vacation by the sea. That is when I work on my programs and prepare the various concertos I am to play the following season."

ERNEST HUTCHESON
[1871-1951]

TECHNIC AND INTERPRETATION

I n Ernest Hutcheson are united the abilities of the concert artist and the artist teacher. It is not easy to take high rank in both the art of playing and the art of teaching, but here is an Australian musician who has been able to do both. In this double capacity he has become noted on both sides of the ocean.

Mr. Hutcheson rightly feels that experience should loom large when estimating the value and usefulness of the teacher. He can often determine at once whether a prospective pupil can work with him to advantage or be better off with some other teacher.

"I would sometimes rather take a beginner," he says, "than one who has played a great deal and is very set in his ways. Various students come to me asking to be coached on the interpretation or pedaling of different pieces. They may not be in any condition, technically, to play those pieces, or to profit by my ideas on the subject, for they have not taken the necessary steps to climb the heights required in such compositions.

"It is surprising how little many people comprehend where they stand in their musical studies. Where they *think* they are, and where they really stand, may be wide apart! A teacher needs large experience and acumen to help him decide quickly just what regimen is best for the pupil, both technically and musically. Some pupils can play a Mozart sonata respectably who would have little idea of the modern tonal coloring required to render even MacDowell's little *Wild Rose*. Or they might play the Reinhold Impromptu with brilliancy, yet would quite fail to give the right atmosphere to the *Water Lily*. Some pieces which seem simple, so far as the notes go, present difficulties of another sort. How is it possible to attempt a Liszt Rhapsodie, when one cannot compass the little Fantaisie in D Minor, by Mozart?

Finding New Music
"My time has become so limited that I have not the leisure to look over quantities of new music. One would need to examine perhaps a hundred compositions to find one which would be acceptable. Of course I make use of the entire standard repertoire in teaching; the ultra-modern things come to me, so to speak. As I find them, or hear them from artists, or occasionally

from pupils, I make a note of them; in this way they come to me.

"I arrange my teaching lists like this," and Mr. Hutcheson showed a little blank book with lists of pieces, from the classics of Bach and Beethoven down to the present hour; certain signs indicated their special technical value.

"No doubt all teachers make such lists. Mine are not arranged in grades, however. I could never see the use of grading pieces. Pupils vary so greatly in comprehension and mentality that the same piece might be difficult for one pupil and very simple for another, both having studied for about the same length of time. This shatters the grade theory. I find myself at sea on the subject, and banish all thought of grades."

Knowing Mr. Hutcheson's wide experience in teaching, both privately and in music schools, in Europe as well as in America, I inquired his opinion as to the relative value of each.

"There is much to be said in favor of the music school. A school is beneficial for its routine work and free advantages. If your pupil needs ear-training you can require her to attend such a class; it is the same with harmony. All pupils need drill in these subjects, and in a school they are included in the tuition. Then there are the opportunities to play in the concerts and musicals, often with other instruments and with the orchestra. If the student intends becoming professional these things are indispensable. In a school they can be obtained free of cost.

Importance of Playing in Public

"The private teacher, though doing excellent work, finds himself at a disadvantage on these points. Playing before others is an absolute necessity. I have always insisted on it with my private pupils. I have had a large studio, seating 150 or 200, and generally have had a musical once a week, the pupils inviting their parents and friends. There is nothing which will take the place of the routine of playing before others. The only way to learn to play in public is—to play. Pupils who play their pieces correctly and well for me, will make shocking mistakes and go all to pieces through sheer nervousness, if playing for the first time in a musicale. They soon get used to it however. Even three or four performances during the season will be of great benefit.

Technical Training

"In regard to technical training there are certain principles underlying all correct teaching and playing. I do not believe in any special method. It is so easy to make a method, if certain phases are held up and magnified, to the exclusion of other phases of the subject. There are so many sides to be considered; they should all be viewed in the right perspective, and in just relation to each other. It is difficult even to speak of certain sides, for fear of seeming to neglect other phases which are equally important.

"Perhaps the three most important principles are: Position, Condition, Action. The first presents the least difficulty. With the second we are first concerned when a new pupil is taken in hand. There is usually stiffness. It may be that nothing can be done till the pupil learns to relax shoulders and arms. Then we come to the piano and touch single tones, using relaxed arm weight and a single finger. There are three different ways of touching a key; we can hit it, press it, or fall on it, The first, of course, is harsh; the second term is sometimes misleading. Playing with relaxed weight of arm and a firm finger seems to express the idea. My old teacher in Leipsic, Zwintcher, used to say legato touch was like walking. As in that movement the weight of the body is transferred from one foot to another, as we take each step, so in playing a smooth legato on the piano, the weight of hand and arm goes easily from one finger to the next as we proceed.

Position and Touch

"When easy, relaxed conditions of arm, elbow and wrist are understood, we secure an arched position of the hand, with rounded fingers. The latter are not to be straightened when lifted, as some are inclined to do, but should preserve their rounded shape. In all the earlier stages of piano study there must be decided finger action, with fingers kept at a medium height above the keys. A too high lift may cause strained conditions and hard tone; a too low position will not give a sufficient clearness and development.

"There are various forms of staccato touch; one is the drawing in of the finger, giving brilliancy and delicacy.

"In chord playing there are many touches, the one chosen depending on the character of the passage. We can use down-arm action, with great weight, or hand action at the wrist, or up-arm touch, always taking care to keep unemployed fingers out of harm's way." Mr. Hutcheson illustrated with a few measures of a Chopin Prelude, a Beethoven Sonata and the Schumann *Grillen*.

"For octaves, after the arched position of the hand has been formed the great point seems to be to touch the white keys up near the black ones, so that the hand shall not zig-zag in and out, but preserve an even line in playing both black and white keys, always keeping the other fingers out of harm's way, by holding them up."

Thoughts on Interpretation: Objective and Subjective

"Interpretation has two aspects, an objective and a subjective. Imagine several fine orators reading the soliloquy from *Hamlet*. In many respects their versions would be identical; all would presumably pronounce the words correctly, give the right accents to strong syllables, punctuate intelligibly so that the sense and construction of the speech would be clear; all would employ certain inflections of tone and rhythm in their effort to express the ideas of the author. That is objective interpretation.

"But each individual orator would probably go farther. He would hardly fail to add touches peculiar to himself: heightened stresses, delicate shades of voice, a barely perceptible dwelling on chosen words, gestures prompted by his own feeling; in short, he would endeavor to add his mental and emotional force, which we may call his artistic personality, to that of Shakspere. This is subjective interpretation. No greater mistake could be made than to suppose that there is a latent antagonism between the objective and subjective sides. It is so in music also; the most 'original' rendering of any work may at the same time show infinite care of the composer's intentions.

Use of Rubato

"One of the most harmful prejudices in regard to interpretation is the prevalent idea that one takes a 'liberty' in adding inflection and rubato not directly prescribed by the author. This is an absurdity, for any performance devoid of such enrichment will inevitably be dry and mechanical, and the most unpardonable liberty one could possibly be guilty of toward a composer is to make his music sound mechanical. Hardly less is the suggestion often made to students that, while rubato may appropriately be used in playing Chopin and Schumann, it is out of place in Bach and Beethoven. The truth is that the degree of rubato necessary to a beautiful performance depends entirely on the character of the work itself, not on the name of the writer or the date of composition. Many of Chopin's and Schumann's works would be ruined by a lavish employment of rubato, and many Fantasias of Bach and slow movements of Beethoven call for as much rhythmical freedom as any modern nocturne or romance. These prejudices, for that matter, are even historically wrong; the old masters all used rubato, and Beethoven's playing, as far as we can judge from reports of his contemporaries, was so extraordinarily free that in all probability it would have been a severe shock to audiences and critics of the present day. Flexibility of rhythm, in fact, is and always has been as logical and correct a means of interpretation as any other, provided always that it be dictated by artistic sense, not by caprice.

Variety of Tone

"Rhythm is but one element of interpretation. Chief among the others are Tone, including accent and shading, Phrasing and Pedaling. In all of these we shall find the same necessity of exercising our own taste and judgment. The composer directly indicates his essential wishes; others he implies; other points again he leaves entirely to the player's discretion. For instance, the author very rarely suggests, except by implication, a difference of tone between melody and accompaniment, yet even a beginner strongly feels the obligation of a marked difference of quality or volume.

"In phrasing, precisely the same principles apply to classical and modern works, but the usage of the classics in regard to legato-slurs differs very widely from that of the moderns. It is necessary, therefore, to interpret phrasing in the light of the composer's idiom. Roughly speaking, it might be said that in classical usage the end of a slur does not necessarily involve an interruption of the legato, while in modern usage (particularly that of Chopin) the presence of a slur does not always preclude such breaks.

Pedaling

"As for pedaling signs, the convention under which they are employed is radically incorrect, and accordingly we have to displace or 'syncopate' every sign in order to realize the writer's intention. Nor is this by any means the only demand customarily made on our intelligence. Beethoven, for example, wrote for an instrument of very small resonance as compared with a modern Steinway. We are told that he played the entire theme of the second movement of his C minor Concerto without lifting the damper pedal; a similar performance on a piano of today would have the most disastrous results.

"While all musical notation, except the mere notation of pitch, is limited and inaccurate, that of the pedal is peculiarly inadequate, and the ear, our only safe guide, must constantly be invoked. The use of the soft pedal is almost always left to the native sense of the pianist; and the sostenuto pedal, found only on instruments of American make, has been practically ignored by living composers.

The Content of a Piece

"The character of a piece is always the real key to its interpretation. We should be careful to seek the essential meaning, not merely display the outward form. Let me give a few instances. In the Berceuse of Chopin the pervading spirit is tenderness, soothingness, the song of mother-love; the conspicuous ornamentation is only incidental and should be veiled, not insisted on; the suggestion (in the left hand) of a persistently rocking cradle is wholly external and should never 'creak.' Take the same composer's Funeral March; here the true character is that of dull, sullen grief, rising to anguish, relieved by hope or sweet memories; the hint of tolling bells and pageantry of woe is material, not spiritual, and should be kept in the background. I once knew a lady who 'quite distinctly saw the carriage wheels go round' when she heard this tragedy of tone! Again, look at the Etude in F minor, Op. 25, No. 2. This is a tiny gem which might be compared to a wandering and wistful breeze, elusive, remote; it should be played in that mood, not as a study in speed and cross-rhythms. Is there any 'moonlight' in the C sharp minor Sonata of Beethoven?

Heaven forbid! It shows us a dark, tormented soul which finds fleeting peace in the Intermezzo, that 'flower between two abysses,' and drives on to a tempest of despair in the Finale.

"It is an excellent exercise in interpretation thus to take a composition, or more often a single theme, and attempt to describe its character in a few words. This does not mean to fit a story to it, to impose on it attributes not necessarily inherent, but simply to fix its indisputable qualities in the mind as a key to the right feeling.

"Let it not be thought, however, that the right feeling for music will alone insure good interpretation. The deepest feelings often fail to find adequate expression; concealed in the player's mind, they reach no listening ear. The mission of the interpretative artist is to communicate music, as he feels it, to others. Our Anglo-Saxon temperament always labors under the artistic disadvantage of a deep-rooted reluctance to show emotion. But emotion must be shown to be shared, and this, I think, is in substance what we usually mean in speaking of musical 'expression.' I am far from decrying the sensuous and intellectual elements of interpretation, though it seems that our modern world derives little satisfaction from these elements when unaccompanied by poetic fervor, and on the other hand will forgive many offenses if once persuaded that a strong imaginative impulse sways its performers.

RAFAEL JOSEFFY

[1852-1915]

BY SOME OF HIS PUPILS

T he name Rafael Joseffy has long been one to conjure with, whether in Europe or America, whether as pianist or as pedagogue. He was by birth an Hungarian, itself a fact of musical significance. He had studied with Tausig and Liszt, and when he came to America, in 1879, in the flush of youthful mastery of his instrument, he created a furore. He was at that time a marvelous virtuoso; he developed later into a poetic genius of the piano.

It would require a readier pen than mine to fitly describe either the manner of playing, or the teaching methods of this piano conqueror. He had many pupils and followers during his long residence among us, and his influence over the development of music in America was important. As the years passed he became more and more a thinker along the lines of music education, as is evidenced by his two valuable works on piano technic. These books prove how carefully he worked out technical problems.

Technic for the piano is such an individual thing. In a sense it must be applied differently to each pupil. This enlists all the resources of the teacher, since the mentality of the student is varied in every case. And if the teacher must adapt his instruction to fit each and every individual, so, on the side of the pupil, there will be found every shade of comprehension and receptivity.

I have been able to confer with several of the American pupils of Rafael Joseffy, and what they have to say will be of deep interest to pianists and teachers.

ROSE WOLF

Mme. Rose Wolf, who was the master's assistant for about fifteen years, brought to her work a wide experience of masters and methods. Born in Russia, a student in the Rubinstein Conservatory, under the famous pianist, she also studied with Klindworth and Scharwenka in Berlin, and with Dr. William Mason and A. K. Virgil in New York. In fact she has investigated all methods, "to see what was in them."

"I had studied with Joseffy, with some interruptions, ever since I was fourteen," she says. "I feel I know his method thoroughly; in fact, his 'new book,' as we called it,—the *First Lessons*, we wrote, so to say, together. He consulted me about every exercise; my knowledge of Mr. Virgil's Method helped to explain many a point. During the past fifteen years I prepared most of the pupils for Joseffy, and alternated lessons with his.

Joseffy's Method

"Here is a model of Joseffy's hand. You see how the fingers are rounded, the knuckles almost level on top; the knuckle of the fifth finger is as high as that of the second; the thumb is curved also; it is an ideal shape. He was very particular about hand position; that must be formed before anything else could be done. He takes up this subject in the opening chapter of *First Lessons*. Then comes finger action. He believed in high, free finger movements, especially at first; later the high action was reduced. Each of the exercises are to be taken in different touches—legato, marcato and staccato; these are for trills and five finger forms, in all keys. Much attention is to be given to chord study; the various positions both in three and four voices to be played in a variety of touches, and always with fingers prepared beforehand for the keys.

Joseffy made much of the staccato touch, both for fingers and wrist. Finger staccato was not played by simply working the fingers quickly up and down, but rather by a slight drawing-in of the finger tip (as Doctor Mason taught). Wrist staccato was executed with the hand, the wrist being free and supple and fingers rounded. He did not advise alternating legato and staccato touches for scales, a few repetitions of each, as is usually done; he considered this method of practice a waste of time. But if staccato scale practice can be kept up for ten or fifteen minutes at a time, great benefit will result.

Fingering

"Joseffy was very exact in all matters of fingering. When possible, a phrase or passage should begin with thumb and end with fifth finger. An ascending scale should end with fifth. Chords following single tones, in bass, should receive, not the fifth finger again, but the fourth or third, when possible. I took him the G minor Ballade of Chopin; he changed the fingering in such a way that I had to learn the piece all over again; but it then sounded like quite a different composition, which shows how fingering can alter interpretation.

Ornaments

"In regard to embellishments, he was particular to preserve the classic spirit, of bringing the mordent or grace note on the beat. This for Haydn, Scarlatti or Mozart, and even for Beethoven. For later composers the modern manner was generally chosen, though taste should decide. His taste was exquisite on all such points.

Choice of Pieces

"One of the most valuable things about Joseffy's teaching was his rare insight into the needs of his pupils. He was able to choose just the musical food they required. If the student lacked expression and a singing tone, he was advised to study nocturnes or other lyric music; if he needed bravoura, he was required to work on brilliant pieces. Sometimes he was allowed to play just the sort of composition that would bring out his best qualities in high relief.

"Joseffy never talked much in the lesson, never played the composition entirely through, only parts of it. The student imbibed more by intuition than in any other way. He made you see what he meant, what the music stood for, its meaning and significance. If the pupil were not advanced sufficiently, he might get but little out of the lessons; but if really prepared, physically and mentally, he could grasp intuitively, a great deal of the higher side of pianism."

ALEXANDER BERNE

Mr. Berne, who is doing excellent work as pianist, teacher and composer, speaks enthusiastically of his lessons with Joseffy, with whom he studied for four or five seasons.

"Joseffy insisted on the following four fundamental principles: 1, Arched Hand; 2, Loose Wrist; 3, Slanting Position (for scales and arpeggios); 4, High Finger Action. He was very particular about position of the hand; that had to be formed before anything else could be done. Accuracy also was one of his hobbies; therefore fingers must be well raised during practice.

"With some pupils, I am told, he did not concern himself so much about technic. He was very exact with me, for which I am grateful, as it has helped me so much in my teaching.

Slow Practice

"Slow practice was greatly recommended, as only in this way could accuracy be acquired. After the piece had been played for him slowly and carefully, he would sometimes say: 'Now play it fast, even if you drop some notes; I want to see what you can do.'

"He required much scale practice. At first we used a short scale of nine notes, for which it was necessary to pass the thumb under twice. This was played in all keys, hands singly and together. He claimed this little figure embodied the whole principle of the scale, without waste of time or energy. Later, scales in four octaves were studied in all keys.

Rhythm

"Joseffy was a great stickler for perfect rhythm. He insisted this principle should be carried into everything. If the scale ended on a third beat, the following repetition, or new scale, must begin on the first beat of next measure, leaving one beat between. The same was true of all technical forms.

The Classics

"With the classic in music Joseffy was in complete *rapport*. He used much Bach, also Haydn, Scarlatti, Mozart, Beethoven. Then came Schumann, Brahms and, most of all, Chopin. His taste did not incline toward the ultramodern school, though he used the two Arabesques of Debussy.

"In Bach, when one voice is in eighths against another in sixteenths, the former was played staccato and the latter legato, unless otherwise marked. This reading gives variety to the parts and preserves the classic spirit. Joseffy used it for the older music.

"After the student had been initiated into technical methods, and had studied some pieces very carefully, he was told to bring several pieces for each lesson. Sometimes I had to prepare thirty or forty pages at a time— during the two weeks' interval; the idea being to play through a number of compositions for smoothness, style and effect.

"At the beginning of his lessons, the student provided himself with a staff-ruled notebook, in which Joseffy indicated the technical matter to be studied. Many of the exercises in his new book,—*First Lessons*—were thus dictated to me before the work was published. This is the book I use in my teaching, although I have adopted Joseffy's method of writing down exercises for my pupils, as it gives peculiar interest to their technical studies."

Mr. Berne relates many incidents, showing the personality of the great pianist and his kindly interest in his pupils. Lack of space prevents their inclusion.

EDWIN HUGHES

Mr. Edwin Hughes, who has been for a number of years—as student and teacher—a leading representative of the pianistic principles of Theodor Leschetizky, was a pupil of Joseffy for a couple of seasons before going to

Vienna. Of the latter's teaching methods he says:

"Joseffy was immensely particular about fingering. I have known the whole lesson hour to be occupied with this subject. He would finger a passage in several ways, telling the pupil to practice them all and then decide which would best fit the hand. In his work as editor, he would spend many hours over the fingering of a single composition. He often hit upon brilliant ideas in this line, though he was apt to be somewhat old fashioned and pedantic. This frequently showed itself in the changing of fingers on keys, for no special reason. With him fingering was almost an art in itself. He worked according to a principle, and always put that first. If a passage ought to be played legato, he would preserve that principle in the fingering.

Inventing Difficult Exercises

"He advised making difficult technical exercises out of pieces; that is to say, selecting the hard parts and then turning them about in different ways, for one hand or the other. This was the idea of Tausig and Liszt, with both of whom Joseffy studied. It is also Rosenthal's plan; he doubtless got it from his teacher, Joseffy. Another technical stunt was to practice with uncomfortable hand positions, such as octaves with very low wrist, for instance. Afterwards the normal position of hands, or written arrangement of notes would be found much easier.

Perfection or Endurance

"He counselled the student to practice either for perfection or endurance. For the former slow practice was necessary, with well-raised fingers and minute attention to every detail. For endurance the opposite course was observed. 'Play for speed, and keep it up, no matter if some of the notes are dropped,' he would say: 'go through the piece several times without stopping, and do not yield to fatigue; overcome fatigue!'

Choosing Suitable Pieces

"Choosing pieces from which one could learn a great deal, technically as well as musically, was almost a gift with him. Take, for instance, two works like the Schumann Fantaisie, Op. 17, and Chopin's Sonata, Op. 35. To the listener these works may sound about the same in point of difficulty, but the pianist will learn much more from the first movement of the Sonata than from the first part of the Fantaisie. For the same reason he did not favor either the Tchaikowsky or Grieg Concertos. 'Any one who can play chords can play those,' he would say. But from a Mozart or a Chopin Concerto one learns much. The Intermezzi of Brahms are more for interpretation than for technical mastery, as few technical problems are involved in them.

Joseffy's Books on Technic

"I make great use in my teaching of Joseffy's treatise on *Piano Technic*; I consider it a great work. He has treated every point exhaustively. Of course it is a book for advanced students, as he accepted no other kind. His *First Lessons*, which was issued later, I do not use. After a careful examination, I found the exercises just as difficult—many of them—as those in the larger work. He intended the *First Lessons* to precede the more advanced work, and started out with a few foundational exercises, but soon leaped ahead to advanced problems. He was very favorable to the Virgil clavier and to the method evolved by its inventor, Mr. A. K. Virgil. A pupil coming to him who had been well prepared in this method, he considered had a thorough foundation. I had been well grounded in this method before I went to him, through my studies with S. M. Fabian, of Washington. I found this preparation of the greatest benefit to me in my later studies.

"Joseffy was one of the greatest teachers of our time. As Rosenthal remarked: 'Why do Americans come over here to study, when they have one of the most remarkable teachers in their midst?' Yet Joseffy himself counselled his students to cross the ocean and learn what Europe could do for them in matters of experience, travel, and musical inspiration."

EDWARD MACDOWELL, AS TEACHER
[1861-1908]

RELATED BY MRS. EDWARD MACDOWELL
[1857-1956]

Each year adds to the fame of our greatest American composer, Edward MacDowell. As his music is more frequently heard, it becomes better understood and loved. The various clubs bearing the composer's name, scattered over the country, are doing their share to familiarize people with his music. Perhaps the most potent factor in spreading this familiarity is the work which Mrs. MacDowell, widow of the composer, is doing. For the past five years she has traveled over the length and breadth of the land— "from coast to coast"—bearing her sweet message of harmony and beauty. As she ministered to her distinguished husband, with the most unselfish devotion, during his life, so she has consecrated her time and talents to the work of spreading broadcast a better understanding of his music, and to the upbuilding of the Peterborough Memorial, which, mainly through her untiring efforts, has come to be a source of help and inspiration to many an artist.

While Edward MacDowell's fame in the future will rest on his many valuable contributions to musical literature, we do not forget he was a brilliant pianist and considered a great teacher. He had the gift of imparting, and numbered among his students some of exceptional talent; musicians who are now making an honorable career in the profession.

In regard to MacDowell's ideals of teaching and piano study, no one could speak with more knowledge and authority than Mrs. MacDowell herself, who studied very seriously with the composer for four years. She has been willing to give some of her valuable time, between lecture recital engagements, to a conference on these subjects, which is here set down with all possible accuracy.

"I began to study the piano when I was ten, though I had picked out many little things for myself before that time," began Mrs. MacDowell. "My first and only teacher in America was a favorite aunt, who, owing to changes of fortune, had come to New York from her home in the South. She was half French, a Jumel,—doubtless one of the original family—and was really a remarkable woman. She was a fine musician, and was able within one year to make a place for herself here, and obtain a large fee for lessons, something unusual for a woman to do in those early days.

"My aunt evidently felt I had some talent that was worth while cultivating, for she took me in hand and taught me thoroughly, for four years. After that I worked by myself for several years, until, under stress of circumstances, it was decided for me to make music my profession, and I went abroad to continue my studies.

"My goal was Frankfort, and my desire was to become a pupil of Clara Schumann. Her daughters acted as Vorbereiters for their famous mother. I learned they were slow, heavy and pedantic, without having inherited the gifts of their distinguished parents. Raff, Director of the Conservatory, seeing how matters stood, said it would be so much better if I could study with a teacher who could speak English, and mentioned the young American, Edward MacDowell, who was then just finishing his studies with Raff. I consented to try this plan for six months, though I confess I was not eager to come to Europe to study with an American teacher; neither was the young professor anxious to accept pupils from his own country. However I began. My teacher put me through a very severe course of training. He has since confessed that he never would administer such Spartan treatment to any one else. He gave no pieces, but many etudes and much Bach. At the end of the half year, I was free to go to another teacher—to Mme. Schumann if I wished. But I had enough good common sense to see that I had made astonishing progress, much greater progress than other students. So I wisely decided to remain with my American teacher.

"We were both working very hard, each in our own way, without thought of any sentiment between us. I well remember my first piece, after almost a year's study. It was the Bach A minor Prelude and Fugue, transcribed by Liszt.

Teaching Material

"What teaching material did Mr. MacDowell use, you ask? I studied Czerny, Heller, Cramer (the original, not the Bülow edition), Clementi's Gradus, and plenty of Bach, the smaller pieces, Inventions and so on. Mr. MacDowell did not give a great many technical forms outside of etudes. His idea was that scales and arpeggios need great concentration in order to render their practice beneficial. Many students cannot concentrate sufficiently, in which case they are apt to lose time over these forms. I mean to say they will practice scales better if they are interestingly treated in an etude than when they are studied alone.

"This was his idea. But Mr. MacDowell never claimed he was always

right in his views, never felt his way was the only way. He was ever broad
minded in such matters. He would say, 'I do not work just that way,' or 'I do
not see it in your light, but yours may be just as good a way as mine.' He had
not very much use for so-called piano methods; he said there was some
good in each, but would not confine himself to any one. He felt that as there
were so many degrees of intelligence, so many sorts of hands, a different
method was required for each mentality. He did not always adopt the
Leschetizky idea of an arched hand—at least for small ones like mine. A
principle of his was to develop the muscles of the palm of the hand,

The Under Side of the Hand
"This principle is one I have never heard spoken of; he made a great point
of it. The under muscles are delicate, and care should be taken not to strain
them; but with judicious training much strength of hand and fingers can be
acquired through development of these muscles. In my own case, I attribute
the ability to regain my technic quickly to this particular principle.

"After my marriage to Mr. MacDowell, I relinquished all thought of
making a career, although he felt I had the necessary talent and ability. For
fifteen years I scarcely touched the piano. I felt it more important to devote
myself to caring for him, saving his time in many ways and shielding him
from unnecessary cares. Then I took up my music after he passed away, and
taught for five years. I have now had five years in the lecture recital field.

"For this work I needed to regain my technic, and what is more, to keep it
up. I find some of my husband's exercises employing the palm or under
muscles of the hand most beneficial. Here are a few of them." Mrs.
MacDowell sat down at the piano, and laying her outstretched hand on the
keys without depressing them, raised the fingers singly and in pairs, and let
them fall softly on their keys, without in the least disturbing or pressing the
other fingers lying at rest. The fifth finger was especially spoken of as needing
this exercise.

"I practice pieces with this kind of touch," commented the speaker, "when
I go over them for technical purposes.

Playing Softly
"One of Mr. MacDowell's ideas was to practice softly, with outstretched
fingers. This did not mean to the exclusion of other forms of touch, else the
player might lose force and vitality of tone. You remind me that William H.
Sherwood also advised soft tone for practice.

"Another quality of tone is secured by a slight drawing in of the finger tips. I was told the other day, by a pedagogical authority, that this touch was no longer in use—was quite out of date. I am glad to know that you and others use it, and that various well-known artists approve of it.

Memorizing

"I do my memorizing away from the piano, and in several ways. Perhaps the most effective way is the mental photograph I make of the printed page. I can really see the notes before me. I can also recite them, thinking or speaking the two staves together, vertically, not one and then the other, singly. I think one should thoroughly know the piece in various ways, otherwise one may meet disaster when playing in public.

MacDowell's Class

"A very helpful means of study—the fortnightly class, gave zest to the student's work. These classes were regular lessons, of course; in them the student was expected to play a piece through, in a semi-public manner. He was not obliged to memorize, though he could, if he wished, play without the notes. The idea was to go through the piece before others, so that the master himself could judge of the effect. Students usually brought something they had been recently working on in the alternate private lesson, or they might be asked to play a selection that had been laid aside for a few months, and needed review.

Interpretation

"Mr. MacDowell had a strong theory that the pupil should use his own innate musical and rhythmic feeling to get at the meaning of the piece. He sometimes gave a composition of his own to two pupils at the same time, to see how they would work it out. He preferred to have them express their own individuality, if they did not offend against any musical law. The first lesson on a piece was always devoted to the technical side; after that came the interpretation.

"In my recital work, I am always asked to play MacDowell's music; this is quite to be expected. I have a vivid memory of how he played his compositions, and I believe I am better able than any one else to give an adequate idea of his own desire as to its interpretation."

GUIOMAR NOVAES
[1895-1979]

THE GIFT OF MUSIC

The most dazzling meteor that shot across the pianistic sky during the past season—1916—was the young Brazilian pianist, Guiomar Novaes. We were quite unprepared for such an apparition; we had heard nothing of her; she came unheralded. In a season filled to the brim with the greatest piano playing the world can produce, she came—and conquered—by sheer force of genius.

The marvel of it! Such a talent in a family where neither the parents nor any of the eighteen other children showed any special musical inclination. Hers is surely a gift straight out of Heaven!

Many of us are familiar with the story of how this slip of a girl developed her gifts, first in her own country and then in Paris, where she took first place over 388 contestants, in the entrance examinations of the Conservatoire. At that examination her performance of Schumann's *Carneval* was so unusual in the mastery of technic, so poetic in interpretation as to greatly impress the jury, composed of Debussy, Moszkowski, Fauré and other distinguished musicians.

The young girl was about fourteen when she arrived in Paris, and began her studies with Professor Philipp, at the Conservatoire. At the end of the second year she received the first honor, a *Premier Prix du Conservatoire.* After this came many engagements to play in Paris, London, Switzerland, Germany, and Italy, which she filled with ever-increasing success.

Then came two years at home in Brazil, which she spent resting, working, thinking, growing and ripening, but playing little in public. Late in the year 1915 she and her mother came to New York, escorted by the Brazilian Ambassador from Washington.

"I think it is time for her to begin her American career," he remarked, after her first New York recital; "and," he added significantly, "I believe she is ready for it."

The young artist indeed proved herself ready. Her first long and difficult program revealed sentiment, power, passion and ripe musicianship. Her success was immediate and complete. These are, briefly, the mere facts. But who can put into words the thrill, the spell of such playing as hers? In London, when she played there, it was chronicled: "She is one of the world's greatest pianists." After her first American appearance, Mr. Finck, in the *Evening Post*, said of her: "She is the greatest woman pianist now before the public, and even some of the men had better look to their laurels." Later, after her fourth triumphant recital in the metropolis, the same critic wrote: "Her tone has the limpid purity and beauty that the world adores in voices like Patti's or Sembrich's or Caruso's; in runs these tones are like strings of perfect pearls. Miss Novaes seems to get her inspiration direct from heaven. One has a feeling, when she plays Beethoven, as if she were in long-distance telepathic communication with him—as if he indeed were at the piano. And if her piece is by Chopin, Schumann or some other master, it is they who apparently are personally guiding her. This is no hyperbole; it is an impression, which makes this girl one of the seven wonders of the musical world."

What are the attributes in the performance of this "superpianist" as she has been called; what are the things that compel admiration, that enthrall alike the unskilled music lover; the trained musician and the exacting critic? If we can discover them, analyze and reduce them to tangible terms, we may be able to apply the principles to the profit of our own studies.

On the technical side we can study the player's manner of tone production. Tone is the medium through which the musical idea is set forth. With Miss Novaes the tone seems to be produced by controlled relaxation. Much is said and written about relaxation in these days. The kind this girl possesses is plastic and beautifully controlled. With the most graceful movements of arm she forms and molds the tone to such quality as she desires. She plays with controlled weight, but it is weight that is *alive*, vital, not lumbering and "dead." With this condition of poise in arm, wrist and hand, every tone she produces, from feathery *pianissimo* to the utmost *fortissimo*, has a searching, vibrant quality, a quality that makes an instant appeal to the listener. Even a single tone has the poignant quality that makes a thrilling effect. She produces these tones without apparent effort; yet they carry a message quite apart from the studied phrases of other pianists.

Technic in her case is an "art in itself." No problem seems too difficult; all are flawlessly mastered. Imagine strings of pearls, large and small; in each string the pearls are exactly the same size, round and perfect; such are her scales. Her glissandi ripple up and down the keyboard with a perfect beauty and smoothness that the hand of no other pianist within memory has surpassed. Her chords are full and rich, her trills like the song of birds. The listener sits aghast at such absolute mastery, and marvels where this girl has acquired such consummate technic. He marvels still more at the interpretative genius, which seizes upon the inherent meaning of the composition, finds its poetic, emotional message, and is able to present it with such convincing, overwhelming conviction and appeal.

I have tried, in few words, to voice some of the causes of Miss Novaes' mastery, some of the means by which she conquers the keyboard, the music and our hearts, because I know she could not do so herself. She could no more explain how she does these things than a flower bud can describe how it becomes a perfect rose. She would only say: "Your praise may apply to a great pianist, but I am not a great artist." Such is her modesty and self-effacement.

We must let Guiomar Novaes say something for herself, however; she will do so in a pretty mixture of English and French, with a few sentences of Spanish thrown in here and there. When she talks one hardly knows which to admire most, the pleasant voice and smile, the dimples that play hide and seek in her cheeks, or the artless sincerity of her words.

"I began to play piano when I was four, by listening and by picking out everything on the piano by ear; I taught myself by the ear. Sometimes it seems I learned to play before I learned to speak; it is true I knew my notes before I had mastered the letters of the alphabet.

"When I was six my studies really began. I was placed with a most excellent teacher, Professor Chiafarelle, an Italian musician. With him I learned a great deal, and began to play in Sao Paulo, my home city, when I was ten.

"He was my teacher seven years. Then our Government sent me to Paris, where I was admitted to the Conservatoire, and became a pupil of Isador Philipp for nearly four years.

Technic Practice

"I practice about three to four hours every day. I no longer practice the technic by itself, outside of pieces, for there is so much technic in the pieces themselves, that I work on that. But when I was a child I had to work on technic and on all kinds of exercises most industriously. I haven't time to do so now, for there is so much music to learn.

"Yes, I play Bach—much Bach, when I have time, but not every day."

"Some artists save their strength by playing with only half force during practice. Do you follow this course?" she was asked.

"No, in practice I use full power; that is, I try to make the piece sound as I want it to sound. If I should play with a weak touch, I would not get the *sonore*, how do you call it? Ah, yes, the sound. I would not get the sound as I want it.

Memorizing

"I really do not know how I memorize; it all comes to me very quickly—the music. I find it very amusing to learn by heart. You think I should not call it amusing you think I should say interesting? Well, then, I think it is very interesting to learn from memory. I can do it away from the piano, by thinking how the music looks when it is printed. I sometimes do this on the trains, when I am traveling. When I was in Switzerland, I found I had to play the Beethoven G major Concerto, in Paris, in a short time. So I learned it all by heart in fourteen days. It is true I had played at it some at home in Brazil; but now I really had to learn it. The Bach Organ Prelude and Fugue, transcribed by Moór, which I played at my third New York recital, I learned in four days. When I did so I was feeling very fresh and well rested, and equal to the task. I might not always feel able to do it so quickly."

Public Playing

"Do you really enjoy playing in public?" she was asked.

"Yes, I do like it. At a recital, I soon become so absorbed in what I am doing that I quite forget the audience; it is as if the audience was not there; it does not exist for me. I cannot say I always feel the same or play the same. The piano may seem different, the hall, the audience, too, and my mood."

"That is what Josef Hofmann says also," I remarked.

"Ah, what a great, big artist Hofmann is!" The dark eyes glowed with inward fire and the dimples deepened. "I think he is so wonderful. Schelling is a big artist, too. He played in my country, *Brazillo*, and had a great success there."

Modern Music

"Do you care for modern music—Schoenberg, Stravinsky, Korngold or Ornstein?" she was asked. The mention of these names awoke no answering gleam in the calm, sweet face.

"I do not know the music you speak of," she said. "I shall play something of Bach arranged by Emanuel Moór. Moór has written much; some fine things for cello, which Casals plays.

"You think I make good progress with English? I have only studied it five months, just since I came to New York. I am really surprised at myself today, that I have had the courage to speak to you in your own language. Usually I speak French, as, naturally I know that much better than English."

LEO ORNSTEIN

[1893-2001]

SANITY IN MUSIC STUDY

L eo Ornstein, an ultra modern pianist and composer, was born in 1895 near Odessa, Russia. After coming to America he was thoroughly trained in the Leschetizky principles of piano playing by Mrs. Thomas Tapper, and in other musical studies at the Institute of Musical Art. Several years ago he went abroad for further study and recitals. He played in London and Norway, and had numerous concerts ahead when the outbreak of the war caused him to return to America.

"You heard me play years ago?" began young Ornstein, as we were seated in my studio for a musical conference. "It must have been about five at least, if it was in the Mendelssohn, G minor. Did I really ever do that? Ah, how long ago it seems! A lifetime appears to lie between that period of my life and today, so much has happened to me—I am another person."

One could easily understand his feeling. For the student had developed into an artist, the fledgling into an aspiring composer, whose daring flights of imagination have already aroused much attention on both sides of the Atlantic. Whether, as some would have us believe, the startling innovations of the young musician are but the ravings of an unsound mind, or are to preach a new gospel of emotional impression and tone color; whether the youth is but a clever juggler with sounds, or is a new and brilliant star arising in the musical firmament, the future alone can decide.

It can be truly said, however, that one cannot talk with Leo Ornstein for five minutes without realizing he is absolutely sincere in his work. His fixed purpose is to express himself and his age with fidelity and honesty, according to his lights, no matter what critics or others may say to the contrary. And he has the courage of his convictions, plus enthusiasm enough to furnish forth a dozen less buoyant and more sedate brothers in art.

"The technical side of piano playing?" he continued; "what is technic but the means by which you can express yourself—it is the outward and material sign through which you are able to say what is in your heart to say; therefore it is subordinate, but must be individual. Do not think that I would for one moment belittle technic; one must have it, it is a necessity; but it sinks into insignificance before the meaning of the message one has to deliver.

"As a pianist I have had most thorough and excellent training, I am thankful to say; I play my Czerny constantly, and know my Bach from cover to cover. I feel Bach is the greatest master of all: his works will never fall into neglect. Still, we must realize we live in a different age; our customs, our manner of living, we ourselves are not at all like the people of Bach's time or Beethoven's, or Haydn's. Look at Mozart; could any music mirror and express the spirit of his age with more charming simplicity and fidelity? I love it; it is a perfect reflection of the time in which he lived. The technic to play Mozart, however, will not answer to play Debussy. Modern music requires an entirely different handling of the instrument. We cannot interpret modern ideas with the old style equipment. To illustrate: none of the older composers would think of making such requirements on one's technic as this, for instance." The young artist went to the piano and played a succession of shadowy, filmy chords. "I must here use the palm of my hand as well as the fingers; the former depresses the white keys below, while the fingers touch the black keys above them. In another chord passage from one of my pieces, I had in mind the falling of blocks of granite, which descend softly with a muffled thud," again illustrating.

As a pianist Leo Ornstein has won high praise from the critics. Huneker says of him: "He is that rare thing, an individual pianist." Others have written that: "his playing has tonal beauty and clarity of style," that "he has a touch on the keys as caressing as it is powerful—with an almost uncanny breathing into and inhaling from them something of inspiration." "He is a born virtuoso, with an ear unparalleled in its sensitiveness for tone color and tone quality. Trills and passages are faultless and are delivered with a freedom and perfection any one might envy."

On a later occasion Mr. Ornstein spoke more freely about technical development. "I have made a good many experiments and discoveries about piano touch and technic, especially when I was living in Paris. After being in Vienna, I went to Berlin and then to Paris, where I literally shut myself up in a garret and worked for about nine months. For one thing I wanted to make a study of some modern French music, for modern tendencies absorb me greatly. I procured a few pieces by Debussy and Ravel and studied them closely. Of course I memorized them in a few days and played them a good deal. But my playing did not satisfy me, though I did not see what was the matter. All at once it came to me that I was trying to make tone color with my fingers, when it should be done with the pedals. The moment this truth was borne in upon me, the problem was solved. I began to study all manner of pedal effects and tonal coloring with the pedals.

"In mastering piano tone and technic, the arm plays a vital role. Naturally, the fingers must be well trained, but in playing they do not need to be lifted high. In fact, the nearer they are held to the keys—provided strength and elasticity have been developed, the better the tone. Strength of finger is the great thing. A firm nail joint is absolutely necessary, quite as much for soft as for loud playing. People think it does not need much strength to play softly; I am sure the reverse is true. Fingers must be very strong and then held close to the keys, for pianissime effects, otherwise the tone will be mushy and uncertain. I have a whole set of technics for strength and agility, which I go through when I am away from the piano; they are specially useful when traveling. Here is one:" he pressed one finger, firmly curved, into the table, and slowly rolled it from side to side. All fingers are to be treated in the same way. Another exercise for strength consisted in lifting one finger in curved position, as high as possible, while the other four were pressed down into the table with strong pressure. In neither exercise should the fingers yield or 'give in,' at the nail joints, but always preserve their rounded form.

When practicing I use full power, or nearly so—play slowly and firmly. When I thoroughly know the piece, I gradually go faster, till I have worked it up to the required tempo. It comes up without much trouble, when one thoroughly knows the notes. Many players make the mistake of at once playing quickly, after the slow practice; I find it much better to acquire speed gradually.

"It is so easy to fall into a rut in regard to interpretation. We grow accustomed to hearing compositions rendered in a certain way; any deviation from that standard startles us. I can feel the shock caused by novelty, go over an audience, when my rendition is not the conventional one of the schools. For instance, in the G minor Ballade of Chopin, I hold pedal through each of those final runs, on through to the chord following; it makes a new and interesting effect. But it surprises the musicians sometimes, and I can see they do not consider it orthodox.

Before a Concert

"It is true that on the day of a recital, I practice for hours—all day perhaps— but do not touch the pieces I am to give for my program. Instead, I practice many other things, often Bach. In this way the program seems to me much fresher than if I had delved on it up to the last moment. I play Bach a great deal; all the Well-Tempered Clavichord, the big organ Preludes and Fugues arranged by Liszt, and of course the Chromatic Fantaisie and Fugue.

"The artist's playing in public is very deceptive, to the student. For the artist conceals the mechanism of his art, and only considers its emotional message before his audience. Therefore it is not always a real benefit to the student to hear a great many artists; that is, not a benefit to his technical development, though it should help him on the interpretative side.

"Let me give you a few words more about my Paris experiences. I brought a letter of introduction to the famous critic and writer, Calvocoressi. There is a wonderful man! He can speak and write eight languages—Greek is one of them. He writes for several English papers and two Russian, besides the foremost Paris magazines. I went to him, told him what I was doing, played for him and showed him some of my stuff. He at once spoke Russian to me, interested himself in me and helped me in a great many ways. He lectured on the music of Schoenberg, Stravinsky and Ornstein in the Sorbonne and other places.

"You have heard the story of my London concerts. It was a terrible experience; I can laugh at it now, but then it was heart-rending. There seemed to be two factions; those who were open-minded enough to listen, who wished to understand what I was trying to do; the others who closed their ears and would have none of me. Well-seasoned concert goers said they had never seen a London audience so stirred and upset.

"A week after my first recital there, I gave a second, with an entire program of my own compositions. That occasion was the most trying one of my whole life. I was hardly conscious of a note I played that day, but I got through the ordeal in some fashion.

"I can well understand how my music must strike people on first hearing. Even good musicians can discover nothing whatever in it when they listen to it once; but I know many cases where they do see the meaning of it after repeated hearings. If they would but reserve their decision till they have heard a piece seven or eight times, they could judge of it better. It has often chanced that they understand it after the eighth time. You know *Pelléas and Melisande*, at its premier, was hissed off the stage and the curtain rung down on the second act. Now it is sung to sold-out houses. So I always feel like asking the listener to bear with me till after he has heard my work a few times. Even the *Wild Man's Dance* has become clear to some after the eighth time!

"As you say, I must always lead up to a piece like that: I could never let it out of a clear sky, so to speak. And I must work up my mood also, in order to be an efficient medium.

"You ask about my manner of composing. I can say I never sit at the piano when I compose, never try the thing over as I write it, and never under any circumstances change a note of the piece after it is written; it must stand or fall as first set down. Perhaps after a few days I may condemn what I have written. If I find it unworthy I say to myself: 'Leo Ornstein, for shame! how could you write like that.' Then I tear it up. Probably I shall never make a second attempt on the same subject—it is gone, passed into oblivion.

"The composition comes into my mind fullfledged and complete as far as it goes. When I hear it, I make frantic haste to get it to paper lest I lose a note. This is a difficult task, because the rhythms are often so intricate, and I must preserve those as well as the harmonies. It is very difficult to decipher the first hasty draft of my pieces; no one can do it but myself, for I have a sort of musical shorthand. Tonic and other regular chords may not be written in at all, but I know what they ought to be. All must be jotted down so quickly there is no time to be careful. It only took about two and a half hours to put the *Wild Man's Dance* on paper. Publishers are asking for more piano pieces; I have composed a number, but oh, the task of copying them!

"When composing, I have often an incident in mind which the music is designed to illustrate; yet I am averse to affixing any special title to the piece, as this may hamper player or listener, who are endeavoring to picture the scene or mood hinted at. To others the piece may suggest something entirely different from the picture or mood the composer had in mind when writing it; these may be quite as appropriate and legitimate as the one he had intended. I might tell you a pretty story about my *Wild Man's Dance*, that is, what the music means to me; to you it may mean an earthquake or a shipwreck. When you hear it you observe that at first there is some confusion, as the men fall into line. But soon the rhythms become very insistent and compelling, as the savages unite in their mad whirl. At last one of them comes out from among the others, and dances alone in the circle. This Dance is one of the most difficult compositions, and requires tremendous power to play. You may have heard about my playing it for Leschetizky. Of course I led up to it with some simpler and more melodious things. When I finished the Dance he seemed quite dazed by it. Then he sprang up, exclaiming, 'You must have lied to me, for no living mortal could put such a thing on paper!' I happened to have the manuscript with me, and showed it to him; he would scarcely believe it even then.

"Another piece that interested me to write was *Impressions of Notre Dame*. I visited the famous church almost as soon as I arrived in Paris. On my return to the hotel the first *Impression* sprang into my mind. A few days later, after another visit to the old pile, the second *Impression, Gargoyles,* was written.

"Some of my recently published compositions include a set of nine piano pieces (Op. 7), two songs, *Mother o' Mine*, and *There Was a Jolly Miller*; also a Sonata for violin and piano, and one for piano and cello."

It is evident that talent for composition went hand in hand with pianistic ability, for the young Russian began to compose at an early age. About four years ago new impulses led him into novel paths; his work began to manifest traits similar to those found in the music of Schoenberg and Stravinsky, although Ornstein was unacquainted with their compositions. As he himself explains: "I do not conceive of music in the way Beethoven did—as a mosaic of themes and motives, each developed and repeated, block-wise. I try to express feelings rather than forms—impressions, emotions, mental states of consciousness."

To quote again from Huneker:

"I never thought I should live to hear Arnold Schoenberg sound tame; yet tame he is, almost timid and halting after Ornstein—who is, most emphatically, the only true-blue, genuine Futurist composer alive."

MARTINUS SIEVEKING

[1867-1950]

THE DEAD-WEIGHT PRINCIPLE

Martinus Sieveking, sometimes known as the "Flying Dutchman," on account of his nationality and his volatile disposition, was born at Amsterdam. He studied music as a child with his father, and afterward became a pupil of J. Rontgen, a graduate of the Leipzig, who settled in Amsterdam in 1878.

In 1895 Sieveking came to America to visit the World's Fair. He played in Boston, and was induced by his friends to remain and make a concert tour, which he did during the following season. This tour was brought to a sudden conclusion by the unexpected disappearance of the pianist, who, it afterward appeared, had taken the steamer for home, being dissatisfied with his own performance.

On his return to Europe he sought Leschetizky and studied with him for some time, after which he set to work to develop a method of his own, and has greatly improved his playing. For some years Sieveking has resided in Paris, and in 1899 he married.

Sieveking is a man of frank and generous disposition. He is full of mechanical ingenuity, and enjoys nothing better than inventing and making ingenious mechanical appliances of various kinds." [Lahee, Henry C., *Famous Pianists*, 1906, p.251-253]

A MAN who has, according to his own account, solved all problems of the keyboard—a man who, during a dozen or fifteen years of unremitting effort has built up for himself a perfect piano mechanism, is truly a unique figure in the pianistic world. Few artists are willing to make, or can substantiate such a claim. Even the greatest of them confess to some limitations; they admit there are some problems a little beyond their reach. The eminent Holland pianist believes he has solved them all; he feels there is nothing on the technical side beyond his ken.

Mr. Sieveking tells us his piano method is founded on scientific principles unknown up to the present time. The most important of these is the principle of dead or relaxed weight. But we, in America, have for over thirty years, been familiar with Dr. William Mason's exposition of the principle of relaxation and devitalization. Some of the most prominent teachers and pianists among us today were students of Mason, use his method and are working along the lines laid down by him. They cannot forget the ease and power this principle gave their master's playing, nor his beautiful touch and tone. Godowsky is a modern master who preaches relaxed, or dead weight of hand and arm upon the key. It is the vital principle of Hofmann's wonderful art. A host of others have testified to its value and necessity—Powell, Carreño, Schnabel, Leginska—to say nothing of the Breithaupt book on weight touch.

And now we are told that the principle of dead or relaxed weight has been unknown up to the present time! What does it all mean?

Thus I mused as I proceeded to keep an appointment with Mr. Martinus Sieveking, who had recently arrived in this country from Paris. It will be remembered that he toured America years ago, and proved himself a brilliant pianist and most excellent musician. I mentally resolved to settle the subject of weight touch with him the very first thing, before taking up other technical points which had occurred to me to question him about.

Let it be recorded at once that I came, saw, and became convinced that here was one who had solved many if not most of the technical difficulties of the piano. While it may be too much to claim that the principle of dead weight has not been fully understood until now, it can be truthfully stated that the Dutch pianist has discovered a means of applying this principle in a manner that will improve touch and tone in a short time. If his directions are implicitly followed, the fingers will almost immediately become stronger while the tone will increase in volume and sonority. His authoritative words and manner bespeak the autocrat, but a man who has spent a good part of his life in devising means to obtain a big, luscious tone, strong fingers, fluent technic, and has succeeded to a remarkable degree, feels he has a right to be autocratic. Details of this conference will surely be of deep interest to teachers and students of the instrument.

I found Mr. Sieveking in his spacious studios, a man of commanding presence, winning manner, and speaking English fluently. Two grand pianos, one of foreign the other of American make, stood side by side in the center of the music room. The French instrument had been built for his special use; not only were the keys wider, but the whole keyboard was tilted a little downward at the back, which he explained was a decided advantage.

His Method

"You want to know about my method of using relaxed weight?" he began. "I will gladly tell you all I can; what is more, I will show you each step. Let us sit here at this piano and demonstrate as we go along." As he spoke he caught my hand by one finger and held it up to test its weight; in fact he let the hand hang by one finger and then by another as he talked.

"Many people think they are using dead weight in playing, when the truth is they do not really understand the principle at all. I could mention a few pianists who do use it. Godowsky does to a considerable extent, Carreño also. It requires absolute concentration from the start, until it has become so much a part of one's being that it is 'second nature.' Its use increases the volume of tone in a wonderful degree."

All this time my hand had been held suspended in air; now he let go of the finger and the arm fell.

"You have an understanding of the dead weight in the arm; now we will see if you can put it into the fingers."

The second finger of the right hand was placed on the key D, in a firmly arched position. The other fingers were well curved and raised, thumb extended from the hand, and arm hung down naturally at the side. Mr. Sieveking believes in arched hand, well curved fingers and high, free finger action, for all technical finger exercises. He says: "The fingers should be raised as high as possible (without strain). I insist on this important point, as I do not believe it possible to develop a fine technic without it. Sometimes the flat finger is employed by virtuosi to secure a beautiful tone, but at first the student should confine himself to the curved finger."

The second finger, resting on the key D and supporting the entire weight of hand and arm, was now tested over and over, by being lifted high and then allowed to fall back on the key. Arm weight increased as thought was consciously directed to this point.

"*Perfectement!* Now you see what I mean—now you have it! With your arm supported on the tip of the second finger, play a down stroke with the third finger, over and over again, always maintaining this heavy, weighted feeling in the hand and arm. Of course you are familiar with the different sets of muscles which work the fingers, some of which lie on top and others on the underside of the arm. The extensors on top of the arm do the lifting, and as lifting is more difficult to accomplish than dropping or falling, we must give greater heed to the raising of the finger, that it may be done with quickness and exactness."

Each Finger by Itself

Each finger in turn was now used as support, while the one next it was exercised with quick up-and-down movements. No weakness or bending, no hesitation in movement, no lifting except in an exactly straight line were allowed. The stroke was made with as much power as possible. Every player and teacher knows how important it is to gain power and clearness, and feels the need of some sure way to acquire these with the right conditions. I had made my own experiments along these lines; now it was a satisfaction to meet with a master who had worked them out so logically.

"We have now done the first exercise I give the students who come to me. The second goes a step further. As you see the first step only employs one finger at a time; for I consider it a great mistake to play so-called five finger exercises, at first. The only sound basis for technic is to begin with one finger at a time. The second step employs two fingers in legato, but always with dead weight of arm, supported on the finger tips. We must be conscious of this condition at all times, which means—at first—constant thinking. One should also play with each hand alone, as concentration is a most important factor of all the work.

The Proof

"A player who has taken the two steps, as we have just done, has already the proof of what this method will do for him. In one hour I can convince him of its benefits. With two hours daily practice for one week, he will find his tone increased and his fingers appreciably stronger."

Octave Training

"What about octaves?" he was asked.

"We need strength, suppleness and rapidity for octaves. I have special training for octaves. They call into requisition the muscles of the forearm; the wrist is but the hinge between the hand and forearm. With the hand in arched form, the playing fingers curved and firm, we cultivate each finger in turn, with quick hand strokes on the key. Of course, for octaves, the first and fifth are most important, but all fingers can come in for this sort of training. At first use four repetitions on each key, and play up and down the keyboard, at least four octaves. Use the diatonic and chromatic scales. After these have been learned, I have invented various exercises which employ 8ths, 7ths, 6ths, 5ths and 4ths, in this way," and he ran over these forms with the greatest ease and speed.

Training the Thumb

"I have also many exercises for training the thumb in scale playing. Here is the first one: With the second finger on a black key and the arm weight suspended on it, the thumb passes from the white key on one side of it to the white key on the other side of it, the thumb describing an arched movement from one key to the other. The thumb is also trained to pass under all the other fingers."

"Have you any special counsel to give in the matter of memorizing?"

Memorizing

"In the first place, try to have the pupil learn something of harmony; even a little is helpful, it is better than nothing. It will enable him to analyze the music sufficiently to give him some little idea of what he is trying to play. Take a small portion of the piece, say two measures at a time, learn one hand and then the other. Know them so thoroughly the notes can be recited or written. Thus one can think out the piece away from the instrument.

"I have had and now have students of great talent studying with me, several of them winners of the *Premier Prix* in Paris. They all testify to the benefits received from careful study of my exposition of the principle of dead weight. I have embodied these principles and exercises into a system; I hope to have the work published later on." Mr. Sieveking took a book from the table and asked me to look it over. The text and musical illustrations were all written by his own hand, the former in clear, elegant English.

"This is a life work," he said. "I have written it to aid teachers and students, for all must learn these principles. I have come to America for this purpose, leaving my home and family in Paris. I intend to return after accomplishing my mission here. Oh, yes, I shall concertize in America; but I especially desire to compose. Here is a little piece, a Nocturne, which I began in Paris and finished in New York. Would you like to hear it?"

He began to play and I was soon absorbed in listening to the quality of his tone, so big, sweet and penetrating. Once he turned to me naively; "Do you like it—it's nice, isn't it?"

After a little he broke off. "I really cannot play on an ordinary sized keyboard, and my French piano is being repaired. On this one my fingers seem to get between the black keys and I can't get them out." And he held up those wonderful hands of his, surely the largest, most muscular and perfectly developed among piano hands.

"You see that photograph of two hands?" pointing to a picture on the wall. "One is Rubinstein's, the other my own—side by side. They are almost identical. Rubinstein's fingers had cushions on the ends; I believe these are necessary to play the piano successfully.

"Oh, yes, I use the metronome; you see I have one of extra size standing there."

The Holland master is a thorough believer in hard work. "I condemn my pupils to hard labor," he says. "Technic is brains, plus rightly trained muscles and nerves. To acquire a technic, keep it up and constantly improve it, should be the aim of every pianist."

A Visit To Sieveking

"Come down and see me next Sunday afternoon—there will be music," wrote Martinus Sieveking, the Dutch pianist and composer, from his sylvan retreat on Long Island. The invitation was alluring; the day proved fair and we went. Mr. Sieveking had chosen to locate for the summer not on the shore but a little inland, where green lawns and shrubbery abound. With him were Mrs. Elliott and Miss Inez Elliott, a young pianist, who had studied with this accomplished teacher for the past ten years. He considers her a thorough mistress of his method, and as yet the only authorized exponent of it in this country.

When we arrived at the villa, sounds of a piano met us before we reached the garden gate. Bach was being played with amazing fluency and velocity. We paused to listen and waited till the tones ceased before pressing the bell. The player responded, opened the door and led us at once into the parlor which served as his music room. It was a square room with several windows looking out to the green. On a small mantle shelf stood a few drawings; prominent among them a photograph of Adelina Patti, sent him in commemoration of her seventieth birthday. Two concert grands took up the major portion of the room, though the whole space seemed dominated by the presence of the pianist himself. One felt here was a big personality; a man who had thought much, studied deeply, had lived and suffered.

In answer to some of my questions regarding his early life and career, the artist said:

"I was surrounded by musical influences from the beginning of my life. My father was a thoroughly trained musician, a conductor and composer, my mother was a singer. I have always lived in a musical atmosphere: I think this is one of the essentials if one would become a musician. At a very early age I began to play the piano; before long I began to compose. At twelve I played organ in a church. Later on I went to Vienna, to Leschetizky. The Professor took great interest in me and was especially kind. There were six of us, chosen out of a class of ninety, to be his special favorites; they were: Hambourg, Gabrilowitsch, Goodson, Schnabel, Newcomb and myself.

"After those happy student days, I concertized everywhere; I came to America also. But I was not satisfied with the success I had won, nor with what I had achieved. I felt there were deeper principles underlying my art which I did not yet understand. So I set to work to discover them. The result is the method I have formulated, which has cost me fifteen years' hard labor. But I am satisfied with the result; I feel I have won out; I feel I have gained the correct principles of true piano technic. Life has been a bitter struggle at times. Sometimes I have had to go hungry—I have even had to starve! Thank

Heaven, all that is over; there are now no financial worries. My aim is to benefit others with my discoveries. I want to help teachers to teach better and players to play better. I often give much time to those with talent who are unable to pay, yet are deserving. I want to be surrounded by talented, congenial people wherever I am."

Yielding to our request, he began to play. First his *Souffrance*, written three years ago, when his son was very ill. It expresses a father's anxiety for the recovery of the stricken one. After this Beethoven, Op. 27, No. 2, the "Moonlight." Then a Bach violin Gavotte, transcribed for piano by himself. Next some Chopin, and finally one of his latest compositions, a Nocturne, embodying a haunting, appealing melody. "Women like this piece," he remarked, in answer to our openly expressed admiration. "This and the *Souffrance* have, I think, the right to exist; they are modern but not futuristic, for I cannot write in that style. The Nocturne is a little after the manner of Chopin—I quite frankly acknowledge it. It certainly does not copy the Polish master, for it is distinctly modern; but it is in his spirit. I wrote it while staying in a beautiful villa, where there was a lovely garden with flowers and fruit. Blue skies overhead and sunshine and moonlight. Who could help being influenced by such surroundings. I have tried to express the feelings the environment made upon me. Some composers write from the heart, like Beethoven; some from the head, like Strauss. Wagner expressed both head and heart."

More about his Method
A little later he brought out the MS copy of his method, placed it upon the piano, and we fell to discussing the material and doing the exercises. After each one had been tried he would say: "Do you approve of this? Do you think it will help? Is it not a good exercise? Any one who can play this with endurance and velocity has technic. These scale exercises will surely help everybody."

The master constantly spoke of the dead weight principle—the weight of arm hanging on the finger tips. While all this is true, the term "dead weight" does not, to my mind, convey the whole truth, and may mislead the uninitiated. It gives no idea, for example, of the extreme firmness of the fingers, nor of the muscular energy used to depress the keys in all finger exercises. It is this element of energy, combined with arm weight, which give power and sonority to the tone. Sieveking insists on high, large movements of fingers for all technical exercises and wants all the sonority that can be brought from the instrument. His whole mentality is built on large lines of thought: even his handwriting corresponds. Yet he can caress the keys most delicately when he wills to do so.

Later in the afternoon we had tea and delicious cakes made by Miss Elliott's fair hands. Sieveking was genial and told many anecdotes. He wished me to examine the hand of his pupil and note its beautiful development. "She plays with the greatest perfection," he said. "You shall hear her; I insist she make a career."

The blaze of a glorious sunset met our eyes as we all left the villa and sauntered through the quiet, hedge-bordered streets, flanked by pretty villas and gardens. Our genial host insisted on accompanying us to the train and seeing us safely aboard. As he stood there on the little platform, waving us a farewell, his tall figure looming dark against the lambent sunset sky, the whole made an "impression" not to be forgotten. Had we only possessed the necessary gift, the scenes of the afternoon might have served as basis for a futuristic tone poem. Fortunately, or otherwise, we could only keep the group of mental pictures to hang on Memory's walls.

MR. A[lmon] K[incaid] AND MRS. [Florence] VIRGIL

[1842-1921] and [1869-1944]

THE NECESSITY OF A THOROUGH FOUNDATION

I f Mr. Virgil were asked for what particular title he would wish to be known to posterity his answer would surely be "as a musical educator." To the cause of Education in Music he has consecrated his life.

It may be of interest to the army of teachers and players who use the clavier, who have found such benefit in the method of piano technic and study combined with it, to know a few facts in the career of the inventor of this remarkable instrument.

Almon Kincaid Virgil is a native of Erie, Penn. His father practiced law until middle life, then studied theology and became a Baptist minister. He was a highly educated man, with an intense love for music, and much natural ability for it. His son Almon was taught to play both cello and organ at a very early age; while occupied with school work, he devoted much time to music. After graduating from a seminary, he entered college, but later was forced to relinquish his studies on account of ill health. To please his father he then took up the study of law at the Albany Law School; but as all his interests tended toward the study and teaching of music, he soon gave up all thought of being a lawyer.

In his early twenties A. K. Virgil, through the influence of a College President with whom he came in touch, became deeply interested in the study of psychology, and its application to correct educational principles in the study of music. From that period he has been a constant student of this subject.

How the Clavier came into Being

When young Virgil began—over fifty years ago in a western town—to teach music, he discovered that most piano pupils had very little idea of what they were trying to do or what they were aiming at. Even then he felt that the study of music should be made as thorough and logical as the study of mathematics or any other science. He began to strive at once to educate pupils to think; to do one thing at a time and do it thoroughly—to do nothing without correct thinking. His desire was to train the mental and physical powers to form a perfect, well-balanced whole.

He discovered in those early days, that the average pupil had a very uncertain touch and poor key-connection. Some tones were likely to overlap, while others would be disconnected. He felt that if attention could be concentrated on a pure legato effect, away from, or quite apart from musical sound, both touch and tone would be greatly improved.

Two keys abstracted from an old piano served for an experiment he had in mind. When the inventor had arranged the action of these two keys to his satisfaction, he allowed one or two of his pupils to practice slow trill exercises on them. These pupils felt the benefit almost immediately, through more exact movements and better piano tone. Other keys were soon added to the first pair, as the idea grew and more improvements resulted. From such small beginnings as these sprang the first early effort called the techniphone, which finally developed into the Practice Clavier, and then into the perfected instrument we now have.

At the root of all this thought and experiment was the vital idea to awaken musical intelligence in the mind of the pupil, and prevent so much indifferent, shiftless, aimless practice. For it is impossible to accomplish anything on the clavier without thought. A second idea of equal importance was to separate, for a time, the so-called mechanical side of piano study from the musical side; in other words to prepare fingers, hands and arms for the work they were to perform, before attempting that work. In every branch of labor the artisan must fit himself for his task before undertaking it; why should not the pianist do the same? Such a logical division of labor reduces measurably the time required to gain control of physical and mental forces.

It would seem both sensible and normal to begin one's musical studies in a way to gain the quickest results. But finger and arm preparation away from the keyboard had been little thought of. The very idea of moving fingers and playing exercises on a table or toneless instrument was considered detrimental. No,—tone must be heard; there could be no playing without tone. The fact that better and purer tones could be produced as the result of proper preparation, was difficult for teacher or student to grasp or believe. Thus an uphill path lay before the inventor, to convince others his ideas were sound and sensible. It has been a long and arduous struggle, but it has not been in vain. The results for good have been wide and far-reaching. Many have come to realize the truth of the principle he has preached and taught for so many years; countless students have been benefited,—many teachers all over America and also in Europe have been able to teach along scientific lines,—have learned what it is to have something definite to teach.

Education in Music

Mr. Virgil and his wife—formerly Miss Florence Dodd of London, who so ably assists him in his musical and educational labors—called at my studio recently. They had just arrived in New York after completing a successful year of musical activity in St. Petersburg, Florida, where they have established a music school, which is already in a very flourishing condition, with a large number of pupils enrolled.

"As yet we have done all the teaching ourselves," said Mrs. Virgil. "You can get an idea of what that means when I tell you I begin at half past seven in the morning and teach right through the day till into the evening. It is absolutely virgin soil down there, they welcome our work with open mind and are eager for it. We are training some young teachers now, who will soon assist us in the work."

"We believe in teaching music and piano playing on educational principles," said Mr. Virgil. "The trouble seems to be that musicians are not educators, therefore they do not teach music along educational lines, nor with the same thoroughness used for other educational subjects. We feel this is quite a false view to take of music study. The foundation must be well laid if good results are to follow, and the only logical time to do this is at the beginning. Many teachers do not insist on this; there is truly great room for reform in music teaching. Personally we are using time, energy and all our skill to institute and spread these necessary reforms as far as we are able.

"There is one point on which I feel very strongly. A great deal of harm is being done by some artists who are not educators but who are besieged for lessons because of their great success on the concert platform. Their teaching experience includes nothing more than that gained from coaching advanced students in the interpretation of compositions. The harm comes when they declare that definite foundational study and strict technical practice are unnecessary, for technic can be mastered through the study of compositions. Artists who insist there is no need for special technical study—doubtless through ignorance of true educational principles, or because they have never taught the average student—are thoughtlessly doing harm to students the world over.

"For their part, the students are eager to catch at this advice, for they usually wish to get to the top of the tree with as little effort as possible. When they at last awake to the fact they have never laid an adequate foundation to build upon, the awakening is a sad one. For they find it disastrous to try to build up a repertoire without a foundation.

"Fifty years' teaching experience has brought me in touch with thousands of students. From what I have seen of the general lack of preparation I steadfastly maintain that thorough technical study and practice are absolutely necessary and I earnestly warn students against contrary advice.

"It is true artists need not teach technic themselves, but I maintain they ought to consider the proper development of the faculties demanded in piano playing sufficiently to see the importance of advising students to do consistent foundational work. I am thankful there are some artists who do this.

"When correct playing habits have been established and a certain amount of technical skill has been positively acquired, and the student has mastered the principal technical forms, he can dispense with the stacks of etudes which some teachers deem necessary. He can economize time by devoting himself to compositions of real musical value, to be included in a permanent repertoire. But I maintain that even advanced students should give some time each day to direct technical study.

"Some of those who now decry technical study forget what they did in early years to acquire their high pianistic skill. Others are endowed by nature with such wonderful genius and natural physical adaptability to the requirements of the piano that they have been able to dispense with much of the technical practice indispensable to the average student."

Intermediate Teachers

"We feel," supplemented Mrs. Virgil, "there is an important field for musical educators of understanding and ability in bridging over, as it were, the wide gap between the foundation of music study and the stage where the student is ready for the artist teacher. A pupil may have started aright and laid a correct foundation, but if the succeeding steps are not logically taken, precepts which were so carefully inculcated in the beginning are neglected and forgotten. So there is an ever increasing demand for intermediate teachers, who understand the principles of a thorough educational foundation, and can apply those principles to pieces of various degrees of difficulty. This naturally includes a large acquaintance with musical literature, as well as much experience in teaching. I might call such an arrangement a division of labor, though the expression smacks a bit of the workroom.

"Live Weight"

"We hear a great deal in these days about the 'dead weight principle.' Mr. Virgil and I have always taught the principle of weight, but we prefer to call it the 'live weight principle,' for it is really vital and alive. It is of course the principle of relaxation, properly applied and adjusted. When you want great depth of tone you let down all the relaxed weight you have, if you wish softer effects some of the weight is suspended, held back, suppressed. We teach easy relaxed movements from the start. The child must learn to do everything easily and gracefully, if it be only standing, walking, or entering a room. For it cannot be expected that a child who is stiff and awkward in everything else, can suddenly become easy and graceful at the piano without proper training."

Character Building

"Music study based upon true educational principles is most assuredly *character building*," remarked Mr. Virgil. "The successful piano student must have purpose, perseverance and will power; but these qualities, with many students, are apparently lacking in the beginning. It is quite wonderful, however, what persistent effort on the part of the teacher will do to arouse the power of thought and determination in his students."

The Clavier

"And this is just where the clavier, properly employed, becomes such an important ally," interposed Mrs. Virgil. "The majority of teachers do not half realize its value. No student can use the clavier under intelligent guidance, without developing mental control. Experience has taught me that the average student will play far more musically if he divides his practice between clavier and piano, than if he uses the piano exclusively,—this is to say, provided attention is given to ear-training and he is taught to listen to his own playing when he uses the piano. With the average student, use of tone the entire time tends to dull his musical sensibilities. We find that musically gifted students need the clavier just as much as others who are less highly endowed. Constant appeal to the emotional sense through tone is very taxing upon the physical condition; gifted students are apt to work a great deal more through their emotions than through their intelligence."

"Yes," added Mr. Virgil, "and you remember what Professor Butler has said: 'Development through the emotions is ultimate weakness; development through the intelligence is ultimate strength.'"

Volumes might be written about the work of these earnest educators and their efforts toward musical preparedness and efficiency. They have accomplished much and the results of their labors are spreading in ever-widening circles, with ever-increasing influence.

Interviews

from

Modern Masters of the Keyboard
1926

ALEXANDER BRAILOWSKY
[1896-1976]

Thought and Feeling in Piano Playing

I t was in a season more or less dominated by Russians [1925], especially
Russian pianists, that I first heard Alexander Brailowsky. November
was at least half over; Medtner had just been heard in recital and with
orchestra. The later arrival, younger and less known, had not yet made his
debut. Under such circumstances, artists are generally loath to be questioned.
But Mr. Brailowsky was most considerate, and, together with his charming
wife, we had a very pleasant and intimate chat.

Early Studies
"I scarcely know just when I began to play the piano; playing, from the
start, seemed to come natural to me. Even technic itself was made a childhood
pastime for me. My father, a musical amateur of fine taste and cultivation,
played the piano well. He showed me the first steps and helped me over the
early stages. I can remember, when I was only five, how my father and I
used to sit at the piano and play scales together, each of us trying to see
which one would get to the top of the keyboard first! What fun we had with
those scales! I would try to beat Father in speed and accuracy, but he was
usually a little ahead. It was splendid drill for me, though, and I believe such
early practise of scales is invaluable for any child who has real musical ability.

"Later on, as it seemed music was to be my lifework, I was sent to a large
music school in Kiev, the city of my birth, to begin the serious study of
music. I was about eight years old at the time. My teacher at this school was
Pouchalsky, a former pupil of Leschetizky. After several years of earnest
study in my home city, I went to Vienna and put myself into the hands of
Leschetizky. I therefore feel that I have, all my life, been under the influence
of this great master and teacher. I remained with him for more than three
years, that is to say, from 1911 to the year the World War began.

"When I went to this master, he seemed pleased with the technic I had so
far acquired, for I had been developing it for years. However, I went to one of
his assistants for a time, to see that everything was as he would like to have it.

"During all my musical studies, from the very beginning, I was never
trained to consider the mechanical side of piano playing of supreme and

overwhelming importance. I was never made to raise my fingers to just a certain height, nor employed the so-called hammer-touch. Neither was I trained to hold the hand after a certain pattern. Leschetizky always said he had no set method himself; he left that side of the work to his assistants, and each one of these had a little different manner of presenting technical ideas and principles. He also said that, as each student who came to him was of a different caliber and mentality, he must necessarily teach each one differently. He desired to create artistic and musical individuality in each student. In my case, we naturally worked on the interpretative side, as illustrated in the compositions of Beethoven, Schumann, Chopin and Liszt."

Technical Practise

Replying to the question of what material for technic practise, and whether he used mechanical forms of pure technic, outside of pieces, the pianist answered in the negative.

"No, I do not use abstract forms—indeed, I have never done so. There is plenty of technical material to be found in pieces, if one is willing to get right to work and master the knotty problems which occur in any large, serious work. Indeed, I cannot always tell—or put into words—just how I shall go to work to master a passage or piece; the mastery seems to come to me of itself. Again, I do not know, to a nicety, just how I shall interpret a composition after I have made it my own. I have no cut-and-dried manner of playing it; if I had, there would be no opportunity for the inspiration of the moment. When I am alone, communing with my piano, poetic fantasy often carries me away, and I play quite differently from what I do before an audience, where everything must be more circumspect and exact. My wife will bear me out in this statement."

"It is quite true," replied Madame. "He plays very differently when he is alone, or for me—I sometimes scarcely recognize his playing in concert."

Inspired by an Audience

"As I said, I cannot tell, beforehand, exactly how I shall play a certain composition at a given time. I am not one who believes a piece must always be played in just one certain way; that having thought out a conception, the player must always slavishly adhere to it. For in this way there would be no room for spontaneous feeling, for emotion or inspiration. Keeping the general trend and idea of the piece before the mind, I must have some chance to play as I feel.

"An audience can have great effect on the sensibilities of an artist. I can feel at once if any of my listeners are sympathetic, if they are with me and appreciate what I am doing. This mentality in the audience is a tremendous help to an artist and urges him to do his best. A cold or unsympathetic audience has, naturally, the opposite effect, and no one is so quick to sense this atmosphere as the player himself.

Amount of Practise

"I do not practise so very much, only about five hours a day; but, as you say, one can do a great deal in that time, with complete concentration. Of course, situated as we are, in a hotel, I can only do an hour or so, and must go out to get the rest of the time at the piano. But one can do much study away from the instrument, in thinking—*thinking* the music; indeed, it is *all* thinking, in reality. Leschetizky's principle was to do much practise away from the piano. For many reasons this is a necessity.

Repertoire

"Of course I play the classics, but am especially partial to romantic music, Schumann and Chopin. I consider Chopin the greatest composer for the piano. I can say, with truth, that I am not only familiar with all that Chopin ever wrote, but that I play all his music. It is hardly necessary to add that I love this music more than the music of any other composer. It has more poetry, more idealism—at least for me. In Paris, before I left, I gave six programs of his music—I might add, to sold-out houses, showing that French people love his music also. On my piano you will notice a rare portrait of Chopin—" pointing to a picture in color. "It represents a likeness of the Polish master when excited or inspired in playing his own music. It is a copy of a painting by de la Croix, and was presented to me by Pleyel in Paris. One of the six programs I mentioned—one given last April—contained both the Concertos, the Andante Spianato and Polonaise, Op. 22; the Variations on Mozart's 'La ci darem la mano,' Op. 2; the Grande Fantaisie on Polish Airs, Op. 13, and La Krakowiak, Op. 14.

"Yes, most certainly there is a special technic needed to play Chopin's music. It should always be very fluent, fluid, delicate, airy and capable of great variety of color. For this reason the player who would interpret Chopin's music most artistically, should choose a piano with a very facile action and not too deep a touch. I use a Pleyel in Paris and wherever I can get it, as that responds to the lightest pressure.

"As to the program for my debut in America, it is one I have used in many countries. It begins and ends with Liszt. I shall start with the Liszt B minor Sonata, which is a great favorite of mine, and I look forward to playing it in America. This Sonata seems to me one of the greatest works ever written for the piano; it is a true masterpiece. I have heard it played by many artists, and each one finds something individual in it and different from others. Each reading, from Paderewski's down, is interesting, for such a great romantic work is susceptible of great variety of treatment.

"Yes, I play much modern music also. We have various composers in Russia today who are doing good work, each in his own manner, in his own sphere of thought. A few have come to live among you, like Rachmaninoff and Siloti, also Godowsky. Others visit you—Medtner, Prokofieff, Stravinsky, Skriabin. I shall play some Moussorgsky pieces on my first program. We all bring of our art to you, feeling assured of your sympathy and your appreciation."

How He Plays

With his tall, slender figure bowed over the keyboard—as though he loved it—Brailowsky sits as though entranced by the music he evolves, as though utterly oblivious to the listeners who sit before him as under a spell. The tones he produces are always luscious in quality, whether they are of feathery lightness or of splendid sonority. Never once are they harsh or strident. Everything he does has the stamp of a poetic individuality. No matter how hackneyed the piece, he seems to create it anew and hold it up in a fresh light—as he did the Chopin A flat Ballade, the D flat Valse and the Nocturne in E flat. These effects he produces by wonderful tone coloring, by varied nuance, by dwelling ever so slightly on a note here and there, by accents and exceptionally artistic control of the pedals. With him the pedal is truly "the soul of the piano." The Liszt B minor Sonata, under his fingers, becomes heroic, tender, appealing, triumphant. He brings out the gentler side at times where others see the bombastic and self-important. Yet there is plenty of power where it is needed. He has indeed a touch "ravishing in the range and character of its expressive dynamics," as one writer expressed it.

One might almost say the caliber of an artist is shown by the character of the encores he grants. Those given by this artist were always dignified, though some were worn threadbare. That made no difference. The listener might feel he had never heard the E flat Nocturne before, it was so tenderly soulful, without being in the least sentimental. Did the Mendelssohn Spinning Song ever ripple and scintillate more beautifully? Or the Traümeswirren of Schumann ever sound so clear and simple, so delicate? As a parting gift came La Campanella, tossed off with astonishing bravura.

It was all enthralling piano playing, from which the student, the young pianist and the teacher could learn much of tone coloring, power and lightness, of accent and rhythmic security, of poetic feeling and true artistic inspiration.

ALFRED CORTOT
[1877-1962]

PRACTICAL ASPECTS OF MODERN PIANO STUDY

W e have come to know, on this side of the water, the art of the eminent musician, pianist, conductor and teacher of France—Alfred Cortot. His first American recital took place on Armistice Day, November 11, 1918. While confusion and jubilation reigned in the streets, those who were seated in the concert hall listened quietly to a comprehensive program, beginning with Vivaldi, continuing through Chopin's Andante Spianato and Polonaise, the Twenty-four Preludes entire and some modern French music, on to Liszt's Second Rhapsodie. We recognized, after the first quarter of an hour, that we were listening to one of the great artists of the world. And since that day, each visit he has paid to America has deepened the first impression. Then, too, it is felt that M. Cortot's art has grown and ripened with the years. It has become more intense, more vital and sympathetic in touch and tone, more noble in conception.

Alfred Cortot is known to us only as pianist and teacher, but in his own country he has equal renown as conductor, and also as founder of the famous Trio, composed of Jaques Thibaud, violin; Pablo Casals, cellist, and himself, pianist, which for a number of years did much for chamber music in France.

The artist's education in piano was gained at the Paris Conservatoire, under Decambes, Rouquon and Diémer. He won First Piano Prize in 1896. Then, after a successful debut as pianist in Paris, he went to Baireuth and made a thorough study of Wagner's scores, remaining several years. Returning to Paris, he conducted the first performance of *Götterdammerung*, and subsequently did much, through his orchestral concerts, to increase French appreciation of the works of Richard Wagner.

Cortot's great gifts as master of the piano and its literature made it imperative for him to return to the concert stage, and he has made frequent tours through many countries of the world. He is a distinguished example of the intellectual pianist who does not allow the academic phases of piano study to overbalance his emotional and sympathetic interpretation.

The writer had sought a conference with the French artist during his first American season, but without success. Subsequently, however, in spite of the overwhelming amount of work undertaken by him, the pianist was willing to grant an hour out of his crowded day, to talk over matters of pianistic and pedagogic interest. An appointment was made to meet in his lair—otherwise old Steinway Hall, of blessed memory, fragrant of reminiscences of famous pianists, from Rubinstein down.

Punctual to the minute, M. Cortot appeared, and, with polished French courtesy, led the way to one of the inner rooms, where we would be undisturbed. He assured the visitor he spoke only French, since he has profited by Maeterlinck's experience, and has not tried to learn English "by the phonetic method," at which witty sally we all laughed heartily. As a matter of fact, however, he understands English very well, and can say little sentences in it.

The Technical Side
"You wish to speak to me about matters pertaining to the technical side of piano playing," began M. Cortot, after he had seen that we were comfortably seated, and he had placed himself on a piano-stool before us. "That is a very important side, especially for the young student. Of course, in the earlier stages, the pupil must be very exact about everything connected with technic—hand position, finger action, relaxation and so on. But, in presenting these fundamental subjects, the student's physique and mentality enter largely into the scheme, so that one might almost say the teacher must have a different method for each pupil. Students cannot all be taught in the same way. I teach in the Conservatoire in Paris, and have ample opportunity to judge of the diversity of gifts. Naturally, I have the advanced students and those especially talented.

"Do not be seated too low at the piano," he went on, continuing the subject we had begun. "The height at which one sits has much to do with tone quality. If one sits too low, and the elbow is below the wrist, the effort to get power often renders the tone harsh; whereas if the arm slopes somewhat down to the wrist, as is the case when one sits higher, the hand and arm are over the keyboard, which fact, of itself, lends weight and strength to the tone."

M. Cortot went to the piano and illustrated his meaning.

Eliminate Unnecessary Practise
"In the early days, the student has to do considerable technic practise, but the material for this should be so carefully chosen as to eliminate all unnecessary effort. Avoid useless repetition; rather get at the principle—the

heart of the thing you want to conquer, and cut away whatever is superfluous. You need practise in scales? Then what is the use of playing them over and over, in rotation, as so many players do. It is only a waste of time. What is the principle of scale playing? Is it not this—putting the thumb under the hand and the hand over the thumb?"

And again the artist turned to the keyboard and played a short exercise, starting on C with thumb, then D with second finger, C again with thumb, B with second finger, and back to C. He illustrated the same principle with other fingers and wider intervals.

"There you have the principle, and it is not necessary to play scales incessantly in order to learn that principle. It is so much better to save one's strength for other things.

"As for variety of material, there is always plenty to be found in pieces. Take the difficult portions and passages of the piece you are studying, one after another, and study them in detail, each hand alone. Best of all, make new material for technic practise out of them. For this work, accents may be varied, rhythms can be changed, and the passage may, in various ways, be developed in such style as to fix it deeply in the mind, besides making it valuable for finger, wrist and arm technic. This manner of study aids concentration and develops the resources of the pupil. It also does away with the mass of studies and books of etudes which some teachers consider so essential. The pupil realizes he is working on repertoire, while, at the same time, he is developing and perfecting his technic. Of course, this especially applies to the advanced worker.

Rhythm Must be Inborn

"I do not consider the metronome at all necessary in piano practise. If used, it is apt to induce mechanical habits. Rhythm must be inborn; the student must feel the beat, the pulse. If he is unable to do so, no amount of mechanical practise will supply this defect."

"Oh, but M. Cortot," we protested. "Just think of all the young people who love music and wish to study it—older people, too—who can get so much pleasure out of a nearer contact with music, but who may not be blessed with this fine, inner sense of rhythm. The metronome would be their only salvation. Through its use they learn what rhythm means. What would they ever do without such an aid and guide?"

"Let them do something else beside music, then," answered the French pianist. "I repeat it—let only those study music who have an innate sense of rhythm. You remember Hans von Bülow's saying, 'In the beginning was rhythm.' "

"And you would not permit the use of the little monitor, even if it brought about the desired result—that is, educated the pupil to a sense of rhythm, which he seemed to lack at the start?"

"No," was the decided answer, "for the reason that it would be an educated, not an inborn, sense.

Teacher Like a Physician

"A thoroughly competent teacher will adapt his work to the needs of each pupil who comes to him. He stands in the place of a physician and should be able to administer the correct remedy for every pianistic ill. He has all kinds of hands and various sorts of minds to deal with. A very long hand, with long fingers, can do quite different things from the short-fingered, plump hand. The weak, flabby hands should have special treatment. Then the mentality of one student is so different from every other. Thus, you see, the resourceful teacher must be ready for every emergency; must be able to teach each pupil according to his needs."

Restoring one's Technic in Fifteen Days

"How are you able to keep your large repertoire in review, while maintaining technic at concert pitch?" he was asked.

"I learn easily, and must remember what I have learned. During the war, I was three years without a piano, and therefore did not touch a note. When I was free and could return to the piano, I was able to bring back my facility and repertoire in fifteen days.

"During the three years that I had no opportunity to use a piano, I was determined to keep my fingers, hands and arms flexible in some way. I did many gymnastics with them, inventing all sorts of forms, so that they should keep in good condition. I also had a silent keyboard to work on, and found it a most helpful and wonderful aid to the keeping up of one's technic. It seemed remarkable to me that I could get back my facility so quickly; it must have been the gymnastic work I did, with the help of the clavier, and the constant mental effort in keeping my repertoire in review. I always learn everything very thoroughly, from the start.

A Piece Learned is a Piece Memorized

"I consider it absolutely essential for the piano student to commit everything he attempts to learn, to memory. If he wishes to enlarge his acquaintance with music by getting the works of various composers and playing them through, there is certainly no harm in that. But this is very different from attempting to learn the pieces. With this end in view, one must study seriously, analyze the music, see how it is made up, consider its form and tone texture, and what the composer evidently intended to convey through it.

"So many points need to be considered in the interpretation of a composition, aside from technical development and performance. One of these aspects is a consideration of the epoch in which the composer lived. The men of a past age surely felt as deeply, as vividly, as we do today, but they had a different idiom of expression. This was partly due to the instruments of former times, which were small and delicate, with little power or tone quality. The technic of those days was adequate for the instruments, but dramatic power was not considered necessary. Therefore we ought to play the older music in the style, tone quality, and with the psychological meaning it had in its own time and epoch. Modern music needs all the resources of the modern instrument, which is capable of expressing both the power and delicacy, the passion and exaltation, that are now deemed essential. The modern piano is a wonderful instrument, and if we understand and can control it, we can express every emotion of which the soul is capable."

ERNO VON DOHNÁNYI

[1877-1960]

TECHNICAL MATERIAL DISCUSSED

A serious, thoughtful, earnest musician is Erno von Dohnányi, Hungarian composer-pianist. He seems to be equally at home in the field of composition and conductorship as when giving a recital on the concert stage. Acknowledged one of the big pianists of the day, he is also a composer who has contributed various graceful as well as grateful pieces to the pianists' repertoire, and last, but not least, he is a conductor of originality and virility.

America has had several visits from this artist. The first came in the season of 1898-9, when he was only twenty-one. He returned two years later for another tour. Then came a long break, of about twenty years, during which Dohnányi continued his European tours, and then was appointed Professor of Piano Playing in the Royal Hochschule, in Berlin, a post he held for eleven years. He now resides in Budapest. Fully occupied with professional duties, composition, and prevented by the World War from leaving home, he was unable to return to America until a couple of years ago. We then found him a matured pianist and composer.

As a Teacher

As a teacher, Dohnányi has a large following, and has directed the studies and developed the talents of various well-known pianists. "Dohnányi is such a wonderful master, and above all such a thorough musician. I know of no greater teacher, if the pupil is well prepared and able to profit by such guidance." This is the testimony of Mischa Levitzki, who was a student of the Hungarian master, in Berlin, for a considerable time. There are other students in this country, and many more who both admire and play his compositions. The four Rhapsodies are becoming familiar in our concert rooms, while the *Winterreigen*, a charming set of piano pieces, was played by Rudolph Reuter a couple of seasons ago in New York. We know that Brahms praised the compositions of Dohnányi. Besides the pieces already mentioned, there is a piano Concerto, which is excellently well conceived for the instrument, and other works of an ideal character.

In a conversation with Dohnányi, some questions were asked in regard to handling various grades of pupils.

"I firmly believe in individuality in piano teaching. Each pupil is a different mentality and forms a separate study. My own ease would not be that of any one elsc. A piano method which works well for one pupil might not be the best for another. It is true a desired result may be attained through different means, and these means should be adapted to the needs of each pupil.

"Of course, in the early stages, one must be well-grounded in finger exercises, scales, arpeggios and octaves. There is nothing that will quite take the place of scales, to gain fluency and command of the keyboard. As the student advances, he should be given a liberal amount of Bach. A selection of Czerny is also indispensable. Then comes Clementi; we cannot do without him either, if we are to help the pupil to build a thoroughly furnished background.

"To this end an adequate familiarity with the classics is necessary. Mozart, Haydn, even Hummel, are not to be neglected. Mozart has left numerous Sonatas, Concertos and several Fantaisies; some of these are very beautiful, especially the Fantaisies, and are of the greatest value in forming the student's taste. The Sonatas of Haydn, also, are perhaps even richer in technical and musical material.

"The keeping up of my own technic and repertoire is perhaps a case of what I do not do. At present I spend little time on abstract routine technical exercises, as so many pianists think they must do, for that seems to me a waste of time, which is so precious to the musician. Of course, as you know, every pianist has some little mechanical forms, which he uses to oil up his machinery, so to speak; but that is an individual matter. I can truly say I have never practised technic exhaustively. I began to play the piano at the age of six, and even in those early days read much at sight and played with other instruments. Thus I gradually evolved a technic of my own at the instrument.

"It goes without saying that one can waste much time over so-called technical material, and not really get anywhere, or make a definite advance. It can be merely useless repetition. Of the books on pure technic, like Hanon and Pischna, I prefer the latter. It has been said a player ought to be able to go through Hanon in one hour—what a grind!

"Everything depends on *how* one practises. One student may spend five hours at the piano and will not accomplish as much or progress as fast as one who spends one hour at work, but concentrates his whole mind on the task before him. The first is a mechanical machine, the second uses his mental powers.

"One of the best ways to keep up one's technic as well as one's repertoire is, I have found, to select the difficult portions of compositions, and make technical studies out of them. The literature of the piano provides such rich material of all kinds that the student or artist need never be at a loss.

As to Etudes

"I should like to offer a protest against using too many etudes, for much valuable time may be thus wasted. Students often think the greater number of etudes they go through, the better players they will be; whereas they had much better put some of that time on mastering repertoire. What masses of etudes have been written! Their name is legion. Von Bülow edited a book of fifty Cramer Studies, selecting those he considered the best. But while the player is learning these, he could put in the time to more advantage on pieces of value, which would add just so much to his repertoire.

"Of course some of the etudes are very nice, but we have grown away, in these modern days, from the older ways of study. We do not seem to need so many studies, nor do we use them in the way a past generation did. If, however, you speak of the Etudes of Chopin, that is quite another matter. Chopin Etudes belong to the repertoire of every pianist; indeed they are not etudes at all but beautiful works of art, which every one must love. In them one finds every form of technical problem, which is necessary for the building up of a virtuoso pianism. Why should one seek afar, when such wonderful material is ready to the hand? Of course, they are not for the immature student. For all who attempt to master them must be prepared through the practise of scales, chords, octaves, and so on."

Although Dohnányi does not concern himself with the technical preparation of the students and players who come to him—artist-teachers are not expected to do this—he is very painstaking and careful in his teaching. He regards the subject of artistic interpretation as of the very highest importance. It is the soul of the music which interests and absorbs him completely, not the body of mere mechanical notes and signs. The meaning and spirit of the music is what he seeks to reveal to the student. Again to quote from Mischa Levitski, his admiring pupil:

"When I went to Dohnányi, he first gave me the smaller things, such as the Kinderscenen of Schumann and the earliest Sonatas of Beethoven. He believes the player should have much more technic than the music one is studying requires, so he usually gives pieces that do not tax too severely the technical ability of the player, in order that he may more fully grasp and master the meaning of the piece. At the lesson he allows the student to play through the work in hand without interruption, listening carefully, and often jotting inaccuracies and corrections on a slip of paper, though he generally tries to remember them. When the composition is finished—not before—he makes the necessary corrections. Finally he himself plays the piece entirely through. As he is such a master of interpretation, this of itself is a great inspiration to the pupil."

Dohnányi is very particular about clearness of touch, requiring slow and careful practise, with fingers well raised. The beginning and finish of a phrase, its shading and climaxes are all carefully considered.

Asked if he were familiar with American music, especially the compositions of Edward MacDowell, he admitted he had seen very little of it, and did not know the Sonatas at all. He had, however, become initiated into the intricacies of American jazz, which, he said, is for the head and not for the heart. He considers it intellectual and not emotional.

The human side of an artist is the side the general public does not guess; in the case of this artist it is a very lovable side. I remember meeting him one evening in the side corridor of Carnegie Hall, at the close of a recital by Levitzki. A long program had been given, with many encores added. The master had remained to hear them all. He wanted to go to the artist's room, greet his popular pupil and then leave. There was an eager look on his tired face. But no, another encore was demanded, and granted; so he turned into the hall again, to wait patiently for the last.

On another occasion, hearing that the music committee of the MacDowell Club had arranged an entire Bach program, he asked if he might contribute something to it. We joyfully consented, of course. He came and played the Chromatic Fantaisie and Fugue, adding another Bach number as an encore. It was a graceful thing to do, and everybody appreciated his kindness.

He has a keen sense of humor, too, in spite of his grave demeanor. Looking from the windows of the office building in which are the rooms of his managers, he spied the Y. M. C. A. Building, on the side wall of which are painted various signs, two of which read: "Men's Bible Class"— "Swimming Pool."

"Where but in America would one see those terms in conjunction?" he remarked, with his faint smile.

IGNAZ FRIEDMAN

[1882-1948]

SELF-DEVELOPMENT A NECESSITY FOR THE PIANIST

Y ou must hear Ignaz Friedman, pianist and composer; for me he is the greatest piano virtuoso," remarked another piano virtuoso, also great, recently to the writer.

"In what way is he the greatest?" was asked.

"In poetic conception especially, though he also has a marvelous technic; indeed he is unique among pianists."

What first impresses in the playing of Friedman, is the intensity of his musical utterance, the poetical imagination, the sense of tone color, raised to its highest emotional power. Later on we begin to realize Friedman possesses a formidable technic, capable of expressing and revealing an intensely artistic temperament, in many and diverse moods.

Piano technic may be acquired with industry and perseverance. When acquired, it can only reflect the individuality of the performer possessing it. The pianist of frigid temperament will reveal himself in a technic corresponding to that temperament. His playing will lack the divine spark, though he may have consummate command of his instrument. The musician of ardent, poetical nature, saturated with poetry and the lyric spirit, will reveal in his technic the qualities peculiar to himself. His playing will be living, vital, and will make an instant appeal. Thus it may be said that artistic technic is not an exterior circumstance, which any one may acquire with sufficient labor, but is in itself an art and provides the means for unfolding the inner life of the artist in all its eloquence.

This idea is aptly illustrated in the piano playing of Ignaz Friedman. With him it is impossible to separate technic from temperament, for they together form a complete musical personality. His technic is nobly expressive of both the greatest delicacy and orchestral power and sonority. Indeed, Friedman rightly deserves the title, Interpreter. For interpretation does not merely signify the slavish mechanical reproduction of a composition, nor is it the capricious disfigurement of the composer's thought, to suit the whim of the player. No, it is something much more noble and sincere. It has been said that the most lovely colors in a score are not those written down in notes. Nor can words express, in any language, the living meanings of music.

For there is much in music which escapes sign or word. The imagination of the artist must penetrate far deeper than these indications given by the composer, must seize and divulge the true spirit of the work.

If the feeling for rhythm and accent indicate a vigorous musical mentality, the poetic use of rubato—as in Chopin—proves the possession of an imaginative, flexible temperament, which preserves the inner rhythm of the music, while expressing every shade of emotion.

When speaking of Friedman the Pole, one instinctively thinks of Chopin the Pole; not because the former fails to interpret other masters, but simply because he seems especially adapted to the music of Chopin.

In the works of Chopin, as in those of all sincere composers, may be traced personal characteristics. Chopin, the delicately organized, dreamer of dreams, was keenly alive to patriotism—a complex, intense nature. This conception of Chopin is divined by Friedman, with a sympathy almost amounting to genius.

If Chopin was one of the greatest geniuses of the piano, preceding modern French, Russian and Spanish composers, the other foundations of piano literature rest in Beethoven, Schumann and Liszt. Friedman, in rendering the works of these masters, deserves the title of super-virtuoso of the piano. He reproduces in Beethoven the rhythmic and melodic beauty, the grandeur of classic outlines, as in Sonatas 57 and 111. In Schumann, the profound poesy and lyricism found in the Carneval and Symphonic Etudes; in Liszt the dizzy heights of dazzling bravura.

The pianistic interpretation of Beethoven has occupied recondite virtuosos and musical philosophers for many a year, each in his own way. From Bülow to Risler, to mention two extremes, the pianists who have devoted themselves to the Master of Bonn, have presented him in the most diverse lights. For Beethoven reveals himself to each mentality in a different way. His art is not like a piece of granite, always the same. Rather it is an aggregate mass of glowing life. Musical art does not become immobile in order to assume one unique aspect, as in painting and sculpture; it is rather the incessant reproduction of forms and ideas.

Friedman presents Beethoven at once as a classicist and romanticist—as form and spirit. Standing as he did at the confluence of two epochs, Beethoven did not cast aside classical material. The spirit of Beethoven, influenced by the parallel which exists between literature and music, glimpsed a romantic world, a world of freedom and independence of thought in music. Yet he remained on the threshold of this new world, not yet entering into its full presence. Beethoven appears to us a romanticist still under the partial influence of classicism.

"To our mind," asserts an excellent musical authority, "this is the manner in which Friedman understands Beethoven. The Polish pianist knows how to express the ardent but new-born romanticism of Beethoven within the symmetrical form of classicism, mingling grace and delicacy with exaltation and ardor—the very soul of romanticism."

After these thoughts on the art of Friedman the artist and musician, let us approach Friedman the man.

In many little, unexpected ways, Ignaz Friedman is unique and individual. For instance: on arriving in America, instead of going at once to one of the great hotels of New York—to some popular hostelry, where he would see the gilt-edged side of the city's life, which eddies about Thirty-fourth or Forty-second Streets—he chose to locate in one on lower Fifth Avenue, which, to be sure, is much nearer the heart of old New York. A short distance away, Paderewski's "Washington Arch" rises above the square, while many little streets lead off into unexpected quaintnesses.

As one approaches the spot through a couple of these old streets, one finds here and there fascinating little shops, filled with wares from many parts of the world. Rare porcelains and bronzes peep out at you from basement windows; quaint signs on doorways invite you to enter and purchase. Odd eating-places along the way tempt you to try them, just to see what they are like. Some other time we will come this way and explore, but not today. For just now we are bound for the hotel where is to be found Ignaz Friedman, the astonishing pianist.

"Yes, Mr. Friedman will see you at once," was the response to our question. And we were scarcely seated in the comfortable little parlor, when the pianist entered with cordial greeting.

A man of kindly and simple manners, inclined to be reserved, yet ready to respond to a sincere desire to know his views on musical subjects, especially on piano study. By way of introduction, he was asked how he happened to locate so far from the city's fashionable center.

"I like it here, it suits me. I would not feel comfortable in a fashionable place; then, too, this is more European. When I walk about in this vicinity, I feel as if I were on the other side of the globe. Yes, I can practise here, all I wish. I have a dumb piano, too, how do you call it—a 'practice clavier'? It may be a Virgil Clavier; it is an American instrument, anyway; I always have it with me."

"It is good to know you approve working on such a mental instrument as the practice clavier," we remarked.

"Oh, yes, indeed, I approve of it. One must do much technical practise each day, if one would not have one's mechanism become rusty. The pianist must have a big technic, in these days of great technical achievements. He must have much more technic than he really needs for the works he plays. Ten times more, you ask? Yes, that is about the proportion. When he possesses such an equipment, then piano playing is an easy matter, for then he has perfect control of himself and his instrument.

"And now as to some of the most important technical principles used in piano playing. Perhaps the first is:

Conservation of Energy

"Learn to reserve your strength. Do not put out any more strength, power or vital force than you absolutely need. Then you do not become so fatigued by much practise or playing.

No Short-cut to Piano Mastery

"I have made myself familiar with the whole literature for the mastering of piano technic. One must do so if one would know whatever has been accomplished along this line. I assure you, at the outset, there is positively no short-cut to the mastering of the piano. If any one affirms there is, he says what is false. Students think if they play a dozen etudes of Czerny, they have acquired all he has said; but they have not. There is a great deal more to Czerny than that. It is the same with many other technical masters who have contributed to the literature for acquiring mechanical perfection.

"When one has worked through all the important material of this nature, it is only the outside shell after all. It is the proper assimilation of all this material which will adequately equip the artist; it is what he makes out of it; it is what the artist does for himself. No one can do this for him; no teacher, no set of etudes, no mass of finger gymnastics. It is self-instruction—self-development.

Principles

"To go back to our enumeration of foundation principles. They can be given in a single sentence. The hand must be arched at the knuckles, the fingers firm at the nail joint, the wrist loose. Clear, articulate finger action is necessary. Arm weight must be under control, so that too much is not allowed to rest on the fingers in passage playing; otherwise a heavy tone is produced, and the player becomes sooner wearied."

Observers of Mr. Friedman's playing have noticed the absolute freedom from effort with which he plays. This consummate ease is doubtless one of his artistic secrets.

The Pedals

"The pedals, too, have a special technic of their own. Sometimes the pedal is taken *before*, sometimes *with*, and frequently *after* the note or chord. Often a fine effect is made by omitting the pedal altogether. The understanding of when and how to use these various effects comes only through a close analysis of the piece, its harmonic structure and the artistic effect which should be produced.

Memorizing

"How do I memorize?" The artist smiled, as though the subject were either too large or too inconsequent to mention. Then he said:

"One must know the piece, its construction and harmony, through careful study. There are four sources of memory: the eye, to see the notes on the page or keys—that would be visual memory; the fingers, to find the keys easily on the keyboard—digital memory; the ear, to hear the tones —auricular memory; and, lastly, though we might say it should be first, the mind to think these tones and keys—or mental memory.

"In the case of young students, they should learn the principal chords of the keys—tonic, dominant and dominant seventh—with their different positions. All these can be found in the simple pieces they are studying. And they ought to analyze the chords and learn how the melodies are formed from them. In this way they discover how the piece is put together, and can better memorize and retain it.

The Trill

"About the best exercise and most useful one, is the trill. It can be employed by each pair of fingers in turn; that is to say, with 1-2, 2-3, 3-4, 4-5. It can be beneficially used by pairing off other fingers, such as 1-3, 1-4, or 1-4, 2-3. The trill gives facility and control to the fingers and should always be kept up.

Applying Technic to Pieces

"In piano playing it is experience that counts for so much. Even if you acquire a good technic, it is not of much use unless you employ those principles in the pieces you study. And so, in the constant effort to do this, experience is gained, also that fine sense of balance and proportion, without which artistic performance is not possible. All this takes time—much time. I began to play the piano when I was three, and have been at it ever since—thirty odd years; I surely should know whereof I speak. Indeed, in all these years I should have learned what there is to learn and know about piano playing.

The Hand of a Pianist

"The formation of the hand of a pianist is a very important part of his equipment; therefore this should be a paramount consideration. The first question is, has he a hand that will reward cultivation? Some persons love music, but are not physically fitted to become pianists; they would be more at home with cello or violin. My hand now," holding up and regarding his own perfectly formed and developed member, "is really fitted to play the piano; I could not handle the violin with any success."

As Ignaz Friedman has related, he began to attempt the piano at the tender age of three; at eight he played exceedingly well, and his musicianship was such that he could transpose Bach's Preludes and Fugues without difficulty. He was at that time a piano prodigy and toured Poland, Russia and the Continent. Later he settled down to very serious study, went to Vienna and remained with Leschetizky for a number of years, finally becoming his assistant.

As a composer, Friedman has almost a hundred compositions to his credit, including a piano concerto, a quintette for piano and strings, three string quartettes, piano pieces and songs.

Further proof of his musicianship is found in his work of editing the entire Chopin and Liszt publications. He is now at work on similar editions of Bach and Schumann.

WALTER GIESEKING

[1895-1956]

RELAXATION A PRIME ESSENTIAL

A new star in the pianistic firmament! Walter Gieseking has been called a musical genius and a pianistic phenomenon at the same time. Also it is said he has the ability, the power, to project the thought and meaning of the music he plays, so that it at once appeals to the listener. Indeed, the critics of Europe have showered unstinted praise upon him, and after his first appearances in America, the most glowing tributes were chronicled.

After hearing the new pianist on each occasion, always with the desire to form an unbiased opinion, it seemed to this listener that he has indeed a very beautiful pianistic mechanism. His arms and hands, from shoulder to finger-tips, seem to be completely relaxed, so that his legato passage playing is smooth as oil, and his manipulation of the keyboard appears to be absolutely effortless. His Bach and Mozart are delicately clear, with each tiny shade and nuance in its appropriate place. His Debussy is all in cool, pastel shades, subtly impersonal. He seems very fond of the most airy qualities of tone color and indulges in these shimmering half-lights and shadows to such an extent that we cannot help wishing, at times, for some rich, vibrant tones by way of contrast. Still, the twilight tints are very alluring and incite to dreams. The pianist enters heart and soul into everything he plays, and while his fingers glide over the keys in this effortless fashion, his head and body reflect the intensity of his thought—especially in rapid passages—by many jerks and movements.

We will let Mr. Gieseking relate, in a few words, some incidents of his musical career, as he told them to me, sitting near his piano, in his hotel suite.

"I was born in Lyons, France, in 1895. My father was a physician and had a post in Italy. So I spent my first sixteen years on the Italian Riviera. I was, from a tiny chap, very fond of music, and picked up my piano playing somehow by myself. I read and played everything I could lay hands on. It was not till we went to Hanover, Germany, to live, in 1911—when I was sixteen—that I really began to study music seriously. I entered the Hanover Conservatory, where I had Karl Leimer for a teacher.

"I was with him three years—then came the war, which put an end, for the time being, to many things I had planned to do, though of course I kept right on with my studies. Leimer was my only teacher, as I never had any other. After these three years with him, I decided to make music my profession and began gradually to appear in recital. I progressed in this line of effort until now, each season, I have more than one hundred concerts to play, so that I have little time for anything else.

Memory Study

"To commit to memory is a very simple matter with me, unless the composition happens to be very difficult. A great deal can be accomplished by reading the music through away from the piano. As I read it the eye takes in the characters on the printed page while the ear hears them mentally. After a few times reading through, I often know the piece, can go to the piano and play it from memory. Take this Concerto of Mozart"—picking up a small 12mo score from the table. "This is simple, so far as notes go, and can be learned in the way I speak of. But the Hindemith Concerto, here, which I played with the New York Symphony Orchestra, is much more difficult. I read this through also, but in small sections—line by line. Afterward I must play it often, too, to fix it in memory. As you see," showing me the music, "it has many uneven and irregular rhythms. We had four rehearsals with orchestra, before the concert, as it was the first performance in America."

Hand Position

If you speak to Gieseking about normal hand position at the piano, he is mystified, for all positions are equally admissible to him, depending on the requirements of the music. Sometimes his hand is high and arched, then it is flat, with wrist dropped far below the keyboard. "I have a good hand for the piano," he says, as he holds it up; "and the fingers are flexible, as you see"— which he proved by bending them far back, at right angles with the back of the hand. It is indeed a wonderful hand, and must resemble Rubinstein's. Indeed, Gieseking has been called the German Rubinstein.

Amount of Practise

"I really need very little practise," continued the pianist, "as I do not forget what I have learned; my fingers don't forget either. In the summer I take a couple of months off for rest and recreation, and often do not touch a piano or even see one, in all that time. But this seems to make no difference with my playing. After the vacation I can return and at once give a recital or play with orchestra without the least difficulty. All of which proves I do not need much visible practise. During my concert season, of course, I have little time for practise, but I can study new works, on trains, as I travel about.

Technical Material

"With technical forms, pure and simple, I have done comparatively little. There is the C major scale, for instance. Its construction is very simple, and this form can be applied to all other scales or keys. The C scale, however, seems to me the most difficult of all, on account of the wider crossing of hand over thumb. As you notice, B, E or others are easier." Mr. Gieseking demonstrated various scale forms, running them up and down the keyboard with amazing swiftness. "Then, after scales come accords—arpeggios or broken chords. These formed from chord positions are simple, too. These few things my teacher required. After these I was given etudes. I think it was the Cramer Studies I had to learn. And after these came the Clementi Gradus, and later I worked on the Chopin Etudes, as every pianist must."

Repertoire

Asked about his repertoire, the artist took several sheets of notepaper from the table: "These are the pieces I play," he said simply. A rapid glance revealed some of the larger Bach compositions, as well as a group of Preludes and Fugues. Numerous Sonatas of Beethoven came next.

"Of course I know all the Beethoven Sonatas, but from those indicated I will choose for my present concerts. As you see, I have the Schubert *Wanderer Fantaisie,* Op. 15, of which I am very fond, besides other compositions of this master. Then some Schumann and much Debussy. Both books of Preludes—twelve numbers each—besides other pieces of the French composer. You doubtless notice an absence of Chopin. I do not play his music, though I know it, of course. But I have refrained from using it to any extent in my recitals, for it is overplayed. Almost every program of every pianist has a group of this music; sometimes it is an 'all Chopin program.' So I want to give other things, that are not so very familiar.

"Do I play American music—MacDowell? I do not know American music—yet; though I am slightly acquainted with some of your MacDowell's shorter pieces—not the Sonatas. Ah, yes, the *Hexen Tanz,* that is a charming composition," and turning to the piano he played it in part, with the fleetness and delicacy for which he is so noted.

Playing with Orchestra

"In playing with orchestra, the quality of tone of the two instruments should blend artistically. If one pianist's scale of dynamics is less boisterous and militant than another, the orchestra should adapt itself to the reduced scale of the soloist. For my part, I feel that the whole conception of performance in these days is too heavy, loud and blatant. I prefer less power, but, instead, more delicacy and ethereal refinement of tone."

In his two New York recitals, Gieseking has chosen compositions with which he feels a peculiar affinity. Of Bach a Partita and the English Suite No. 6 in D minor. Then the Schubert Wanderer and Schumann's *Kreislerianna*, and finally Debussy's Twenty-four Preludes, equally divided between each list. This music does not make much noise. It is introspective, intimate, refined, poetical. And the choice of it and the interpretation of it reveal the qualities of this master pianist.

MYRA HESS

[1890-1965]

GLIMPSES OF PRESENT-DAY PIANO STUDY

M yra Hess is spoken of as an English pianist. As a matter of fact her parents were German, though her rich coloring gives one the impression of an Oriental. She is rather slight of figure and one sometimes wonders where the power she occasionally employs comes from. It is well known, however, that when conditions are correct, power can be expressed by simple means and through slight physique.

Miss Hess retires into the background when the subject of personal methods of study or of piano mastery is brought up. She is not anxious to talk about herself, or her particular ways of doing things. "It is so difficult," she says, "to put into words the ways and means one uses to acquire what one seeks. Words are often misleading, and do not express just the shade of thought one desires to give.

"To begin with, I had a wonderful teacher in Mr. Tobias Matthay, of London. He is such a thorough musician, from every point of view. He sees the subject from all sides, and is so broad and comprehensive in his attitude toward all forms of art. I was placed under his guidance when I was thirteen, and he has trained me entirely ever since. I feel I owe everything to him. I am afraid he spoils me when he speaks so well of me, as he has in the letter you have mentioned. But I always appreciate it very deeply.

Form and Shape

"When I take up a new work, I try to see it from all sides. By this I mean that I study out the harmony, the chord and key progressions, the technical requirements, then the meaning and necessary interpretation. Some players go about the work in quite a different way. Perhaps they take up first the technical side and make an exhaustive study of that, or they may work a great deal each hand alone, learning each one straight through. The fact is, different pieces ought to be treated differently, each in its own way. In a composition where technical problems predominate, one must of necessity give more attention to that.

"How does one arrive at the understanding of Form and Shape? Through analyzing the composition, finding the phrases and half-phrases, and keeping those patterns intact, that is to say, not breaking them up. The phrase is the basis of musical meaning and content, the backbone, as it were, of music itself. Very much has been written about musical form, but very little about its shape, which is just as important. To understand and explain the shape, we must go back to the phrase, and preserve its melodic line.

Balance and Proportion

"In regard to balance, I would say that, to attain an understanding of correct balance in a composition, we should first learn what phrases are more important than others. These are to be brought forward into higher relief, while less important ones drop back into the shadow. A correct comprehension of the phrase and its meaning enables the player to balance all parts artistically. Then there is the balance of tonal values and dynamics, which is an equally fascinating study.

"Again, one of the most important points in the interpretation of a piece is the idea of Proportion, which really means a just balance of all parts and their relation to each other. Matthay is such an authority on this subject. How seldom young players have any exact idea or definite plan for proportion and for balance in their playing! They may produce the tones correctly, may have a good technic and get over the keys quite fluently, in fact; but the meaning of the music they endeavor to interpret lies beyond their grasp, often for lack of any conception of the significance of Proportion, Balance and Shape. Each one of these terms carries a world of meaning with it, as every one knows who has studied at all into the subject. Mr. Matthay gives unceasing care and attention to these things.

"Of what use are correct notes when the form and shape of the phrase are all out of gear? Inexperienced students who accent, phrase, increase and diminish the tone, hurry or retard the tempo in wrong places, disturb the proportion and shape of what they play, and by so doing often miss entirely the meaning of the composition they attempt to interpret. If one does not mentally understand what one is trying to do, one can never really do it. For it is the mind that does the work always. If these subjects of which we have been speaking were more emphasized in teaching, or if teachers had greater knowledge of them, there would be more artistic players in the world, which is a self-evident truism after all," added the pianist with a smile.

Memorizing

"How do I memorize? Fortunately, I am blest naturally with an excellent memory, and after I have made a careful study of the piece, noting the points we have dwelt upon, I nearly know it already, without giving special attention to that side of the work. As is well known, there are three kinds of memory training: that of the eye, the ear and the fingers. Although I use all three, I depend, I think, more on the first than on either of the others. I can really see the printed page before me, mentally, and can actually read it as I play, just as though it were on the music-desk before my eyes. There have been times of great stress, when I was mentally agitated and could neither see the notes before me nor even hear them, yet my fingers would go on and continue to play of themselves. Can you imagine it? This fact only proves that one must have keyboard memory as well as both the other kinds. As I seem to depend more frequently on visual memory, I do not like to be long away from the notes of my repertoire, for I must refresh my memory with frequent references to them. Of course I can, and often do, work away from the keyboard, when analyzing and committing to memory.

How to Obtain Both Power and Delicacy

"I do not practise in any special way for the purpose of gaining power. If tone production is legitimate and correct, one can command the necessary power the moment it is needed. Power is a matter of relaxation; it is not force alone, nor is it only muscular; it is nervous control as well. And thus it is a mental concept, a mental force. If one is able to play softly, with beautiful quality of tone, one should be able to give out a *forte* or *fortissimo* when necessary. Articulation that is soft and at the same time clear, is more difficult to achieve than mere loud playing. It seems to me that the player who has clearness and delicacy, together with good tone, will naturally have necessary power.

"As for using full power during practise, it is something I seldom do. Indeed, it seems to me quite wrong. Especially is it injurious to the ear. One cannot continually listen to such a din, without its deleterious effect on ears and nerves.

The Classics

"Yes, I play much old classic music. On the modern grand piano, of course, one loses the tinkling quality of tone obtained from old instruments, but something of the effect is preserved by playing lightly and using the pedal sparingly. I want my classics unadulterated, and always prefer to use the original editions rather than those that have been 'edited' or improved upon. I am especially fond of Bach, and there is so much of him! I should like to take a year off, sometime, and do the whole two books of the Preludes and Fugues; it would be great fun! Yes, I would always play the Fugue corresponding to the Prelude. I cannot imagine playing the Prelude alone: it would be like having a body without feet.

"While I love Bach, I am extremely fond of the Scarlatti music, as well as pieces by the old French classicists, Rameau, Lully, and the rest. This music is being 'rediscovered,' as it were, in these days. Players are delving into these forgotten riches and bringing forth fascinating things. I have put some of these little-known pieces of old masters on my programs this season, and intend to prepare many more for use next year. Such compositions seem more modern now than one would imagine, especially when played on our present-day grands.

Modern Piano Music
"Do not think that I give myself over to the charms of old music to the exclusion of the new.

I play much Debussy, Ravel, and other French music, not forgetting modern Russian. I also want to bring out and make familiar to American audiences some up-to-date British music—pieces by Arnold Bax, Delius, Bridge, and others. A humorous little incident, anent modern music, happened recently. I was engaged to play a program for a club, and was asked to make my scheme very modern. I did so, choosing largely from the music of Debussy, Ravel, Scriabine and the like. I imagined it might be too stiff for them. Can you guess my surprise when it was returned to me with the request that I give them something much more modern than that! So I had to set to work on the very latest things obtainable.

"Yes, I am somewhat familiar with the MacDowell Sonatas. Besides being modern, they are very interesting works in the sonata form. While I like certain parts and movements in each one immensely, I do not find the complete work, as a whole, exactly adapted to public performance; the interest is not sufficiently sustained for a composition of such length. I have had a great deal of American music sent me to look over, though when I am on the wing so constantly, there is very little time to attend to its consideration. I shall take back some of it with me, that I may go through it when I have a little leisure. A part of it interests me very much.

Broadening One's Views
"Although the pianist is deeply engrossed in his work, he must not forget that there are other branches of art to be studied and loved. I find the greatest help and inspiration in studying fine paintings and in watching the trend of art in painting and sculpture. I visit art galleries and exhibitions of pictures whenever I have opportunity, or in whatever city I happen to be; for it is

indeed an education for the musician to study this side of art.

"But if one thinks of sources of inspiration for the pianist, what can compare with the inspiration nature can give, in all her aspects? What can be more refreshing, after hours of hard study, than to escape to woods or fields, and enjoy nature's loveliness. And I am very fond of animals, too. After a trying rehearsal it is a complete mental diversion to visit a zoological garden and study animal life there. I did this on one occasion this season, after a hard afternoon, and found real delight in it. So much so, that I returned to the garden the next morning to have another look at the llamas. One may smile at this confession, but, to my mind, the musician should be many-sided, in order to put much into his music.

"It is difficult to secure any time for quiet work when one is engrossed in public playing. People in America have literally overwhelmed me with kindness; I cannot begin to accept all that is showered upon me. I never expected anything like it. I expected and hoped audiences would like certain things, it is true, but I was unprepared for their liking everything as they do, and with such understanding. It is indeed a great pleasure and inspiration to play for them."

WANDA LANDOWSKA
[1877-1959]

THE CHARMS OF OLD MUSIC

W anda Landowska, patron saint of the harpsichord and its wealth of rare old music, is herself a charming personality. To come in touch with her is like meeting with a musician from the time of Bach and Scarlatti, who in some mysterious fashion appears to belong to the present, though revealing the spirit of the past.

As one enters her artistic studios high up in one of New York's residential hotels, situated in the heart of the city, one comes upon a beautiful harpsichord, made by Pleyel of Paris especially for this unique artist. A little farther away stands a modern grand piano. It is pleasant to imagine her at work on one instrument or on the other, sitting in the brilliant sunshine, which on bright days floods the rooms. "I adore New York, with its beautiful sunshine," she says, with an expressive gesture.

Mme. Landowska, at home, flitting about her rooms, touching lovingly her treasured instruments and souvenirs, seems a different person from the dignified figure, clad in seventeenth century trailing garments, who comes before her audiences to play music of bygone days. Today she wears a simple house gown; her manner is cordial and unaffected, putting her visitors at once at ease. We feel the friendly atmosphere and sip our tea, as we listen to Madame's fluent French, interspersed with German words and phrases, with here and there a touch of English.

"In studying the technic as well as the music for the harpsichord, I had to rely greatly on myself and my own researches," she began. "I had already made a thorough study of the piano and its literature, and we know that technical material for that instrument is endless. But for the clavichord and harpsichord there is nothing, or next to nothing. So I was forced to invent, as it were, my own technical material. If there ever had been works treating of this subject they have long since disappeared. So I had to feel my way and learn through the best means one can have, through experimenting and experience, how to play and interpret the old music.

"Old music has always appealed to me, even as a little child. The other day I played for a whole audience of young students. I looked into the eager faces and said to them:

" 'I began to play the piano when I was four years old. My first teacher was a kind and indulgent man, who allowed me to browse freely amongst the music which pleased me, which was always music of olden times. I can still remember the delight with which I first heard Bach's Prelude in C major. But, alas, I was soon obliged to change teachers, and the new master proved to be stern and tiresome. I was made to play twenty-five times, each hand separately, the studies of Kalkbrenner and Thalberg, instead of the delightful gavottes and bourrees of Bach, which I loved. Alas, I was very unhappy and homesick for my beloved old-time music. And then I made a vow that I would, one day, when I was grown up, play a program devoted entirely to Bach, Rameau, Haydn and Mozart. I wrote this vow and the program neatly on a sheet of paper, decorated with Christmas pictures, and sealed it in an envelope, on which I wrote "To be opened when I am grown up."

" 'This program and these very pieces are the pieces I am going to play for you today. Do not think that because this music is very learned it must therefore be without feeling. Follow carefully the themes in each hand and you will see how it all sings.

" 'Then listen with all your hearts! Perhaps this learned but divinely simple music will awaken in you, or in some of you, the same gentle flame that burns in me. Do not be afraid of the grave manner and big wig of Father Bach. Draw near in thought and let us group ourselves about him. You will feel the love, the generous goodness, which fill every phrase of his lovely music. They will unite us by strong and warm ties and enkindle what is good and human within us.'

"And these young people to whom I spoke, listened to the music as I played it, with the greatest interest and attention and seemed to enjoy every note of these compositions of the old masters.

Are Touch and Technic Different on the Harpsichord from the Piano?

"You ask if the touch is different on the harpsichord from what it is on the piano? And in what way? The technic for the harpsichord is much more difficult than for the piano. First of all the touch. Test it for yourself. You see there is great key resistance on the harpsichord. Play a scale now, and you will realize how much more strength of finger is needed and what precision and exactness the player must have.

"The instrument has, as you see, seven pedals, which help to create the seventy-five varieties of color—*Klangfarben*—of which it is capable. There are two keyboards, of five octaves each, which can be used singly or coupled together. Many people, even those at work in music, do not seem to understand the difference between the clavichord, clavicembalo, harpsichord, clavicin and spinet. The clavichord has but one keyboard, and the old-fashioned square piano is its descendant. Clavicembalo is one of the Italian names for the harpsichord. As I said a moment ago, there are no modern books explaining the manner of playing these old instruments. I had no teacher to help me master their intricacies. I was so anxious to learn that I began a thorough search for old manuscripts, and I found, amid the dust and forgotten tomes of old libraries and museums, much information and knowledge that helped in my quest for technical material and for a comprehension of conditions under which Bach wrote. In this way I caught glimpses of the spirit which animated him and the meaning of his work.

"As to the instrument itself, I conceived that a modern-built harpsichord, which should be reconstructed after the authentic instrument of Bach, ought to be brought out, if we are to make the old music live again. The house of Pleyel, in Paris, met my wishes, and the result is a very beautiful instrument, such as you see here. There are three of these instruments in America now; this one, which I use in my concerts in New York and vicinity; one in Philadelphia, and one in Washington. The instrument in Philadelphia has black keys where these are white, while the original black keys are a deep citron yellow. The harpsichord kept in Washington has keyboards like this one here; the case, however, is of rich red wood.

Modernizing Bach

"Many authoritative musicians and pianists have elected to edit Bach's music, with a view to modernizing it and making it more playable for today—so they say. Ah, the pity of it! How dare any one mangle and mutilate these perfect scores! On this subject I have said in my book, *Music of the Past,* 'Change a syllable in a verse and you make the poem limp.' These editors efface the image of the most marvelous genius, on the pretext of bringing it down to date, and making it more modern.

"Every time a publisher proposes a new edition of a piece on my program, he advises me to make some changes in it, *so the work may become our property.* What is even more humiliating is when an unhappy arranger tries to make us believe that he has made improvements, has renovated a work of Mozart's, sparkling with youth and genius.

"It is really regrettable that even great musicians have been guilty of this offense against genius. Von Bülow said: 'Bach's harpsichord works are the pianist's Old Testament; Beethoven's Sonatas are the New; we should believe in both.' In spite of which he adds measures to the Chromatic Fantasy, and enlarges others; he changes the responses of the Fugue and doubles the basses. Thus, failing to recognize the noble transport and measured passion of the work, he has impregnated it with an alien and theatrical character.

"I do not make these strictures against the transcribers of Bach's organ music for the modern piano, for that is quite another matter. Liszt has greatly contributed to our wealth of piano music by placing these fine works, originally composed for organ, in our hands, and we certainly owe him gratitude for doing so.

Editions of Bach

"I am often asked what edition of Bach I use. I say at once, none of the modernized publications, in which editors have endeavored to adapt this lovely ancient music to the present-day grand pianos, by making it more sonorous and powerful. No, my Bach must be as pure, as near the spirit in which the master conceived it, as possible. I find the most complete and perfect edition is that of the Bach Gesellschaft, which comes in fifty-six volumes. This I own and it is indeed a treasure."

The Instrument

To hear Mme. Landowska describe her instrument is inspiring. She says:

"The harpsichord which has been built for me is a wonderful instrument. It has, besides the two keyboards, a great number of registers, imitating the flute, the violin, oboe and even the bagpipe, which vivify the compositions played upon it with the glowing colors of old stained glass. Its deep registers make us feel the dark profoundness of certain preludes and fugues of Bach. The joyous brilliance of its two keyboards, in their struggle with one another, flash and sparkle into flame, and impart to the sonatas of Scarlatti just the right touch of Neapolitan verve. The miracles of jocund grace and of melancholy tenderness which speak to us from the pages of Couperin and Rameau, find again their authentic poetry in that diaphanous sonority."

Thus spoke this remarkable and unique artist, and we listened with rapt attention—over the tea cups. Then, rising, at our request for a portrait, she went to her desk and handed up a photograph of herself, seated before a small upright piano, one of the treasured specimens in her own private collection. It is the instrument which once belonged to Chopin and was used by him during his sojourn at the island of Majorca. As Madame seated herself to write the inscription she had graciously promised, her secretary, a devoted young girl, standing at her elbow, stooped and pressed her lips to the dark head bent over the writing. A pretty touch and one not easily forgotten.

It would be hardly fair to close this brief glimpse of Wanda Landowska without adding a few words about the great work she has done and is now doing for the cause of old-time music. We should not forget that she was first of all a fine pianist, and is now indeed one of the finest we have, a real princess of the keyboard. About her piano playing, one of the critics has said: "To hear her play a Mozart Concerto for the pianoforte is to hear a veritable evocation of the marvelous boy of Salzburg. The perfect continence of her playing, her extraordinary musicianship and finesse, the justness of her accents, her chiseled phrasing, the variety and delicacy of her shading, the soft iridescent coloring of her tone, unite in a magic that transports the listener to a higher and purer region of sound."

As a harpsichordist she is the most distinguished of the present day. And when she is spoken of as an executant of these two instruments, one does not at once consider the enormous amount of study, the deep erudition, the passionate love of the work, which have carried her to such heights.

She has published several books on her chosen subjects. One, *Ancient Music,* which appeared in Paris in 1909, has been translated into English with the title *Music of the Past,* and is published in New York. Mr. Richard Aldrich remarks of it: "Madame Landowska here makes an eloquent defense of the old music. She urges the claims of the elder art, so distinguished by elegance, suppleness, purity of taste, moderation and serene nobility. She dislikes the overwhelming sonorities of these latter days and is not for innovations, for she has sharp words for the way the 'knights of transcription' have taken liberties with harpsichord music."

Among the chapters in *Music of the Past* that will appeal to present players and teachers are probably those on Style, Tradition, and Interpretation, although every page is interesting and full of suggestion.

BENNO MOISEIWITSCH

[1890-1963]

THE STUDY AND ART OF PIANO PLAYING

A t this particular stage in world history, can it be imagined just what would be the emotions of a great artist of the keyboard, on arriving in America on a first visit, with the avowed object of making his art known to an entirely new world? Everything must be novel and strange. To a sensitive, artistic nature the experience is little short of epochal. Doubtless he would like to ask endless questions as to the why and wherefore of things that are different. It may be he wisely refrains at first from asking too many, for in a short time the objects and things about him begin to assume normal relations to each other, and true perspective appears.

I had the privilege of greeting Mr. Moiseiwitsch before he had been on American soil twenty-four hours. He had had a rough, uncomfortable trip, and was as yet hardly recovered from the effect of the inconvenience he had experienced. He was located in agreeable quarters, a little apart from thoroughfares usually frequented by foreign visitors, and in his pleasant sitting-room, with its grand piano standing ready for his hand, we had an intimate talk about the study and art of piano playing.

The young Russian artist meets the visitor with simple, unaffected friendliness, in which there is no posing nor striving for effect. Slender and pliant in figure, with wonderfully supple hands, his dark, expressive face, with its large eyes, reflects a poetical spirit. One feels here is a rare mentality, one which will feel the meaning of the music and will possess ample resources through which to reveal this meaning to the listener.

"I do not care for fireworks in piano playing," he began; "at least I am not that kind of player; I want to get at the meaning of the composition and reveal that; I want to say what is in my heart to say about the music, without bombast of any kind. In short, the virtuosity side of piano playing does not appeal to me. Although, for example, Liszt's music tends to that side of pianism, I am devoted to some of it—to the B minor Sonata in particular, and to some of the transcriptions of songs. A few of the Rhapsodies I do not care so much for, though some others I admire greatly.

The Subject of Technic

"You ask me about the technical side of piano study. Technic is a difficult subject to define; it depends so much on correct understanding of conditions—of the *feeling* one experiences while employing the fingers. It is knowing how to use one's hands; it is control. Before I went to Leschetizky, I had never studied technic for itself alone—in fact I had never thought much about the subject. I had always played the piano for the sheer pleasure of playing. But when I went to Vienna I had to get right down to rock bottom, drop all my piece-playing and simply work at technic. For several months I did nothing but that, working with Fraulein Prentner, one of the strictest of the assistant teachers. I studied very hard at that time to master technical principles, conquer my shortcomings and gain the necessary control of the piano and of myself. For control is required by the pianist—he must have it.

"When I at last finished the preparation and began work with the master himself, I found him to be a wonderful teacher. He would often allow the student to play through the composition without interruption, until it was quite finished. Then came the criticism. He seemed to dissect a piece as a botanist picks a flower to pieces. For he had the gift to discover just what was wrong with one's fingers, and could point out the way to correct the student's faults and show him exactly how to get the right results. He would illustrate at his own piano the desired effect, and then show just how it could be attained.

"One of the wonderful things about his teaching—the thing I am most grateful to him for—was the light he threw on the subject of tone color and variety of tonal dynamics. I now began to learn what tone color really meant. That, too, is such a matter of physical feeling and the manner of touching the keys. The size and formation of hand has much to do with the manner in which one handles the keyboard. A master teacher may play a passage and ask the student to repeat it in the same manner. Perhaps one player can do so; another is quite unable to manage it. Why? Often from physical causes. For no two hands are exactly alike; neither is mental ability the same.

Technical Practise

"When I start the day, I do not begin with a lot of scales and exercises, as so many players do, thus using the precious hours of the morning for mechanical study. No, I desire to enjoy my piano at all times, especially in the early part of the day. I begin with a piece, one that I know; it may be a Prelude and Fugue of Bach, from the Well-tempered Clavichord. I play it through, without stopping. If there are places in it which do not go as they should, owing to a certain finger, or fingers, which do not act correctly, I return to these portions, see what the trouble is, and discipline the intractable fingers with improvised exercises. I also take the passages in question and make special studies out of them, using a variety of rhythms, accents and fingerings. Advanced technique should consist largely in making studies from difficult passages in pieces.

Speaking of Memorizing
"Another difficult subject is to explain just how one memorizes the music one plays. Each pianist seems to have his own method of committing music to memory. It has always been very easy for me, so perhaps that is why I have no cut-and-dried manner of doing it.

"I generally do memory work at the piano, by playing the piece in sections and studying them out in details. For a concerto I must know the whole orchestral score as well as my solo parts. A little illustration of how quickly I can memorize when obliged to do so, was on the occasion of my playing the Tscherepnine Concerto with Sir Henry Wood's Orchestra in London. They had asked me to play something new, and three modern works had been submitted to me to look over: namely, the aforesaid Concerto, one by Prokofieff, and one other. I preferred the first to either of the others, but the orchestral parts for it were not at hand. As the concert was not to take place for several months, the matter was left in this rather vague way, and I had quite forgotten it, as I was busy with concerts in different parts of the country. Just nine days before the concert was to take place, I happened to read an announcement that I was to play the Tscherepnine Concerto on this occasion. This was a surprise, to say the least. I at once began to work on the Concerto, committed it to memory and played it on the appointed date. It is a work of about eighty pages, with a cadenza of about fifteen pages in length. This Concerto is as yet quite unknown in America, and I hope to play it during my visit here."

At that time doubtless Mr. Moiseiwitsch did not realize the difficulty of bringing out new works which are unknown to orchestras and conductors.

"As to keeping up my repertoire, of course I go over my pieces very carefully before a recital, to see that all is well with them. It is interesting to test them out in my own studio, without referring to the score, to see how they have been preserved, and whether I remember them perfectly. When one goes minutely over a composition, one discovers new beauties each time, new effects which can be made. Yes, I travel with copies of the pieces I am to play, so that I can refer to them at any time. The only time I study the printed page away from the piano is when I am on the road, between concerts."

The pianist again reverted to his master, Leschetizky.

"He was a wonderful teacher in so many ways. He was a great reader of character, and could appraise the student's mentality with psychological accuracy. For instance, he would hear the same piece from two players and would teach it differently to each one of them. Again he was able to apprehend just the difficulty the student was laboring under—as I have said—and could tell one what to do to remove it. On one occasion I was playing the G major Prelude of Chopin. He seemed satisfied with the performance until I came to the last line, where the arpeggio passage for two hands occurs. This did not seem to suit him. Instead of saying, 'No, that is not good, you must improve it,' as so many masters would do, he simply remarked, 'Why don't you loosen your arms and make an undulating movement as you go up the keyboard?' for he saw I was a little stiff and constrained when playing that ascending passage. The simple remark was a revelation to me. I found I could now render the passage with the utmost ease."

Mr. Moiseiwitsch moved from his chair to the piano and played the Prelude in question (so familiar to all piano students) with a clarity and fluidity of utterance, a variety of tonal color, a freedom of movement, truly ravishing.

"Of course," he said, "one must use care not to overdo this undulating movement, as it might easily be abused."

The artist was much interested to know the inclinations of American audiences, in regard to classical and modern music. He expressed his preference for Schumann's music, and has given several entire programs of this master's compositions. "I do not think a large auditorium is suitable for my instrument," he said; "I would prefer to play in smaller spaces; if I could have my way, I would play in a room of this size. I prefer intimate surroundings, not a great stage and the big spaces of a vast concert hall."

In this regard, Mr. Moiseiwitsch agrees with Chopin, who was averse to exhibiting his delicate art to great audiences. And, indeed, the Russian artist appears to have many points of resemblance to the Polish master. One cannot help feeling he must also be—as he later proved himself—"a poet of the piano."

The Russian pianist has just completed a second visit to America. When he came to us three years ago, we found him a cultured musician who played both classic and modern music with technical command and poetic insight. At his single recital in New York on this second visit, the critics found he had made tremendous strides in absolute command of all pianistic resources;

in short that he had returned "a digital and technical giant—a real virtuoso."

"What is the difference between an artist and a virtuoso—or what is the true meaning of virtuoso?" I put the question to Mr. Moiseiwitsch at our little conference, a day or two after his recital.

"I hardly know how to define the term *virtuoso*," he answered thoughtfully. "The word means something out of the ordinary, something unusual, dazzling, magical, to attract the crowd. This attracting force is liable to be focused on technic; for supreme agility in manipulating the keyboard is what first impresses the superficial. This may, or may not, be quite apart from the meaning of the music. The musical and emotional import of the composition is what should concern the interpreter, and that is the only side which interests me.

"How have I gained increased facility? A musician must continue to grow, if he keeps on working. I know I have gained in command of my instrument, in the greater understanding of the means used to obtain pianistic effects, and in control of myself and my resources.

Technic

"Naturally one must have some daily technical routine, and must in time discover what technical forms are best for him, and go to the root of the matter most completely and quickly. As he advances in absolute control and mastery, technical tasks become effortless, a part of himself, and he seeks more and more to voice the higher, the spiritual, meaning of the music he plays.

"Some of the critics have mentioned velocity. Well, why should there not be velocity, if it does not interfere with form and shape?" Turning to the keyboard, the artist illustrated convincingly. "Suppose I play Chopin's Etude on the Black Keys, like this, at a moderately quick tempo. Then suppose I play it now much faster; there is no harm in this, if I keep everything clear and well balanced. The Bach Chromatic Fantaisie can start off at a lively pace; later it becomes more introspective and dreamy. It is a rhapsody all through. And then the wonderful Fugue! There seems to be a genuine Bach revival going on; we see evidences of it on all sides, even to entire Bach programs being played.

Pedaling

"One very important factor in piano playing one that is often much neglected—is pedaling. The pedals are as important as the fingers; we have the hands, the feet, the head, with which to make music. The third pedal? No, I never use it. I really see no use for it at all, for I can make all the effects I need with the two pedals. I make great use of the left, the so-called soft pedal, combining it with the damper pedal, even in passages that are marked *forte*; it creates shimmering effects of color when used with the so-called loud pedal.

Brahms

"Yes, I play much Brahms—of course, the Handel Variations, though I omit a very few of them, and many of the shorter pieces. No, I do not play the Variations on a Schumann Theme. I am now making a record of the Brahms Valses, from which I select about ten or so, and arrange them in a different order from that found in the printed copy. Naturally, I try to select the most characteristic ones. Many are charming and I do not consider it does them any harm to be rearranged.

Modern Music

"Do I play modern music? I only care to learn what is worth while, what appeals to me as having something to say, as having vitality and meaning. From this viewpoint it doesn't matter whether the music is new or old. Some modern compositions are interesting. You mention the Sonata by Frank Bridge, which Myra Hess played at her recital here. I have heard her do it in London. It is not a work to attract the listener at first hearing. As I have heard it several times, I begin to be somewhat attracted to it. I think she is very brave to play it here, when she must realize it would not *take* at one hearing. It would be unwise, too, to attempt to play it from memory, since one would not use the work often enough to compensate for the time it would consume to commit it.

A Program of Etudes

"I have in mind a program made up entirely of Etudes, which I hope to bring out here. Such a program would consist largely of the Twenty-four Etudes of Chopin, entire. I don't think they have been played here as a complete whole. But I should not play them in the order they appear in the book. I would begin and end with those originally placed first and last, but others would be arranged differently. I have given much thought to placing them according to type and meaning. Of course these pieces are not studies at all, in any sense, but wonderful works of art, compositions of the highest order. By constant study new beauties are revealed, new ways of interpretation, new atmosphere and tonal coloring.

"Take the Etude in A minor, Number 2, for instance. If I play the right hand like this" (illustrating) "and slightly stress the first sixteenth note in each group of four, a little melody is developed, as you see. It gives variety and meaning to the ascending and descending passages, like a faint pattern in the web of tone weaving. Whenever we can discover a melodic voice, it is our privilege to reveal and bring it out.

"My program of Etudes can begin with the Etudes Symphoniques of Schumann—again a set of pieces, etudes only in name. After these I would place a few of the Liszt Etudes, the Gnomenreigen, Waldesrauschen, Etude in D flat, and a couple of others. I do not want to make the list too long; the Chopin pieces require an hour and five minutes to play, the Schumann about twenty minutes; I would not weary the listener."

VLADIMIR DE PACHMANN
[1848-1933]

A Distinctive Method of Piano Playing

I f you were to come in touch with that superlative pianist and unique personality, Vladimir de Pachmann, you would not soon forget the experience. More than this. If you were permitted to sit beside the piano as he played for you, now this beautiful bit or that—just as they came into his mind—you would feel you were getting a very near and intimate view of a many-sided artist. If a music lover, you would enjoy the shifting web of tone colors he wove for you alone. A pianist—you would like to capture, imprison and make your own the secrets of tone and touch he illustrated for your benefit. A teacher—the wonderful technical control would appeal to you, which this wizard of the keyboard possesses in such a marvelous degree.

I had the privilege of spending over an hour with the Russian pianist, on two different occasions, shortly after he arrived in America for his last tours. The first afternoon several friends were present. He was in rather a gay mood. He had left the steamer but a few hours before, and still felt the throb of the machinery. He was glad to be in our country, where people were so sympathetic to his art, and so on. After a while he brought out one of his most treasured possessions, which he exhibited for our admiration. This was nothing less than a coat which had once belonged to Chopin. It was of mohair of a chocolate brown color, with large collar and long skirt. Some one requested him to put it on. Then the piano was surreptitiously opened, and he was induced, still wearing the coat—which was much too large for him—to seat himself at the keyboard. Almost before he was aware of it he was improvising tiny little stray tone-thoughts. Continually protesting that he could not play that day, that he had not touched a piano for two weeks, he began the D flat Nocturne of Chopin.

It was a memorable performance, or rather it was a poetical inspiration in tones. One felt it was the last word in the interpretation of this exquisite night song. He accompanied the playing with a little by-play of remarks as he went along. "This is Caruso," he said in one place; again, "These tones are sung by Patti." The pairs of intervals toward the close, given to the right hand, he called bells. When it was over, he explained that the beauties we admired were due to a new method of playing which he had discovered about five years ago [ca. 1918]. What this method is has been subsequently much misunderstood, one writer going so far as to say it consists in holding the wrist stiff and high. Nothing could be farther from the truth. He explained his ideas to me the following afternoon, when I spent another hour with him. Calling me to sit beside him at the piano, he began:

"My Méthode, ah yes, I discovered it five years ago. It was a revelation; it came to me from Heaven. It does not consist of high, stiff wrists; that would be very bad—abominable! You see I move my wrists up and down freely when I play. But my hand and arm I hold quite level, with the outside of the hand on a line with the arm, not turned in or out at the wrist.

"In order to preserve this position of hand and arm in different parts of the keyboard, the use of the fingers, or I should say, the choice of them, must be very carefully considered. I must use special fingering for everything I play. Fingering, anyway, is a very important factor in great playing. Take von Bülow, for instance: he did much for fingering in his editions of Beethoven and Chopin. But I do not feel he has solved all the problems, by any means. He always tried to make things more difficult through constant change of fingers, thereby turning the hand from side to side and twisting the fingers out of shape. I make things easy by using fingers that will not throw the hand out of shape and that will always preserve the correct relation of hand to the arm, of which I have spoken. Yet Bülow was a great man, a most excellent pianist, thinker and philosopher. I say all this for him, though I don't approve of his fingering. I care still less for Klindworth's, for he tried to make things more difficult than they need be, in order to keep all fingers employed.

"Look at this passage from Chopin's Third Impromptu. Here is Bülow's fingering; you see how it throws the hand out of shape? Here is mine, which keeps the hand quiet and in natural position.

"The first benefit of my Méthode to the player is that he can produce a *natural tone*, made without effort. I can play hours and hours without fatigue. I could play the whole twenty-four if I didn't have to eat a little and sleep some. But the pianists of today, especially the younger ones—see with what effort they play, and with what a hard tone! How can they ever make natural tones and play from the heart, when they are punching and beating the piano at the rate they do? Ah, the poor piano! But *my* piano will yield lovely tones because I treat it in the right way. Why not caress it like this? Listen to these little upward passages; how delicate and shadowy! How ethereal they can be made if the heart speaks through them by means of the fingers! And the fingers, doing their part through right adjustment and correct choice, glide up and down the keyboard with little or no effort or exertion. "Do you think all this is easy? Of course it looks perfectly so—and it is easy, for me. But each of these passages has cost me months of study. Some of them I have played thousands of times. And even yet they do not quite suit me; they can still be improved with more labor, till they become superlatively perfect.

And the artless pianist, simple as a child, listened intently, with head on one side, to the exquisite tones he produced.

"When I made the discovery of my Méthode, I soon found that to play my pieces in the new way they must all be revised and fingered anew. Many passages written for one hand I now use both hands for; thus keeping the hands in a more natural position and making things easier for both."

Mr. de Pachmann illustrated his remarks with various passages, most of them taken from the music of Chopin.

"Some pieces do not lend themselves to such changes as are required by my Méthode, and those I shall not play in my recitals.

"Of Beethoven I shall not give the Appassionata, for I know it has been done to extinction; every student brings it out. Neither shall the Waldstein appear on my programs. Op. 90 is nice in the First Movement; see how this opening theme can be transfigured by beautiful tone. Is it not heavenly? But the last movement I don't care for, and it's too long, as you say. I shall only put the Sonata Pathétique on my programs.

"Of Chopin I shall select only the special and least-known pieces. Not the Polonaise Op. 53 or the Scherzo Op. 31. I can't hear these any more; they are played ad nauseam. No, I will choose the Fourth Scherzo and two Polonaises, the small one in C sharp minor and the wonderful one in F sharp minor, Op. 44, one of the greatest compositions ever written on this little planet. It is truly inspired. Then I shall give the little-known Allegro de Concerto and a few other things.

"Brahms' Valses will be heard in one of my New York recitals. How light and beautiful is Number One; listen to it! Ah, and I will play it in tempo, too—no hesitation, no lagging. With my Méthode I can play it that way. Then hear Number Six; note the lightness of the skips! They should ripple and dance like tiny fairies. Do you remember the run in thirty seconds in Number 14? You will see I can play it in time. See, I beat the time with my hands and then play. Ah, you don't hear it played like that, with such swiftness, lightness and precision.

"Then there is the music of Godowsky, the greatest since Brahms. He is a great genius, Godowsky; such a thinker, contrapuntalist, composer and pianist all in one. I have talked with him already about my Méthode. When he heard what it really was he understood at once and exclaimed, 'Ah, Pachmann, you have found out something really fine; in this way one can make a true, natural tone.'

"What has Godowsky written for the piano? First, there is a wonderful Sonata in five movements; a great work, finer than Brahms' Op. 5. It is grander, more majestic than that, and exceedingly difficult. Then there is the Walzer-Masken, a set of twenty-four pieces—*beautiful!* I shall play seven of them in my American concerts. They are finer than the Trikatammeron, the set of thirty pieces of more recent date—at least *I* think so. These I do not play—nor the Sonata—in public; my Méthode is not adapted to them.

"Yes, I intend to write out my Méthode; it shall be set down in an orderly manner, for the benefit of those who come after me. But not yet—I have no time; I must go on tour. After all that is over—then—perhaps ——"

After two very successful seasons of concertizing in America, separated by a summer of rest and quiet, the venerable musician decided he must return to his European home. New York had the opportunity to hear him once more before he departed, in a last recital which was called "A farewell for all time."

The last view of a renowned artist—the last time one comes under the spell of his particular form of art—is always memorable. The last American recital of de Pachmann makes history. At least once before he had seemed to take final leave of us, notably in 1912. But the very last "for all time" occurred April 13, 1925.

Many years lay between his early recitals here and the very last of all. Some of us recall the days when he used to play in old Chickering Hall, Fifth Avenue and Eighteenth Street. Many other artists played there in those days, including von Bülow, Carreño and Scharwenka.

Pachmann was ever erratic and talkative during recital, even in those days. On one occasion, during a long composition, his thought wandered, perhaps from too many side remarks, and he seemed suddenly to have a lapse of memory—or was it a cramp of the wrist, as he indicated it was; we could not quite tell which. He sprang from the chair, clasping his wrist, as though the next moment the hand would drop off, all the time talking very fast.

Pacing up and down the platform, still holding his wrist, he slowly indicated that he was recovering the use of his hand. He then went to the piano, made several attempts to use his fingers, and finally told us he would try to continue the composition. He began the interrupted piece at the beginning, and this time went through it in safety.

At the *really* farewell recital, Carnegie Hall was quite filled, and several hundred were seated on the stage. We all waited as patiently as we might, till long past the hour, remembering it was the last time. Finally a small figure threaded its way to the front of the stage, smiling, bowing, and talking as it came. When the piano was reached, the piano-stool proved to be intractable, and an orderly was summoned to adjust it. Meanwhile the eccentric pianist explained to the audience that the fingers and wrist of his right hand were troubling him; it was strenuous business to play a whole recital, at his age, too. He might get through all right; if he did, it would all be due to his wonderful Méthode and Heaven's blessing on his work.

With many glances Heavenward and at the audience, he seated himself before the instrument. It was an "all Chopin" program, and even the severest critics concede that de Pachmann, at his best, can be inimitable in the smaller Chopin pieces. For the greater Chopin he never had, even in his prime, sufficient virility and power. And on this final occasion the strength of former days was lacking. But there were compensations—unforgettable moments, when we listened almost breathless to the fine-spun, gossamer delicacy of the F major Étude, or to the ethereal loveliness of the D flat Nocturne. Some of the shorter Valses and Mazurkas were equally enthralling. Together these blossoms of delicate memory formed a nosegay of rarest fragrance, whose aroma is a lasting memory.

Let us close eyes and ears to those eccentric grimaces and the running fire of comment; for both these are distracting whenever we allow them to divert our attention. But let us rather treasure the remembrance of the few but exquisite tone pictures which Vladimir de Pachmann has left us as a rich legacy.

SERGE PROKOFIEFF
[1891-1953]

FUTURISM IN MUSIC

A few facts about that remarkable pianist and composer, Serge Prokofieff, have been furnished by V. G. Karatygin, Professor of Musical History, in Leningrad. The Professor, glimpsing the achievements of his subject from early years, said in part:

Serge Prokofieff was born in the estate of Sontsovka, South Russia, April 11, 1891. He showed evidence of natural musical ability at the very earliest age—a "leitmotiv" of all famous musicians. His mother was his first teacher, who later passed him on to Professors Janeieff and Glière. His first manuscripts belong to the age of six!

In 1904 young Serge, then only thirteen, entered the St. Petersburg Conservatory, from which he was graduated with highest honors, winning the coveted Rubinstein prize. Here he studied composition under Rimsky-Korsakoff and Liadov, piano with the famous pianist, Annette Essipoff, and conducting with Tscherepnine. Due to the technical possibilities in the construction of his hands, with their long, tenacious fingers, Prokofieff soon became a remarkable pianist. His ease in managing the piano induced him to first compose for that instrument. He also tried his hand at opera at the tender age of seven, and again at nine. At the age of eleven he composed a Symphony in four parts, at twelve a third opera. As he grew older his imagination worked even more energetically. During the first years at the Conservatory he wrote over one hundred works, a fourth opera, *Undina*, another Symphony in three parts, six piano Sonatas, and over ninety other piano pieces. One of these early Sonatas was revised and published in 1909 as Opus 1. In 1911 the First Concerto for piano appeared, and in 1912 the Second Sonata. The next year the Second Concerto saw the light; in 1917 came the Third and Fourth Sonatas.

There is no musician who does not know the originality of Prokofieff's music—daring, turbulent and full of life and power as it is. It is true many musicians cannot accept this music because it frequently, in impassioned moments, oversteps the rules of harmony and counterpoint. But Prokofieff, while violating academic laws, is always logical. His music is marked by genuine truth and sometimes you will discover moments of revelation. He does not care to follow well-beaten paths, but prefers to force his way through virgin forests, putting aside all obstacles with masterful hand, breaking trees and jumping over broad streams. Much noise and rumbling accompany him in his wandering toward new shores. His daring has always a strong and convincing logic. The course of his ship is straight and determined, and leads toward the sun, toward the fullness of life and joy of existence.

In listening to this music we feel its invincible strength, enormous temperament, rich thematic imagination, remarkable harmonic inventiveness. It is painting with broad strokes—even touching the grotesque. There is astonishing boldness and energy in it, alternating with flashes of humor. It is quite wonderful music! You are bitten, pinched, burnt, but you do not revolt. He has some kinship with the American, Edgar Allan Poe. But here and there you will be touched by something tender, gentle, sweet. There are occasional pearls of fine musical poetry, especially precious when contrasted by some of the boiling, rushing music. This lyrical current is to be felt in the Sonatas. The lyrical theme of the Third Sonata is one of the composer's most fortunate achievements.

Besides the Sonatas, Prokofieff has written many shorter pieces for the piano. There are some twenty *Moments Fugitifs*, a set of Etudes, some Miniatures, some Preludes, a Scherzo, a charming Gavotte, five *Sarcasms*, and more than a score of vivid tone pictures and Dances.

Knowing all this before the arrival of the brilliant Russian, for his first concert tour in America, his first appearance as pianist was an event of musical importance.

Prokofieff the Pianist

The large audience sat waiting expectantly—waiting for what? A new light from Russia, it was said. One was inclined to ask: Can anything great come out of Russia *now?* From out all that chaos and red-handed turmoil, shall we get sweet harmonies, pleasant thoughts and sounds? Or will the music of Russia reflect the present conditions of the country? We shall soon know.

Meanwhile the house filled with the cream of Metropolitan musical life. Composers were there, and conductors, pianists and singers. There were many others who did not belong to these divisions, but looked as though they had come out of Russia, Japan or some other country on the opposite side of the globe. One saw many nationalities represented; also many of our teachers were in its makeup as well. It was indeed a cosmopolitan audience—all waiting for a new sensation.

What will he look like, this new light, and how will he play? Like a composer or a virtuoso? Will his music have the flavor, the qualities, of the Russian music with which we are already familiar? Will it be anything like the music of Rachmaninoff, who is in the audience today? For we have grown somewhat accustomed to his idiom by now. Or will it be strange, weird, cacophonous? We shall know what it will be like in a few moments.

Ah, the stage door opens—the door which separates the newcomer from the New World to which he is to lay siege. If that small door could only speak, what could it not reveal of shivering suspense and shaking nerves— of brave determination to do, or—

A young man steps out briskly from the doorway and marches to the instrument. He evidently believes in the old axiom, which may apply to the concert platform as well as to any other spot or situation in life: that time and tide the audience—wait for no man.

He seats himself as quickly as he came, and plunges at once into work, without hesitation or delay. Four Etudes of his own follow each other in quick succession; then a big Sonata, in four movements. The instant the last note is struck, the pianist-composer rises abruptly and retires as briskly as he has come.

As soon as the audience could recover breath, it began to consider what had been happening, what had been heard. A buzz of voices could be heard all over the hall; the critics gathered in small groups, shaking their wise heads and consulting in undertones. No one could deny that here was a composer of torrential temperament, who feared not to assail the ears of the listeners with the most complex dissonances, if he cannot secure the effects he seeks in any pleasanter way. Power of tone he has in abundance, also marvelous velocity. But it is also true that quality of tone is often more potent to conquer and enslave the hearer. He has scarcely arrived at the point where he believes that after the whirlwind may come "the still small voice." Doubtless one day the fiery young artist may discover the potency of this small voice, and then his playing will take on a delicacy and tenderness not at present discoverable. For now he is all fire and flame, though at rare moments, when he did play softly, he secured an excellent singing tone; we longed for more of those moments.

But his playing and his music made an undeniable appeal, through its very daring and bizarre strangeness. It was like tasting a new kind of spice which bit the tongue. The tang was pungent, but not altogether unpleasant; one was not averse to tasting again, and then again. At least the audience seemed to think so, for it remained to applaud and call for encores after the long all-Russian program was finished.

The critics departed to write wisely, about "biceps," "triceps," "wrists of steel" and other things they thought they discovered in the new pianist. The conservatives decided his music was all dreadful cacophony, and they resented having their eardrums assailed so mercilessly. Those with ears open to new ideas, new effects, new surprises and sensations, rather liked it all and were quite willing to listen further—were open to conviction. They had faith to believe that future hearings would reveal new excellences and beauties hidden on first acquaintance. For had it not been said by an authority in his own country:

"It is from Serge Prokofieff that we can expect new ideas in musical art, more and more deep and individual."

Taking this to heart, we resolve to endeavor to understand this strange music and its remarkable interpreter.

The Pianist-Composer at Home

Serge Prokofieff has a studio in a hotel in the heart of the metropolis. Here are his piano, his music and manuscripts—his tools.

He entered this workroom to greet the visitor, one afternoon, with the same *presto* movements that he makes when he walks out on the stage to play a recital. He is quick-spoken, too, with a surprising facility in English, considering the short time he has had at his disposal to become familiar with it. "I speak six languages— French, Italian, Spanish, German, Russian and some English," he asserted calmly, with his pleasant, broad smile, as though to know six tongues were the easiest thing in the world.

"How did you acquire your wonderful piano technic?" he was asked.

"What is?"

"Your piano technic—how did you get it ?"

"Oh, yes, I will tell you. There are some pianists who must practise many hours every day; again there are some others who do not work very much—technic to them seems to be a gift of the gods. I think I must belong to the latter class, for I do not need so much to practise; my hands do not forget," and he held up a wonderful hand, with long, supple fingers.

Then the fiery young Russian took a few turns up and down the room, just to work off superfluous energy, before settling down again in his chair.

"You see," he continued, "it took me some time to reach here after I left my home in Russia; it was a long, roundabout journey. So, for over five months I was without a piano at all. Then, after arriving in America, I had only a short time to prepare the program for my first recital; maybe but two weeks to learn those Rachmaninoff Preludes—three of them. I was very anxious about them, and a bit nervous, when I knew the composer himself was in the audience at my debut.

"Yes, I have read many of the criticisms. Some of them say my music is cerebral; that is said in Russia, too. But about 'biceps' and 'triceps,' I do not quite understand. What is? Can you explain those words, applied to piano playing?"

Criticism an Art in Russia

Without waiting for a specific reply, he went on:

"When a critic in my country has to write about the music of a new composer, or a new pianist, he considers it a really serious matter. He makes it his business to learn all he can about that pianist or that music, in the first place. Then he calls upon the musician, asks him to describe the pieces and play them for him. He will hear them three—four—five times; so he has a very good idea of their form and meaning, also the playing of the pianist, before attempting to say anything about them in print. All this is not too much trouble for the conscientious critic, for he wishes to give the artist the best possible review in his power. But such does not seem to be the method of the critics in your country."

He broke off and looked searchingly at the visitor.

"About composing. I hardly know when I began to compose. When I was seven I wrote an opera, for a little family fête-day. It had no orchestra, only a piano accompaniment. The words were by our greatest poet, Pushkin. We all had much pleasure out of this little story set to music. My next effort in this direction happened two years later, when I wrote another opera, a little bit more elaborate, but still without orchestra.

"When I was eleven, I composed a symphony in four parts, and at twelve a third opera, which this time had an orchestral background. For by this time I had begun to study theory and composition. I made those studies with Glière, Rimsky-Korsakoff and Liadoff. When I was thirteen, I entered the Petrograd Conservatory, and from then on my whole time was given to musical and other studies. I really studied seriously. Mme. Annette Essipowa was my teacher in piano there. You, of course, know her in your country, as she once toured America.

"From the formation of my hand and fingers, I always found it very easy to play piano. And as it was so easy to play piano, I wrote quite a good deal of piano music. I have already four piano Sonatas, and a number of groups of short pieces. You heard my Second Sonata; I shall play the others later. I am always working, always composing—thinking out new effects, new forms of expression. They say my music is material rather than spiritual; perhaps they mean it is subjective; I seem to embody in music real people, real scenes and episodes."

The above is a brief glimpse of the personality and work of the Prokofieff who came to America five years ago. Later he came to direct his fantastic opera, *The Love of the Three Oranges*, which was given by the Chicago Opera Company and was also seen in New York.

Serge Prokofieff, the Rubinstein prize-winner, the militant virtuoso, composer and performer, is one of the remarkable figures in contemporary Russian music. To repeat the words of Professor Katarygin:

"It is from Serge Prokofieff, more than any one else, that Russia will look for new ideas in musical art—more and more deep and individual."

SERGEI RACHMANINOFF
[1873-1943]

SERIOUS PIANO PRACTISE A NECESSITY IN AMERICA

R achmaninoff! The man whose art is as pure gold; the sincere artist, equally admired by musicians and the public. He is indeed simple, unassuming, truthful, generous."

These words of Josef Hofmann are a high estimate of one artist by another of great renown.

Sergei Rachmaninoff, composer and pianist, whose art was so much admired on his first visit to America, in 1909-10, has been for several years a resident of this country; he has made his home here, living in the metropolis in winter and voyaging to the other side in summer. During each season he is active in the concert field, bringing his polished art to music lovers in many cities, from coast to coast. His reserved yet intense personality seems to exert a peculiar fascination on the crowded audiences which always greet him.

What is the Spell?

For here is no spectacular exhibition of mere piano virtuosity, no long-haired sensation. The great Russian comes upon the platform with most serious mien and seats himself at the instrument as though quite unaware of the audience, waiting in breathless expectancy for the piano to awake under his touch. His tall figure bends over the keyboard, as he sits a few seconds in utter stillness before beginning. Then his large hands, with their long, shapely fingers, find the desired keys with no perceptible effort, and weave for the listener enchanting pictures, now bright, now sad and filled with longing. Yet Rachmaninoff is not a pianist who wears his heart upon his sleeve; he is always reserved, self-contained, wrapt in serious thought, or so it seems. And each year when he reappears, his art has ripened, his vision is broader, more searching, comprehensive and vital.

The boy Sergei very early showed signs of sympathy with and feeling for music. Even in his fourth year this aptitude was observed by his mother, who began to teach him the piano, and continued to do so until he was nine, when an efficient woman pianist and teacher carried the work further. These two early teachers laid the foundation of the musical structure, which gradually rose later to such imposing proportions.

In 1882 the family moved to St. Petersburg, and the boy was at once placed in the Conservatory, where he studied industriously for three years. Then came another move, this time to Moscow, where the lad had the advantages of the great Conservatory and the musical atmosphere of this exceptional musical center. As he himself puts it: "My grandfather was a notable pianist, my cousin, Alexander Siloti, was of Liszt's pupils and is still a prominent figure among present-day Russian musicians. Thus my boyhood was spent among musicians and in a musical atmosphere."

It is said that Rachmaninoff belonged to the old aristocratic order in Russia. The grandfather did not play professionally, but there is tradition that the art of the elder musician has never been surpassed by the pianistic art of the younger.

And this younger Rachmaninoff, now a man of genius, a pianist of the highest attainments, a composer of numerous works for his chosen instrument, for voice and orchestra, a conductor of renown, is living quietly among us here in the new world. The public knows him as composer-pianist, and many young people all over the land struggle to play his famous Prelude in C sharp minor, or perhaps the later one in G minor. But the public has no part in his home life: that is sacred. Few interviewers ever cross the threshold, for it is known that he has an inborn dislike to have his privacy invaded.

It had long been an ardent desire of mine to gain a more intimate view of this distinguished musician than could be obtained from across the footlights. I wanted to speak with him face to face, to inquire his ideas of music study and practise. But season after season passed without my wish coming any nearer fulfillment. Then, suddenly, one day the summons came to go to him.

The handsome residence, which is the home of the Russian master, is situated on Riverside Drive, and overlooks a wide expanse of the Hudson with the Palisades beyond. From midday until late afternoon—on fine days—the rooms are flooded with sunshine, turning everything to gold.

One feels a sense of peace and quietude on entering this abode. The colors of furnishings are soft and rich, in artistic blues and deep reds. Floors and stairways are covered with thick, soft velvets, upon which footfalls are noiseless. As we ascend the stairs, sounds of a piano come floating down to us. The master is playing, or rather is at work on some knotty passage which he repeats over and over with the utmost patience. As we enter he rises to greet us with kindly manner, but with grave, austere expression, as though loath to be disturbed, or to leave the musical train of thought, even for a few moments.

Daily Practise
To the question as to how the artist keeps his technic in repair and up to concert pitch, he said:

"The pianist must play much technic and many technical exercises outside of pieces. He has been trained to do so, for he started out with this idea and these principles from the beginning— that is, if he is a Russian. In my native country music is taught much more thoroughly than it is in America. When a student enters the Conservatory in Russia, he is expected to remain nine or ten years. If talented and able to work quickly, he may be able to cover the ground in eight years, though this is seldom done. Of course, you understand he takes other studies along with music: history, literature, languages, philosophy and other subjects.

Pure Technic
"The study of pure technic includes scales, chords, arpeggios, trills and octaves. How can the student expect to learn difficult pieces without a background of technical forms, well digested and mastered? It is perfectly impossible. And if this technical drill and routine are necessary for the student, shall the concert player cast them aside as useless? Not at all; he would be very foolish to do so. If I wish to keep my playing mechanism in condition, I, too, must practise scales, arpeggios, trills, chords and octaves. There is no other way to keep fit.

Students not Sufficiently Serious
"As I travel over your great country and observe conditions, it seems to me the students of music do not study seriously—not with whole heart and soul. There may be several causes for this condition of things; the entire blame cannot be placed on any one of them. For one thing, there seems to be a lack of good teachers. The best teachers here in America are excellent, but there are too few and they are generally found in the music centers and large cities. Smaller places are obliged to get along with a much poorer quality, though they, too, need the best.

The Need of the Hour
"You ask what I consider this country's greatest need, the need of the hour. I answer without hesitation—intelligent, industrious practise. Students of music, in this particular, are indifferent, or, shall I say it frankly? they are downright lazy. They don't give their minds to the work they have taken up—they don't give sufficient time to their studies; they fritter away precious

moments and hours on superficial things, instead of devoting their time to mastering the beautiful art they have undertaken to study. Technical mastery of the piano cannot be won in a month or a year; it is the result of many years of ceaseless study. But even if the student does not wish to enter a public career, there is no reason why piano study should not be pursued along correct lines. Why should not the student go thoroughly even a part of the way? If he attempts the study at all, he should bend all his mental powers to the tasks he has set himself.

"As you suggest, there may be some reasons why American pupils are inclined to slight the study of music and become superficial. There are many distractions."

One of these is surely the radio, was remarked, which he agreed could be very distracting, if the whole family were interested in listening to it. And yet it was sadly evident that really good music was all too seldom heard over the radio, which fact was the more unfortunate, he thought, if the students were obliged to listen to much of it.

Modern Music
"What do I think of modern music? I am free to admit I do not think highly of it. There is very little—indeed but a small proportion of what is composed today—that is attractive or that has any lasting value. What is the use of this constant struggle after originality—of the great effort to dress up the musical idea in unusual form and shape, if the thought itself has little meaning or vitality? Music is a spiritual art; it should elevate and enrich life with beautiful thoughts, feelings and experiences. These vital things seem to be lacking in most modern music.

"The music of MacDowell? He has done interesting things. I am somewhat familiar with the Sonatas and some of the shorter pieces. But his music is not much known abroad, at least not in Russia.

"In Russia we have a number of composers whose works are not known on this side. One of them is Nikolai Medtner, a really great composer. Some have called him the 'Russian Brahms,' yet this a wrong name for him. He is individual and does not pattern after any one else. He is also called a modernist, yet Medtner hates modernism. His music is always true music. Possibly in that sense it is modern, but it never is meaningless and discordant. In addition to being a great composer, Medtner is a wonderful pianist. I trust that when he comes, both his playing and his compositions will be appreciated in America.

"Reverting to American music once more, I would like to say that I recently heard a composition by an American, that pleased me greatly; it really is a

fine piece of work. It is in the form of an orchestral Suite and the composer
is Deems Taylor. Its title is—as you suggest—*Through the Looking-Glass.*
I hope Mr. Taylor has done, or will do, other things, for he has great ability.

"This composition was played by the Philadelphia Orchestra, an extremely
fine organization. Indeed, the orchestras of America—the best of them—
lead the world in excellence and high ideals.

Artistic Outlook in America

"America has almost unlimited possibilities and potentialities, and can
eventually develop into a great musical nation. You have made immense strides
forward ever since I first came here, fifteen years ago. There is really now no
necessity for the American student to go abroad for music study, for you have
every requisite in your own country for the training and perfecting of great
musicians. You have public-spirited men, too, men of wealth, who seem ready
and willing to devote their means to the fostering of music and art. There is no
doubt that one day you will have a great music school or conservatory, which
will train your talented youth to do high things in music, both as executive
and creative artists. And I believe it is much better, for many reasons, for the
music student to receive his training in his native land, *if* he can only receive
training of the right sort. The strength and vitality of your social, home and
outdoor life should influence the student in his musical and artistic expression.

"No, I do not teach piano, as I have no time. I shall start very soon on a
long tour of several months' duration. My summer vacations I usually spend
on the other side. Whenever and wherever there is time and opportunity for
quiet thought and study, I turn to composition."

Beginners should have the Best Teachers

In speaking further of the need for good teachers for those just starting in to
study music, he said:

"It frequently is affirmed that an indifferent teacher will do just as well to
start with. Never was there a greater mistake. The child who shows signs of
musical aptitude should be allowed the very best teacher it is possible to
secure. Do not place a child of even five years old under a poor, inefficient
teacher. Else what is poorly done will have to be done all over again—a
difficult matter, for early impressions are most lasting, as we all know.

"It is to be hoped the day will come when there will be no more poor
teachers, for they will all be trained for the great work of teaching, and will
realize their high calling and wonderful opportunities."

MORITZ ROSENTHAL

[1862-1946]

BUILDING A CONCERT TECHNIC

Moritz Rosenthal is indisputably a true giant of the keyboard. Born in Lemberg, in 1862, he had made such progress under Mikuli, pupil of Chopin and then Director of the Lemberg Conservatory, that he played the Chopin Rondo for two pianos, with his teacher, in public, at the age of ten. Later his parents moved to Vienna and he became a pupil of Joseffy, and the Tausig method. At fourteen he made his debut in Vienna, which was followed by a phenomenal tour through Roumania. From 1876 to 1878 he was with Liszt in Weimar and Rome. After making a sensation in Paris and St. Petersburg in 1878, he withdrew from the concert field and devoted himself to classical and philosophical studies, keeping up his piano practise at the same time. When he emerged to continue his concert career, in 1884, he caused amazement by his marvelous technic and endless physical endurance. Since then he has concertized in many parts of the world. Five tours in America have been made; the fifth one separated about seventeen years from the fourth.

It was during his last tour that I had the pleasure of meeting the artist, and conferring with him on things pertaining to his art.

Just before starting to keep my appointment, I said to one of my students: "And what shall I ask the master, when I come face to face with him?" as I was a bit curious as to how she would answer.

"Ask him how he has acquired his marvelous technic," was her reply.

It is a curious fact that to think of Rosenthal is to think of stupendous technic and great physical endurance. It is said of him that when he appeared in Vienna, in 1884—he was only twenty-two then—he astounded his listeners by his performance, the critics declaring him to be the greatest living technician. And at first that is a frequent impression. But it is soon discovered that, in his case, stupendous technic is only a means to an end, only a legitimate vehicle of musical expression. It is recognized then that Rosenthal is a musician of intellectual power and keen penetration. His playing gives ample proof of the perfect balance of the technical and intellectual in whatever he does.

There are some who assert that the sort of technic this pianist employs is of the old-fashioned Leipsic order, the old German school, though brought to highest perfection. They have not observed, perhaps, that the artist at times uses some of the arm-weight movements, which formerly did not belong to that school of piano playing. These movements and conditions aid in the beautiful tones which he generally draws from the instrument. All must agree he is a truly great and unique artist.

Arriving at the appointed hour of my visit, I was shown to the luxurious study occupied by the pianist, in one of the newest uptown hotels. He was at work at the piano as I entered, but rose and received me graciously. Near his grand piano stood his practise keyboard. It was propped up on two chairs, and was rather a thin, simple affair, which was hinged in the middle, and could fold up in order to be tucked away in a trunk or traveling-case. It had no regulated action or touch, and seemed to be just a "dumb keyboard."

"It was made especially for me, to my order," remarked the artist, pressing the keys here and there with his wonderfully developed hands. "Yes, it accompanies me on all my tours," he added,

A Concert Technic

"And you want to know how I acquired my technic, or, to put it more impersonally, what are the essentials of a concert technic today?

"It would be very difficult for me to say how and where I acquired my technic, as it has come from many sources, and, latterly, from the study of difficult portions and characteristic passages in pieces.

"First of all, I am not favorable to a great deal of time being given to finger exercises, so called. They can be interminably repeated, ad nauseam, without intelligence and without imagination. Such useless repetition is for many pupils as though they were in a boat, rowing aimlessly about, not knowing whither—having no destination. Young people often take up the study of music with no natural ability and no aim in view. It would be more profitable for such students to undertake some other branch of study, as with no innate ability they will only make a failure of music.

"It requires both intelligence and imagination to grasp technical principles and to work them out. Each player's hand is more or less individual, and he must adapt technic to his needs. He must imagine the kind and quality of tone required for every effect, and how to produce and develop that tone to the best advantage. He thus requires both these mental qualities to seize on the right means to develop his technical apparatus, to prepare his tools, if you will, to be used to the highest achievement.

Legato Touch

"A necessity for the pianist is a correct understanding of the legato touch. In reality we seldom find it understood by the general student. Legato does not mean holding one key tightly till the next is struck, although many players think it does. Artistic legato means that the keys are to be depressed in such a manner and with such a quality of tone that the sounds seem to be connected, even though there may be a very slight separation between them. Imagination here plays a large role in securing this result.

Technical Material

"In early stages the pupil should naturally learn principles of touch and movements for arm, wrist and fingers, and how to apply them in trills, scales, chords, arpeggios and octaves. For the last—the octaves—I advise both elevated and low wrist, after the manner shown by Kullak in his Octave School.

"When these principles are understood and are somewhat under control, Czerny can be taken up. Here again use intelligence and imagination, and study those etudes most appropriate to your needs. So, whether it be the School of Velocity, Op. 299, the School of Virtuosity, Op. 740, the School of Legato and Staccato, or any of the other sets—I no longer remember the opus numbers—choose intelligently what is best to study. Through conscientious study of these various forms, you will gain the things necessary for your development. But, if you merely run through them for the sake of practising technic, you will again be like the rudderless boat, aimlessly drifting and arriving nowhere.

"When I have a little leisure—not now, of course, when I am on tour—but at some future time, I intend to write out a set of exercises for the complete development of the hand. The principles of technic thus set down will be illustrated by certain etudes, which I shall select for the further development of the player. This idea has been in my mind for some years, waiting for time and opportunity to carry it out.

"To continue with our technic building. After Czerny, Clementi, in the Tausig edition, will be found useful in forming a concert technic. This does not mean, I take it, that the student should master every one of the Clementi Etudes, but only those found to be the most improving and valuable to his own particular development.

"Henselt has put forth some valuable study material, especially in etudes built on widely extended chords and arpeggios; these are really difficult. Also Moscheles ought not to be forgotten, for there is much good material to improve a concert technic in his collection of Twenty-four Characteristic Studies, Op. 70.

"It is a wide jump from the material I have enumerated to the two books of Etudes by Chopin. He has taken up the principal technical points, and illustrated them in incomparable studies, such as the Double Thirds, the Etudes in Sixths and in Octaves, chromatic runs as in Number Two, staccato intervals, as in Number Seven, arpeggio forms, as in the first and last Etudes, and many other necessary technical points. And while the student is mastering technical difficulties, he is also working on the musical and interpretative side, for both go hand in hand, through the study of these wonderful etudes. In this way one combines technic study with repertoire. Here one learns to mold beautiful tones, to infuse poetry and feeling into these phrases. And as a result of mastering various kinds of pianistic difficulties, one has also a command of two dozen beautiful compositions, each one unique of its kind.

"As I said a moment ago, the difficult passages in pieces also form excellent material for technical study. There are countless such passages in Chopin and Liszt, so that one need never lack an objective for study. For octave practise it is a good plan to select octave passages from certain pieces, and keep them in constant review. Such, for instance, would be the pages of octaves in Liszt's Sixth Rhapsodie. Or the Finale from the same composer's Fourth Rhapsodie, though I consider this piece inferior to the Sixth. Perhaps this is the reason we so seldom hear it.

Modern Music

"I am sometimes asked if I am in sympathy with modern music, and if it finds a place on my programs. If 'modern music' really means ultramodern music, I answer emphatically in the negative. Much of this extremely modern so-called music is poor stuff indeed, lacking in form, shape, melody and harmony. It amazes me that such distortion and cacophony can be set down and performed in the name of music, and that people should ever consider it seriously. There are a few modern composers who have put forth some interesting music for the piano. I play some Skryabin, though not his later compositions—not beyond Opus 40. I also play some Albeniz and Debussy, though not a great deal of the latter.

"But there are worthy modern works that are unknown, simply for lack of the public's interest, or of the manager's either. To mention one composer whose work is little known as yet, is to speak of the Polish master, Xaver Scharwenka. He has written several concertos which are excellent, but they are seldom heard, and are quite unknown in America. I consider them finer than the Saint-Saëns concertos. I have proposed the Fourth Concerto by Scharwenka to orchestral leaders here, but they refuse to put it on their programs. I suppose they don't want to take time to study a new work of that kind.

"It is a great pleasure for me to renew my impressions and friendships in America, as I have not had the opportunity of doing so for seventeen years. Yes, I find many changes, and great progress in many ways. And, though the increase in musical knowledge and activities is marked, yet I had always found, on my previous visits, a great deal of understanding on musical subjects. I have never been one to decry the musical intelligence of this country, for I have always found appreciation here, and have the pleasantest recollections of the treatment I have always received in your hospitable land. Before I leave its shores, I must make the trip to California, which will be my fourth visit to the coast."

❧

ALEXANDER SILOTI

[1863-1945]

GLIMPSES OF RUBINSTEIN AND LISZT

Alexander Siloti, the eminent Russian pianist and musician, a favorite pupil and friend of Liszt, a relative of Rachmaninoff, whose name —known everywhere—stands for what is dignified, noble and best in musical art, is living among us, walking our streets, visiting our concert halls, and learning—we hope—to feel at home in the new land. He does not, however, assimilate the language of the country of his adoption, for he insists he cannot learn English. But he converses readily in German, and is full of reminiscence of the many wonderful musical experiences of an eventful life, a few of which he has imparted to me at different times and occasions.

"Some of the happiest, although some of the most strenuous, days of my student life were spent with the master, Franz Liszt, in Weimar. I was but a lad of nineteen, and not long before had finished my course of study at the Conservatory of Moscow. At the completion of this course I was to have some lessons with Anton Rubinstein, who offered to give me occasional lessons whenever he came to Moscow to conduct the symphony concerts.

"Those lessons were very strenuous, to say the least. I heard I was to prepare four great works for my first lesson. They were: Schumann's Kreisleriana, Beethoven's Emperor Concerto and Sonata Op. 101, and, to cap the climax, Chopin's Sonata in B minor. I knew none of these works and had but about six weeks to prepare them. At the end of that time, by practising seven or eight hours a day, I really learned the notes at least, if not much of the meaning.

"The events of the first lesson are stamped on my memory. The master was not alone, but a number of society ladies were present. 'Play,' said Rubinstein. I chose the Kreisleriana, and began, expecting him to stop me at any moment. He never said one word, but allowed me to continue through the whole piece, of eight parts. When I finished at last, there was absolute silence, which made me feel as though I had lost everything.

"At last he rose and came to the piano. 'Kreisler was a wonderful man who possessed great poetic feeling, combined with a tremendous amount of "temperament." What you have to do is to play these pieces so that every one will realize this fact.' Then, seating himself at the instrument, he played the Kreisleriana as one inspired. The young student was entirely forgotten: he was too insignificant to take any notice of. I felt as though I should give up the study of music for all time. I could not help contrasting this treatment with the manner of Nicholas Rubinstein, who had also been my teacher. His method was to play to his pupils in such a way that they were able to realize the ideal he set before them. He took into consideration the amount of talent each student possessed, and inspired him with the hope that he would be able, one day, to play as well as his teacher.

"There were other lessons of the same sort with Anton Rubinstein, which, as I look back on them, seem like nightmares. If the desire to learn was not killed in me it was due to my happy disposition.

"At last it was made possible for me to go abroad for further study, which I hoped might be with the great master Liszt. Even Anton Rubinstein felt that the greatest thing for me would be to be accepted as a pupil by Liszt.

"A couple of friends traveled with me, and we arrived in Leipsic in time for the Music Festival, in which Liszt himself was taking part. I met him and he asked me to come to Weimar and study with him. As soon as the Festival was over, my friends went with me to Weimar, and engaged a room for me there. By this time I was horribly homesick, for I knew not a word of German. After my first lesson with the master, however, this feeling left me and I threw myself into my studies with the greatest ardor. For three years thereafter I had the infinite privilege of coming into close contact, both as pupil and friend, with this wonderful man, who showed me many marks of his kindly interest and affectionate regard.

Characteristics of Liszt's Playing

"I am asked sometimes what were the distinguishing characteristics of Liszt's playing, and why it was so remarkable. The question is somewhat difficult to answer. His piano tone was not so big; some of the rest of us had as much; but it excelled in a marvelous searching quality, the poignancy of which I have never heard from any one else. In fact, it could not be said that he merely played the piano, but rather that he played *music*. For the terms are widely different. He would sit at the very same piano which we students would thump with our playing, a very mediocre, unreliable thing; yet he would produce music from it such as we, none of us, had dreamed of. Apropos of Anton Rubinstein, Liszt once told me a story of a banquet given to Rubinstein in Vienna, at the close of his series of historical concerts there,

Liszt himself being present. One of the committee gave 'Rubinstein' as the first toast. Rubinstein became very restless during the speech, and as soon as it was finished he sprang to his feet, exclaiming, 'How can you drink to my health, or honor me as a pianist, when Liszt is sitting among us. Compared to him we are all corporals and he is the one and only Field-Marshal!'

"Whoever heard Anton Rubinstein has heard a fine artist—a great artist. I studied with him and know whereof I speak. Compared with the rest of us, he towered far higher. We were pigmies and he the stalwart man. But when one speaks of Liszt, then Rubinstein sinks into insignificance. He is then the pigmy and Liszt the giant. As much difference between them as between black and white. While Rubinstein had a fine tone quality, which he diligently cultivated, Liszt's tone was memorable, unforgettable. I shall never forget how he intoned the theme of the first movement of Beethoven's Moonlight Sonata. The memory of those tones will remain with me for life; I can hear them now and always try to reproduce them when I play the work.

Liszt's Music

"It is the fashion to play Liszt's music, and many treat it very superficially, as though it were merely meant for the salon. But there is usually a deeper meaning than appears on the surface. The master generally had some special thought or experience, which influenced or compelled him to compose as he did. The interpreter of his music must bring to it a many-sided experience of life in order to fathom its depths.

"Take, for instance, that short composition of his, Il Penseroso. To many pianists it means little or nothing; just a 'harmony of sweet sounds.' When he wrote it, Liszt had in mind that masterpiece of Michael Angelo, the statue of Lorenzo di Medici, in the Church of San Lorenzo in Florence. It will be remembered that he sits, a heroic figure, plunged in deep reflection, above two recumbent figures at his feet. The work is termed 'Meditation,' and is one of the great marbles of the world of art. So with Liszt's Sposolizio, an embodiment, in tones, of Raphael's masterpiece of the Madonna. One has only to turn to these pieces, to which Liszt has given titles, to realize the poetical significance of the poetical nature of the compositions. I carry photographs of these masterpieces with me as reminders of the master's intentions.

"In my long life I have met many interesting and remarkable personalities, but never have I seen any one as impressive as Liszt. One felt the instant one came in touch with him that there was something majestic, god-like in him; one felt that here was an all-embracing spirit. He impressed people that way and he played music in that spirit—the spirit of a conqueror.

Liszt the Teacher

"Liszt taught in quite a different way from any one else. He generally sat beside, or stood opposite to, the student who was playing, and indicated by the expression of his face the nuances he wanted brought out in the music. For the first few months I had lessons with the others in class; afterwards I had lessons alone. Of course I knew each work I brought to him, so that I was able to watch his face for signs of interpretation.

"No other master could indicate musical phrasing as he could, merely by the expression of his face. If the student understood these fine shades, so much the better—for him. Liszt felt he could explain nothing to pupils who did not understand him from the first. Each student brought whatever composition he wished, as Liszt never told us what to work on.

"There were two pieces we were not allowed to bring, however; the Moonlight Sonata, of Beethoven and Liszt's Second Rhapsodie. Another one he did not care for was Chopin's Scherzo in B flat minor, which he jestingly called the 'Governess Scherzo.' Everything else of Chopin's, especially the Preludes, he delighted to hear. He insisted on a poetical interpretation, and it irritated him when groups of small notes were played too quickly.

The Music of Bach

"How Liszt loved the music of Bach, and taught us all to love it with him! I am still a student of this great music, for I do not yet know all of it, by any means. I am only beginning to realize and feel its deep, inner meaning. I was over forty years old before I arrived at an understanding of the true greatness of the master, and learned to play his music more in the way it should be played. Young pianists nowadays are fond of placing some of these big works on their programs. Well and good; if they play the notes with clearness and precision, and give a general idea of the form of the compositions. When I see these programs I say— if the player is young— no, he has not *lived,* he has not the life experience to play such music. When one is twenty one cannot fathom the mysteries of Bach. Neither at thirty. At forty, one begins to understand; at forty-five—yes, at forty-five, one should have arrived at years of experience—of life. But, lest these words should discourage young students and players who like to play Bach's music, I hasten to say that I encourage them to study much and deeply into the works of this great master, for this study will bear rich fruit one day, when experience has prepared the soil and fertilized it.

America Should Develop Great Music

"I feel, when I come to America, this great young country, that its people are strong, full of fire and vitality; for this reason they should also develop great music. In the Old World all depends on tradition; the people are bound and held back by it. They speak, act and feel as their parents, their grandparents, their great-grandparents felt and acted. They are held back by barriers and obstacles of custom. Young America meets the obstacle fairly, gives it a blow, pushes it aside and rushes on. Because their ancestors, in the old country, heated their houses very inadequately and froze in cold weather, their descendants do the same. America is more progressive and aggressive; the present generation will not follow in the steps of its forbears, but believes in progress. I love this freedom to progress, to constantly climb higher, and I feel this spirit will animate the art-life of the nation.

Manner of Practise

"Yes, I practise slowly. It is true that fast practise is the bane of many a young student. Slow practise, with medium power, not full power. I do not now practise scales and finger exercises, but rather passages from pieces— difficult portions and places from the whole literature of the piano, or, perhaps I should say, from my own repertoire. Take the C sharp major Prelude, from Bach's Well-tempered Clavichord; that makes a fine finger study. Then parts of the Chopin Preludes, octaves from Tschaikowsky, or anything that exercises the various muscles, or bits that need constant repetition. One must always be at work—always practising; an artist can never get away from that.

"As it may have been noticed from my recital programs, I have edited and revised many compositions, adapting them in various ways to the needs of the modern pianist. I have a large hand, with a wide span, and do not need to resort to the necessities of small hands in playing. For instance, take the little Gigue in B flat, by Bach. It will be remembered that this short piece requires constant crossing of left hand over the right, in order to bring out the melody. This effort is really not necessary, if one has a hand capable of reaching the intervals. I have altered the manner of performing the notes between the two hands, so there is seldom any crossing of hands necessary. In this way the piece is quite simple, and there is no change in the notes themselves. In fact the theme sings itself more connectedly through this manner of playing. Many compositions gain in ease of delivery by forethought in making them more pianistic and helping them to lie better under the hands.

Thorough Study of Music

"I have very definite ideas as to how music should be taught. Let me tell you how we do it in Russia, in the great Conservatories there.

"Everything goes by system. There are two classes of students, the Lower and the Upper; there are also two classes of instructors. Those for the earlier grades must understand the foundation very thoroughly, and must carry the student from the first beginnings up to a certain point, when he is ready to enter the higher classes. The Lower Class instructor may or may not be a player; he can cover the elementary work without ever having come before the public as a pianist. His office is that of a teacher.

"The Upper Class master is called a Professor. He must be a concert artist, either actively before the public, or one who has done concert work at one time of his career. He builds up the student on the foundation laid by the assistant teacher, and aims to turn the student out an artistic player and good musician. The Professor trains him in advanced repertoire, forms his taste, and should be able to act as an interpretive model worthy of imitation.

"There is also system in the study of repertoire. Take the Lower Class, for instance. It has several divisions. For each of these a certain number of compositions must be studied, such as are suitable for that degree of advancement. Small programs, for each division, can be made from these earlier lists. As the student advances, his repertoire grows with his progress. He must study for two years before he attempts anything of Chopin. As for Beethoven—with the exception of the little Sonatines and small pieces—a full-fledged Sonata is not to be thought of for a number of years. Thus the student is carefully grounded, grows slowly but surely, and advances gradually into the stature of a well-rounded musician.

"Perhaps you may think this sounds too slow and pedantic for the rapidly moving American. It may be somewhat slow, but it is thorough; it forms sound musicianship and produces capable artists. Russia is not alone in desiring thoroughness, for these methods are followed in other European music schools. The result of this artistic completeness is that Americans, in many cases, have felt it necessary to come to Europe to study. Why do they do so? Because they realize that there is more thorough and artistic training to be had abroad than at home. But there is really no need for this condition to exist. If Americans felt they could get equally sound, thorough and artistic culture at home, there would be no reason for them to seek it elsewhere.

The General Music School

"It seems to me we have to look deeper than the curriculum of the foreign music school—deeper even than its artistic ideals, to find the cause of its artistic standing and success. The crux of the matter really is that the big European music schools are not run for pecuniary profit; they do not exist to make money. There is always a deficit at the end of the year. If the school is subsidized, the Government attends to the deficit; if not, wealthy individuals or a committee in charge of school affairs looks after it. It is art first with us in Russia, not to see how much money can be made out of teachers' labor, or out of students' fees.

"The case is different in America, is it not? There may be a few endowed music schools with you. But the general run of conservatories follow the plan of building upon a financial foundation—in other words, of *making it pay.*

"I have conferred with some of the heads of flourishing schools in this country, and they all tell me the same thing. They say: 'Our school is on a firm financial basis; it brings in large sums each year; we never have a deficit.' And I say to them: 'It is not possible to run a school with the highest ideals, which will do justice to its professors, its teachers and students, and yet make money. The money you make comes out of the teacher, who slaves day in and day out, in order that the institution may take half the fee he earns from the student, and thus make money for it.' I say to them frankly: 'I cannot teach in any institution under such conditions, Not that I wish to make large sums for myself; I am satisfied to earn enough for daily needs.'

"It is the same with orchestras everywhere. They cannot be run for profit; there must always be sound financial backing. An illustration from my own experience might be apropos. I arranged a performance of a large work of Ducasse for chorus and orchestra. In order to secure musicians, hall, advertising and rehearsals, the expenses were 11,000 rubles. Tickets brought 5,500 rubles, leaving half the expenses to come out of my own pocket.

"Therefore, I repeat, it is impossible to give concerts of the highest class, or run an ideal music school, at a profit. Have the latter endowed; found it on the highest ideals, and you would have supreme institutions right in your midst.

"I am very glad to say a few words on this question; for I feel it is a vital one in the cause of music in this country."

Index

Memory
  Away from the piano: Mrs. MacDowell 128, Gieseking 175
  By analysis: Goodson, 44, Hughes 52, Sieveking 143, Cortot 162,
    Friedman 172, Hess 180
  By "ear": Schelling 71-72, Friedman 172
  By transposing: Goodson, 44
  "Finger memory": Hughes 52, Schelling 71-72, Friedman 172
  James, William, Talks on Psychology recommended: Stojowski 78
  Mental practice: Hughes 52, Stojowski 79, Friedman 172
  Phrase by phrase: Goodson 44, Leginska 56, Moiseiwitsch 190
  Use score if needed: Grainger 101; must memorize: Cortot 162-163
  Visual memory of keyboard: Hughes 52, Friedman 172, Hess 180
  Visual memory of notes: Gabrilowitsch 38, Hughes 52, Schelling 71,
    Mrs. MacDowell 128, Novaes 132, Friedman 172,
    Gieseking 175, Hess 180
Mendelssohn
  Capriccio op.22: Bülow 27, Carreño 33, Hofmann 108
  Comments on selected works of: Bülow 27,
  Concerto in G minor: 108, 133
Mental processes, see Musicianship
Methods, see Pedagogy
"Modern Music"
  Disinclination: Hofmann 111, Joseffy 122, Rachmaninoff 209,
    Rosenthal 214-215
  Enthusiasm: Stojowski on Paderewski 13; Ganz 42,
    Hutcheson 113-114, Ornstein 133-138, Hess 181
  Indifference: Novaes 132
Moiseiwitsch, Benno, 188-194
Moór, Emanuel: Novaes 132
Motion, dramatic significance of: Paderewski 12;
Mozart: Gabrilowitsch 39, Hutcheson 113, Ornstein 134, Dohnányi 165
Musicianship
  Education, importance of all-around: Tapper 81
  Emphasized (theory, ear-training, analysis): Tapper 83
  "Hear all the music you can": Pugno 69
  Mental processes: Stojowski 78
  Self-criticism, value of in: Bülow 25, Carreño 33;
    is often inaccurate: Hutcheson 113
  Transposing, value of in: Carreño 33, Friedman 173

228   *Piano Mastery*

A CATALOG OF SELECTED DOVER
BOOKS IN ALL FIELDS OF INTEREST

CONCERNING THE SPIRITUAL IN ART, Wassily Kandinsky. Pioneering work by father of abstract art. Thoughts on color theory, nature of art. Analysis of earlier masters. 12 illustrations. 80pp. of text. 5⅜ x 8½. 23411-8

ANIMALS: 1,419 Copyright-Free Illustrations of Mammals, Birds, Fish, Insects, etc., Jim Harter (ed.). Clear wood engravings present, in extremely lifelike poses, over 1,000 species of animals. One of the most extensive pictorial sourcebooks of its kind. Captions. Index. 284pp. 9 x 12. 23766-4

CELTIC ART: The Methods of Construction, George Bain. Simple geometric techniques for making Celtic interlacements, spirals, Kells-type initials, animals, humans, etc. Over 500 illustrations. 160pp. 9 x 12. (Available in U.S. only.) 22923-8

AN ATLAS OF ANATOMY FOR ARTISTS, Fritz Schider. Most thorough reference work on art anatomy in the world. Hundreds of illustrations, including selections from works by Vesalius, Leonardo, Goya, Ingres, Michelangelo, others. 593 illustrations. 192pp. 7⅛ x 10¼. 20241-0

CELTIC HAND STROKE-BY-STROKE (Irish Half-Uncial from "The Book of Kells"): An Arthur Baker Calligraphy Manual, Arthur Baker. Complete guide to creating each letter of the alphabet in distinctive Celtic manner. Covers hand position, strokes, pens, inks, paper, more. Illustrated. 48pp. 8¼ x 11. 24336-2

EASY ORIGAMI, John Montroll. Charming collection of 32 projects (hat, cup, pelican, piano, swan, many more) specially designed for the novice origami hobbyist. Clearly illustrated easy-to-follow instructions insure that even beginning papercrafters will achieve successful results. 48pp. 8¼ x 11. 27298-2

THE COMPLETE BOOK OF BIRDHOUSE CONSTRUCTION FOR WOODWORKERS, Scott D. Campbell. Detailed instructions, illustrations, tables. Also data on bird habitat and instinct patterns. Bibliography. 3 tables. 63 illustrations in 15 figures. 48pp. 5¼ x 8½. 24407-5

BLOOMINGDALE'S ILLUSTRATED 1886 CATALOG: Fashions, Dry Goods and Housewares, Bloomingdale Brothers. Famed merchants' extremely rare catalog depicting about 1,700 products: clothing, housewares, firearms, dry goods, jewelry, more. Invaluable for dating, identifying vintage items. Also, copyright-free graphics for artists, designers. Co-published with Henry Ford Museum & Greenfield Village. 160pp. 8¼ x 11. 25780-0

HISTORIC COSTUME IN PICTURES, Braun & Schneider. Over 1,450 costumed figures in clearly detailed engravings–from dawn of civilization to end of 19th century. Captions. Many folk costumes. 256pp. 8⅜ x 11¾. 23150-X

CATALOG OF DOVER BOOKS

STICKLEY CRAFTSMAN FURNITURE CATALOGS, Gustav Stickley and L. & J. G. Stickley. Beautiful, functional furniture in two authentic catalogs from 1910. 594 illustrations, including 277 photos, show settles, rockers, armchairs, reclining chairs, bookcases, desks, tables. 183pp. 6½ x 9¼. 23838-5

AMERICAN LOCOMOTIVES IN HISTORIC PHOTOGRAPHS: 1858 to 1949, Ron Ziel (ed.). A rare collection of 126 meticulously detailed official photographs, called "builder portraits," of American locomotives that majestically chronicle the rise of steam locomotive power in America. Introduction. Detailed captions. xi+ 129pp. 9 x 12. 27393-8

AMERICA'S LIGHTHOUSES: An Illustrated History, Francis Ross Holland, Jr. Delightfully written, profusely illustrated fact-filled survey of over 200 American lighthouses since 1716. History, anecdotes, technological advances, more. 240pp. 8 x 10¾. 25576-X

TOWARDS A NEW ARCHITECTURE, Le Corbusier. Pioneering manifesto by founder of "International School." Technical and aesthetic theories, views of industry, economics, relation of form to function, "mass-production split" and much more. Profusely illustrated. 320pp. 6⅛ x 9¼. (Available in U.S. only.) 25023-7

HOW THE OTHER HALF LIVES, Jacob Riis. Famous journalistic record, exposing poverty and degradation of New York slums around 1900, by major social reformer. 100 striking and influential photographs. 233pp. 10 x 7⅞. 22012-5

FRUIT KEY AND TWIG KEY TO TREES AND SHRUBS, William M. Harlow. One of the handiest and most widely used identification aids. Fruit key covers 120 deciduous and evergreen species; twig key 160 deciduous species. Easily used. Over 300 photographs. 126pp. 5⅜ x 8½. 20511-8

COMMON BIRD SONGS, Dr. Donald J. Borror. Songs of 60 most common U.S. birds: robins, sparrows, cardinals, bluejays, finches, more—arranged in order of increasing complexity. Up to 9 variations of songs of each species.
Cassette and manual 99911-4

ORCHIDS AS HOUSE PLANTS, Rebecca Tyson Northen. Grow cattleyas and many other kinds of orchids—in a window, in a case, or under artificial light. 63 illustrations. 148pp. 5⅜ x 8½. 23261-1

MONSTER MAZES, Dave Phillips. Masterful mazes at four levels of difficulty. Avoid deadly perils and evil creatures to find magical treasures. Solutions for all 32 exciting illustrated puzzles. 48pp. 8¼ x 11. 26005-4

MOZART'S DON GIOVANNI (DOVER OPERA LIBRETTO SERIES), Wolfgang Amadeus Mozart. Introduced and translated by Ellen H. Bleiler. Standard Italian libretto, with complete English translation. Convenient and thoroughly portable—an ideal companion for reading along with a recording or the performance itself. Introduction. List of characters. Plot summary. 121pp. 5¼ x 8½. 24944-1

TECHNICAL MANUAL AND DICTIONARY OF CLASSICAL BALLET, Gail Grant. Defines, explains, comments on steps, movements, poses and concepts. 15-page pictorial section. Basic book for student, viewer. 127pp. 5⅜ x 8½. 21843-0

THE CLARINET AND CLARINET PLAYING, David Pino. Lively, comprehensive work features suggestions about technique, musicianship, and musical interpretation, as well as guidelines for teaching, making your own reeds, and preparing for public performance. Includes an intriguing look at clarinet history. "A godsend," *The Clarinet,* Journal of the International Clarinet Society. Appendixes. 7 illus. 320pp. 5⅜ x 8½. 40270-3

HOLLYWOOD GLAMOR PORTRAITS, John Kobal (ed.). 145 photos from 1926-49. Harlow, Gable, Bogart, Bacall; 94 stars in all. Full background on photographers, technical aspects. 160pp. 8⅜ x 11¼. 23352-9

THE ANNOTATED CASEY AT THE BAT: A Collection of Ballads about the Mighty Casey/Third, Revised Edition, Martin Gardner (ed.). Amusing sequels and parodies of one of America's best-loved poems: Casey's Revenge, Why Casey Whiffed, Casey's Sister at the Bat, others. 256pp. 5⅜ x 8½. 28598-7

THE RAVEN AND OTHER FAVORITE POEMS, Edgar Allan Poe. Over 40 of the author's most memorable poems: "The Bells," "Ulalume," "Israfel," "To Helen," "The Conqueror Worm," "Eldorado," "Annabel Lee," many more. Alphabetic lists of titles and first lines. 64pp. 5$\frac{3}{16}$ x 8¼. 26685-0

PERSONAL MEMOIRS OF U. S. GRANT, Ulysses Simpson Grant. Intelligent, deeply moving firsthand account of Civil War campaigns, considered by many the finest military memoirs ever written. Includes letters, historic photographs, maps and more. 528pp. 6⅛ x 9¼. 28587-1

ANCIENT EGYPTIAN MATERIALS AND INDUSTRIES, A. Lucas and J. Harris. Fascinating, comprehensive, thoroughly documented text describes this ancient civilization's vast resources and the processes that incorporated them in daily life, including the use of animal products, building materials, cosmetics, perfumes and incense, fibers, glazed ware, glass and its manufacture, materials used in the mummification process, and much more. 544pp. 6⅛ x 9¼. (Available in U.S. only.) 40446-3

RUSSIAN STORIES/RUSSKIE RASSKAZY: A Dual-Language Book, edited by Gleb Struve. Twelve tales by such masters as Chekhov, Tolstoy, Dostoevsky, Pushkin, others. Excellent word-for-word English translations on facing pages, plus teaching and study aids, Russian/English vocabulary, biographical/critical introductions, more. 416pp. 5⅜ x 8½. 26244-8

PHILADELPHIA THEN AND NOW: 60 Sites Photographed in the Past and Present, Kenneth Finkel and Susan Oyama. Rare photographs of City Hall, Logan Square, Independence Hall, Betsy Ross House, other landmarks juxtaposed with contemporary views. Captures changing face of historic city. Introduction. Captions. 128pp. 8¼ x 11. 25790-8

AIA ARCHITECTURAL GUIDE TO NASSAU AND SUFFOLK COUNTIES, LONG ISLAND, The American Institute of Architects, Long Island Chapter, and the Society for the Preservation of Long Island Antiquities. Comprehensive, well-researched and generously illustrated volume brings to life over three centuries of Long Island's great architectural heritage. More than 240 photographs with authoritative, extensively detailed captions. 176pp. 8¼ x 11. 26946-9

NORTH AMERICAN INDIAN LIFE: Customs and Traditions of 23 Tribes, Elsie Clews Parsons (ed.). 27 fictionalized essays by noted anthropologists examine religion, customs, government, additional facets of life among the Winnebago, Crow, Zuni, Eskimo, other tribes. 480pp. 6⅛ x 9¼. 27377-6

CATALOG OF DOVER BOOKS

FRANK LLOYD WRIGHT'S DANA HOUSE, Donald Hoffmann. Pictorial essay of residential masterpiece with over 160 interior and exterior photos, plans, elevations, sketches and studies. 128pp. 9¼ x 10¾. 29120-0

THE MALE AND FEMALE FIGURE IN MOTION: 60 Classic Photographic Sequences, Eadweard Muybridge. 60 true-action photographs of men and women walking, running, climbing, bending, turning, etc., reproduced from rare 19th-century masterpiece. vi + 121pp. 9 x 12. 24745-7

1001 QUESTIONS ANSWERED ABOUT THE SEASHORE, N. J. Berrill and Jacquelyn Berrill. Queries answered about dolphins, sea snails, sponges, starfish, fishes, shore birds, many others. Covers appearance, breeding, growth, feeding, much more. 305pp. 5¼ x 8¼. 23366-9

ATTRACTING BIRDS TO YOUR YARD, William J. Weber. Easy-to-follow guide offers advice on how to attract the greatest diversity of birds: birdhouses, feeders, water and waterers, much more. 96pp. 5³⁄₁₆ x 8¼. 28927-3

MEDICINAL AND OTHER USES OF NORTH AMERICAN PLANTS: A Historical Survey with Special Reference to the Eastern Indian Tribes, Charlotte Erichsen-Brown. Chronological historical citations document 500 years of usage of plants, trees, shrubs native to eastern Canada, northeastern U.S. Also complete identifying information. 343 illustrations. 544pp. 6½ x 9¼. 25951-X

STORYBOOK MAZES, Dave Phillips. 23 stories and mazes on two-page spreads: Wizard of Oz, Treasure Island, Robin Hood, etc. Solutions. 64pp. 8¼ x 11. 23628-5

AMERICAN NEGRO SONGS: 230 Folk Songs and Spirituals, Religious and Secular, John W. Work. This authoritative study traces the African influences of songs sung and played by black Americans at work, in church, and as entertainment. The author discusses the lyric significance of such songs as "Swing Low, Sweet Chariot," "John Henry," and others and offers the words and music for 230 songs. Bibliography. Index of Song Titles. 272pp. 6½ x 9¼. 40271-1

MOVIE-STAR PORTRAITS OF THE FORTIES, John Kobal (ed.). 163 glamor, studio photos of 106 stars of the 1940s: Rita Hayworth, Ava Gardner, Marlon Brando, Clark Gable, many more. 176pp. 8⅜ x 11¼. 23546-7

BENCHLEY LOST AND FOUND, Robert Benchley. Finest humor from early 30s, about pet peeves, child psychologists, post office and others. Mostly unavailable elsewhere. 73 illustrations by Peter Arno and others. 183pp. 5⅜ x 8½. 22410-4

YEKL and THE IMPORTED BRIDEGROOM AND OTHER STORIES OF YIDDISH NEW YORK, Abraham Cahan. Film Hester Street based on *Yekl* (1896). Novel, other stories among first about Jewish immigrants on N.Y.'s East Side. 240pp. 5⅜ x 8½. 22427-9

SELECTED POEMS, Walt Whitman. Generous sampling from *Leaves of Grass*. Twenty-four poems include "I Hear America Singing," "Song of the Open Road," "I Sing the Body Electric," "When Lilacs Last in the Dooryard Bloom'd," "O Captain! My Captain!"—all reprinted from an authoritative edition. Lists of titles and first lines. 128pp. 5³⁄₁₆ x 8¼. 26878-0

THE BEST TALES OF HOFFMANN, E. T. A. Hoffmann. 10 of Hoffmann's most important stories: "Nutcracker and the King of Mice," "The Golden Flowerpot," etc. 458pp. 5⅜ x 8½.   21793-0

FROM FETISH TO GOD IN ANCIENT EGYPT, E. A. Wallis Budge. Rich detailed survey of Egyptian conception of "God" and gods, magic, cult of animals, Osiris, more. Also, superb English translations of hymns and legends. 240 illustrations. 545pp. 5⅜ x 8½.   25803-3

FRENCH STORIES/CONTES FRANÇAIS: A Dual-Language Book, Wallace Fowlie. Ten stories by French masters, Voltaire to Camus: "Micromegas" by Voltaire; "The Atheist's Mass" by Balzac; "Minuet" by de Maupassant; "The Guest" by Camus, six more. Excellent English translations on facing pages. Also French-English vocabulary list, exercises, more. 352pp. 5⅜ x 8½.   26443-2

CHICAGO AT THE TURN OF THE CENTURY IN PHOTOGRAPHS: 122 Historic Views from the Collections of the Chicago Historical Society, Larry A. Viskochil. Rare large-format prints offer detailed views of City Hall, State Street, the Loop, Hull House, Union Station, many other landmarks, circa 1904-1913. Introduction. Captions. Maps. 144pp. 9⅜ x 12¼.   24656-6

OLD BROOKLYN IN EARLY PHOTOGRAPHS, 1865-1929, William Lee Younger. Luna Park, Gravesend race track, construction of Grand Army Plaza, moving of Hotel Brighton, etc. 157 previously unpublished photographs. 165pp. 8⅞ x 11¾.
                                                                              23587-4

THE MYTHS OF THE NORTH AMERICAN INDIANS, Lewis Spence. Rich anthology of the myths and legends of the Algonquins, Iroquois, Pawnees and Sioux, prefaced by an extensive historical and ethnological commentary. 36 illustrations. 480pp. 5⅜ x 8½.   25967-6

AN ENCYCLOPEDIA OF BATTLES: Accounts of Over 1,560 Battles from 1479 B.C. to the Present, David Eggenberger. Essential details of every major battle in recorded history from the first battle of Megiddo in 1479 B.C. to Grenada in 1984. List of Battle Maps. New Appendix covering the years 1967-1984. Index. 99 illustrations. 544pp. 6½ x 9¼.   24913-1

SAILING ALONE AROUND THE WORLD, Captain Joshua Slocum. First man to sail around the world, alone, in small boat. One of great feats of seamanship told in delightful manner. 67 illustrations. 294pp. 5⅜ x 8½.   20326-3

ANARCHISM AND OTHER ESSAYS, Emma Goldman. Powerful, penetrating, prophetic essays on direct action, role of minorities, prison reform, puritan hypocrisy, violence, etc. 271pp. 5⅜ x 8½.   22484-8

MYTHS OF THE HINDUS AND BUDDHISTS, Ananda K. Coomaraswamy and Sister Nivedita. Great stories of the epics; deeds of Krishna, Shiva, taken from puranas, Vedas, folk tales; etc. 32 illustrations. 400pp. 5⅜ x 8½.   21759-0

THE TRAUMA OF BIRTH, Otto Rank. Rank's controversial thesis that anxiety neurosis is caused by profound psychological trauma which occurs at birth. 256pp. 5⅜ x 8½.   27974-X

A THEOLOGICO-POLITICAL TREATISE, Benedict Spinoza. Also contains unfinished Political Treatise. Great classic on religious liberty, theory of government on common consent. R. Elwes translation. Total of 421pp. 5⅜ x 8½.   20249-6

MY BONDAGE AND MY FREEDOM, Frederick Douglass. Born a slave, Douglass became outspoken force in antislavery movement. The best of Douglass' autobiographies. Graphic description of slave life. 464pp. 5⅜ x 8½. 22457-0

FOLLOWING THE EQUATOR: A Journey Around the World, Mark Twain. Fascinating humorous account of 1897 voyage to Hawaii, Australia, India, New Zealand, etc. Ironic, bemused reports on peoples, customs, climate, flora and fauna, politics, much more. 197 illustrations. 720pp. 5⅜ x 8½. 26113-1

THE PEOPLE CALLED SHAKERS, Edward D. Andrews. Definitive study of Shakers: origins, beliefs, practices, dances, social organization, furniture and crafts, etc. 33 illustrations. 351pp. 5⅜ x 8½. 21081-2

THE MYTHS OF GREECE AND ROME, H. A. Guerber. A classic of mythology, generously illustrated, long prized for its simple, graphic, accurate retelling of the principal myths of Greece and Rome, and for its commentary on their origins and significance. With 64 illustrations by Michelangelo, Raphael, Titian, Rubens, Canova, Bernini and others. 480pp. 5⅜ x 8½. 27584-1

PSYCHOLOGY OF MUSIC, Carl E. Seashore. Classic work discusses music as a medium from psychological viewpoint. Clear treatment of physical acoustics, auditory apparatus, sound perception, development of musical skills, nature of musical feeling, host of other topics. 88 figures. 408pp. 5⅜ x 8½. 21851-1

THE PHILOSOPHY OF HISTORY, Georg W. Hegel. Great classic of Western thought develops concept that history is not chance but rational process, the evolution of freedom. 457pp. 5⅜ x 8½. 20112-0

THE BOOK OF TEA, Kakuzo Okakura. Minor classic of the Orient: entertaining, charming explanation, interpretation of traditional Japanese culture in terms of tea ceremony. 94pp. 5⅜ x 8½. 20070-1

LIFE IN ANCIENT EGYPT, Adolf Erman. Fullest, most thorough, detailed older account with much not in more recent books, domestic life, religion, magic, medicine, commerce, much more. Many illustrations reproduce tomb paintings, carvings, hieroglyphs, etc. 597pp. 5⅜ x 8½. 22632-8

SUNDIALS, Their Theory and Construction, Albert Waugh. Far and away the best, most thorough coverage of ideas, mathematics concerned, types, construction, adjusting anywhere. Simple, nontechnical treatment allows even children to build several of these dials. Over 100 illustrations. 230pp. 5⅜ x 8½. 22947-5

THEORETICAL HYDRODYNAMICS, L. M. Milne-Thomson. Classic exposition of the mathematical theory of fluid motion, applicable to both hydrodynamics and aerodynamics. Over 600 exercises. 768pp. 6⅛ x 9¼. 68970-0

SONGS OF EXPERIENCE: Facsimile Reproduction with 26 Plates in Full Color, William Blake. 26 full-color plates from a rare 1826 edition. Includes "The Tyger," "London," "Holy Thursday," and other poems. Printed text of poems. 48pp. 5¼ x 7. 24636-1

OLD-TIME VIGNETTES IN FULL COLOR, Carol Belanger Grafton (ed.). Over 390 charming, often sentimental illustrations, selected from archives of Victorian graphics—pretty women posing, children playing, food, flowers, kittens and puppies, smiling cherubs, birds and butterflies, much more. All copyright-free. 48pp. 9¼ x 12¼. 27269-9

PERSPECTIVE FOR ARTISTS, Rex Vicat Cole. Depth, perspective of sky and sea, shadows, much more, not usually covered. 391 diagrams, 81 reproductions of drawings and paintings. 279pp. 5⅜ x 8½. 22487-2

DRAWING THE LIVING FIGURE, Joseph Sheppard. Innovative approach to artistic anatomy focuses on specifics of surface anatomy, rather than muscles and bones. Over 170 drawings of live models in front, back and side views, and in widely varying poses. Accompanying diagrams. 177 illustrations. Introduction. Index. 144pp. 8⅜ x11¼. 26723-7

GOTHIC AND OLD ENGLISH ALPHABETS: 100 Complete Fonts, Dan X. Solo. Add power, elegance to posters, signs, other graphics with 100 stunning copyright-free alphabets: Blackstone, Dolbey, Germania, 97 more–including many lower-case, numerals, punctuation marks. 104pp. 8⅛ x 11. 24695-7

HOW TO DO BEADWORK, Mary White. Fundamental book on craft from simple projects to five-bead chains and woven works. 106 illustrations. 142pp. 5⅜ x 8. 20697-1

THE BOOK OF WOOD CARVING, Charles Marshall Sayers. Finest book for beginners discusses fundamentals and offers 34 designs. "Absolutely first rate . . . well thought out and well executed."–E. J. Tangerman. 118pp. 7¾ x 10⅝. 23654-4

ILLUSTRATED CATALOG OF CIVIL WAR MILITARY GOODS: Union Army Weapons, Insignia, Uniform Accessories, and Other Equipment, Schuyler, Hartley, and Graham. Rare, profusely illustrated 1846 catalog includes Union Army uniform and dress regulations, arms and ammunition, coats, insignia, flags, swords, rifles, etc. 226 illustrations. 160pp. 9 x 12. 24939-5

WOMEN'S FASHIONS OF THE EARLY 1900s: An Unabridged Republication of "New York Fashions, 1909," National Cloak & Suit Co. Rare catalog of mail-order fashions documents women's and children's clothing styles shortly after the turn of the century. Captions offer full descriptions, prices. Invaluable resource for fashion, costume historians. Approximately 725 illustrations. 128pp. 8⅜ x 11¼. 27276-1

THE 1912 AND 1915 GUSTAV STICKLEY FURNITURE CATALOGS, Gustav Stickley. With over 200 detailed illustrations and descriptions, these two catalogs are essential reading and reference materials and identification guides for Stickley furniture. Captions cite materials, dimensions and prices. 112pp. 6½ x 9¼. 26676-1

EARLY AMERICAN LOCOMOTIVES, John H. White, Jr. Finest locomotive engravings from early 19th century: historical (1804–74), main-line (after 1870), special, foreign, etc. 147 plates. 142pp. 11⅜ x 8¼. 22772-3

THE TALL SHIPS OF TODAY IN PHOTOGRAPHS, Frank O. Braynard. Lavishly illustrated tribute to nearly 100 majestic contemporary sailing vessels: Amerigo Vespucci, Clearwater, Constitution, Eagle, Mayflower, Sea Cloud, Victory, many more. Authoritative captions provide statistics, background on each ship. 190 black-and-white photographs and illustrations. Introduction. 128pp. 8⅞ x 11¾. 27163-3

CATALOG OF DOVER BOOKS

LITTLE BOOK OF EARLY AMERICAN CRAFTS AND TRADES, Peter Stockham (ed.). 1807 children's book explains crafts and trades: baker, hatter, cooper, potter, and many others. 23 copperplate illustrations. 140pp. 4⁵/₈ x 6. 23336-7

VICTORIAN FASHIONS AND COSTUMES FROM HARPER'S BAZAR, 1867–1898, Stella Blum (ed.). Day costumes, evening wear, sports clothes, shoes, hats, other accessories in over 1,000 detailed engravings. 320pp. 9⅜ x 12¼. 22990-4

GUSTAV STICKLEY, THE CRAFTSMAN, Mary Ann Smith. Superb study surveys broad scope of Stickley's achievement, especially in architecture. Design philosophy, rise and fall of the Craftsman empire, descriptions and floor plans for many Craftsman houses, more. 86 black-and-white halftones. 31 line illustrations. Introduction 208pp. 6½ x 9¼. 27210-9

THE LONG ISLAND RAIL ROAD IN EARLY PHOTOGRAPHS, Ron Ziel. Over 220 rare photos, informative text document origin (1844) and development of rail service on Long Island. Vintage views of early trains, locomotives, stations, passengers, crews, much more. Captions. 8⅞ x 11¾. 26301-0

VOYAGE OF THE LIBERDADE, Joshua Slocum. Great 19th-century mariner's thrilling, first-hand account of the wreck of his ship off South America, the 35-foot boat he built from the wreckage, and its remarkable voyage home. 128pp. 5⅜ x 8½. 40022-0

TEN BOOKS ON ARCHITECTURE, Vitruvius. The most important book ever written on architecture. Early Roman aesthetics, technology, classical orders, site selection, all other aspects. Morgan translation. 331pp. 5⅜ x 8½. 20645-9

THE HUMAN FIGURE IN MOTION, Eadweard Muybridge. More than 4,500 stopped-action photos, in action series, showing undraped men, women, children jumping, lying down, throwing, sitting, wrestling, carrying, etc. 390pp. 7⅞ x 10⅝. 20204-6 Clothbd.

TREES OF THE EASTERN AND CENTRAL UNITED STATES AND CANADA, William M. Harlow. Best one-volume guide to 140 trees. Full descriptions, woodlore, range, etc. Over 600 illustrations. Handy size. 288pp. 4½ x 6⅜. 20395-6

SONGS OF WESTERN BIRDS, Dr. Donald J. Borror. Complete song and call repertoire of 60 western species, including flycatchers, juncoes, cactus wrens, many more–includes fully illustrated booklet. Cassette and manual 99913-0

GROWING AND USING HERBS AND SPICES, Milo Miloradovich. Versatile handbook provides all the information needed for cultivation and use of all the herbs and spices available in North America. 4 illustrations. Index. Glossary. 236pp. 5⅜ x 8½. 25058-X

BIG BOOK OF MAZES AND LABYRINTHS, Walter Shepherd. 50 mazes and labyrinths in all–classical, solid, ripple, and more–in one great volume. Perfect inexpensive puzzler for clever youngsters. Full solutions. 112pp. 8⅛ x 11. 22951-3

PIANO TUNING, J. Cree Fischer. Clearest, best book for beginner, amateur. Simple repairs, raising dropped notes, tuning by easy method of flattened fifths. No previous skills needed. 4 illustrations. 201pp. 5⅜ x 8½. 23267-0

HINTS TO SINGERS, Lillian Nordica. Selecting the right teacher, developing confidence, overcoming stage fright, and many other important skills receive thoughtful discussion in this indispensible guide, written by a world-famous diva of four decades' experience. 96pp. 5⅜ x 8½. 40094-8

THE COMPLETE NONSENSE OF EDWARD LEAR, Edward Lear. All nonsense limericks, zany alphabets, Owl and Pussycat, songs, nonsense botany, etc., illustrated by Lear. Total of 320pp. 5⅜ x 8½. (Available in U.S. only.) 20167-8

VICTORIAN PARLOUR POETRY: An Annotated Anthology, Michael R. Turner. 117 gems by Longfellow, Tennyson, Browning, many lesser-known poets. "The Village Blacksmith," "Curfew Must Not Ring Tonight," "Only a Baby Small," dozens more, often difficult to find elsewhere. Index of poets, titles, first lines. xxiii + 325pp. 5⅜ x 8¼. 27044-0

DUBLINERS, James Joyce. Fifteen stories offer vivid, tightly focused observations of the lives of Dublin's poorer classes. At least one, "The Dead," is considered a masterpiece. Reprinted complete and unabridged from standard edition. 160pp. 5³⁄₁₆ x 8¼. 26870-5

GREAT WEIRD TALES: 14 Stories by Lovecraft, Blackwood, Machen and Others, S. T. Joshi (ed.). 14 spellbinding tales, including "The Sin Eater," by Fiona McLeod, "The Eye Above the Mantel," by Frank Belknap Long, as well as renowned works by R. H. Barlow, Lord Dunsany, Arthur Machen, W. C. Morrow and eight other masters of the genre. 256pp. 5⅜ x 8½. (Available in U.S. only.) 40436-6

THE BOOK OF THE SACRED MAGIC OF ABRAMELIN THE MAGE, translated by S. MacGregor Mathers. Medieval manuscript of ceremonial magic. Basic document in Aleister Crowley, Golden Dawn groups. 268pp. 5⅜ x 8½. 23211-5

NEW RUSSIAN-ENGLISH AND ENGLISH-RUSSIAN DICTIONARY, M. A. O'Brien. This is a remarkably handy Russian dictionary, containing a surprising amount of information, including over 70,000 entries. 366pp. 4½ x 6⅛. 20208-9

HISTORIC HOMES OF THE AMERICAN PRESIDENTS, Second, Revised Edition, Irvin Haas. A traveler's guide to American Presidential homes, most open to the public, depicting and describing homes occupied by every American President from George Washington to George Bush. With visiting hours, admission charges, travel routes. 175 photographs. Index. 160pp. 8¼ x 11. 26751-2

NEW YORK IN THE FORTIES, Andreas Feininger. 162 brilliant photographs by the well-known photographer, formerly with *Life* magazine. Commuters, shoppers, Times Square at night, much else from city at its peak. Captions by John von Hartz. 181pp. 9¼ x 10¾. 23585-8

INDIAN SIGN LANGUAGE, William Tomkins. Over 525 signs developed by Sioux and other tribes. Written instructions and diagrams. Also 290 pictographs. 111pp. 6⅛ x 9¼. 22029-X

CATALOG OF DOVER BOOKS

ANATOMY: A Complete Guide for Artists, Joseph Sheppard. A master of figure drawing shows artists how to render human anatomy convincingly. Over 460 illustrations. 224pp. 8⅜ x 11¼. 27279-6

MEDIEVAL CALLIGRAPHY: Its History and Technique, Marc Drogin. Spirited history, comprehensive instruction manual covers 13 styles (ca. 4th century through 15th). Excellent photographs; directions for duplicating medieval techniques with modern tools. 224pp. 8⅜ x 11¼. 26142-5

DRIED FLOWERS: How to Prepare Them, Sarah Whitlock and Martha Rankin. Complete instructions on how to use silica gel, meal and borax, perlite aggregate, sand and borax, glycerine and water to create attractive permanent flower arrangements. 12 illustrations. 32pp. 5⅜ x 8½. 21802-3

EASY-TO-MAKE BIRD FEEDERS FOR WOODWORKERS, Scott D. Campbell. Detailed, simple-to-use guide for designing, constructing, caring for and using feeders. Text, illustrations for 12 classic and contemporary designs. 96pp. 5⅜ x 8½. 25847-5

SCOTTISH WONDER TALES FROM MYTH AND LEGEND, Donald A. Mackenzie. 16 lively tales tell of giants rumbling down mountainsides, of a magic wand that turns stone pillars into warriors, of gods and goddesses, evil hags, powerful forces and more. 240pp. 5⅜ x 8½. 29677-6

THE HISTORY OF UNDERCLOTHES, C. Willett Cunnington and Phyllis Cunnington. Fascinating, well-documented survey covering six centuries of English undergarments, enhanced with over 100 illustrations: 12th-century laced-up bodice, footed long drawers (1795), 19th-century bustles, l9th-century corsets for men, Victorian "bust improvers," much more. 272pp. 5⅜ x 8¼. 27124-2

ARTS AND CRAFTS FURNITURE: The Complete Brooks Catalog of 1912, Brooks Manufacturing Co. Photos and detailed descriptions of more than 150 now very collectible furniture designs from the Arts and Crafts movement depict davenports, settees, buffets, desks, tables, chairs, bedsteads, dressers and more, all built of solid, quarter-sawed oak. Invaluable for students and enthusiasts of antiques, Americana and the decorative arts. 80pp. 6½ x 9¼. 27471-3

WILBUR AND ORVILLE: A Biography of the Wright Brothers, Fred Howard. Definitive, crisply written study tells the full story of the brothers' lives and work. A vividly written biography, unparalleled in scope and color, that also captures the spirit of an extraordinary era. 560pp. 6⅛ x 9¼. 40297-5

THE ARTS OF THE SAILOR: Knotting, Splicing and Ropework, Hervey Garrett Smith. Indispensable shipboard reference covers tools, basic knots and useful hitches; handsewing and canvas work, more. Over 100 illustrations. Delightful reading for sea lovers. 256pp. 5⅜ x 8½. 26440-8

FRANK LLOYD WRIGHT'S FALLINGWATER: The House and Its History, Second, Revised Edition, Donald Hoffmann. A total revision–both in text and illustrations–of the standard document on Fallingwater, the boldest, most personal architectural statement of Wright's mature years, updated with valuable new material from the recently opened Frank Lloyd Wright Archives. "Fascinating"–*The New York Times*. 116 illustrations. 128pp. 9¼ x 10¾. 27430-6

PHOTOGRAPHIC SKETCHBOOK OF THE CIVIL WAR, Alexander Gardner. 100 photos taken on field during the Civil War. Famous shots of Manassas Harper's Ferry, Lincoln, Richmond, slave pens, etc. 244pp. 10⅝ x 8¼. 22731-6

FIVE ACRES AND INDEPENDENCE, Maurice G. Kains. Great back-to-the-land classic explains basics of self-sufficient farming. The one book to get. 95 illustrations. 397pp. 5⅜ x 8½. 20974-1

SONGS OF EASTERN BIRDS, Dr. Donald J. Borror. Songs and calls of 60 species most common to eastern U.S.: warblers, woodpeckers, flycatchers, thrushes, larks, many more in high-quality recording. Cassette and manual 99912-2

A MODERN HERBAL, Margaret Grieve. Much the fullest, most exact, most useful compilation of herbal material. Gigantic alphabetical encyclopedia, from aconite to zedoary, gives botanical information, medical properties, folklore, economic uses, much else. Indispensable to serious reader. 161 illustrations. 888pp. 6½ x 9¼. 2-vol. set. (Available in U.S. only.) Vol. I: 22798-7
Vol. II: 22799-5

HIDDEN TREASURE MAZE BOOK, Dave Phillips. Solve 34 challenging mazes accompanied by heroic tales of adventure. Evil dragons, people-eating plants, blood-thirsty giants, many more dangerous adversaries lurk at every twist and turn. 34 mazes, stories, solutions. 48pp. 8¼ x 11. 24566-7

LETTERS OF W. A. MOZART, Wolfgang A. Mozart. Remarkable letters show bawdy wit, humor, imagination, musical insights, contemporary musical world; includes some letters from Leopold Mozart. 276pp. 5⅜ x 8½. 22859-2

BASIC PRINCIPLES OF CLASSICAL BALLET, Agrippina Vaganova. Great Russian theoretician, teacher explains methods for teaching classical ballet. 118 illustrations. 175pp. 5⅜ x 8½. 22036-2

THE JUMPING FROG, Mark Twain. Revenge edition. The original story of The Celebrated Jumping Frog of Calaveras County, a hapless French translation, and Twain's hilarious "retranslation" from the French. 12 illustrations. 66pp. 5⅜ x 8½.
22686-7

BEST REMEMBERED POEMS, Martin Gardner (ed.). The 126 poems in this superb collection of 19th- and 20th-century British and American verse range from Shelley's "To a Skylark" to the impassioned "Renascence" of Edna St. Vincent Millay and to Edward Lear's whimsical "The Owl and the Pussycat." 224pp. 5⅜ x 8½.
27165-X

COMPLETE SONNETS, William Shakespeare. Over 150 exquisite poems deal with love, friendship, the tyranny of time, beauty's evanescence, death and other themes in language of remarkable power, precision and beauty. Glossary of archaic terms. 80pp. 5³⁄₁₆ x 8¼. 26686-9

THE BATTLES THAT CHANGED HISTORY, Fletcher Pratt. Eminent historian profiles 16 crucial conflicts, ancient to modern, that changed the course of civilization. 352pp. 5⅜ x 8½. 41129-X

THE WIT AND HUMOR OF OSCAR WILDE, Alvin Redman (ed.). More than 1,000 ripostes, paradoxes, wisecracks: Work is the curse of the drinking classes; I can resist everything except temptation; etc. 258pp. 5⅜ x 8½. 20602-5

SHAKESPEARE LEXICON AND QUOTATION DICTIONARY, Alexander Schmidt. Full definitions, locations, shades of meaning in every word in plays and poems. More than 50,000 exact quotations. 1,485pp. 6½ x 9¼. 2-vol. set.
Vol. 1: 22726-X
Vol. 2: 22727-8

SELECTED POEMS, Emily Dickinson. Over 100 best-known, best-loved poems by one of America's foremost poets, reprinted from authoritative early editions. No comparable edition at this price. Index of first lines. 64pp. 5³⁄₁₆ x 8¼. 26466-1

THE INSIDIOUS DR. FU-MANCHU, Sax Rohmer. The first of the popular mystery series introduces a pair of English detectives to their archnemesis, the diabolical Dr. Fu-Manchu. Flavorful atmosphere, fast-paced action, and colorful characters enliven this classic of the genre. 208pp. 5³⁄₁₆ x 8¼. 29898-1

THE MALLEUS MALEFICARUM OF KRAMER AND SPRENGER, translated by Montague Summers. Full text of most important witchhunter's "bible," used by both Catholics and Protestants. 278pp. 6⅝ x 10. 22802-9

SPANISH STORIES/CUENTOS ESPAÑOLES: A Dual-Language Book, Angel Flores (ed.). Unique format offers 13 great stories in Spanish by Cervantes, Borges, others. Faithful English translations on facing pages. 352pp. 5⅜ x 8½. 25399-6

GARDEN CITY, LONG ISLAND, IN EARLY PHOTOGRAPHS, 1869–1919, Mildred H. Smith. Handsome treasury of 118 vintage pictures, accompanied by carefully researched captions, document the Garden City Hotel fire (1899), the Vanderbilt Cup Race (1908), the first airmail flight departing from the Nassau Boulevard Aerodrome (1911), and much more. 96pp. 8⅞ x 11¾. 40669-5

OLD QUEENS, N.Y., IN EARLY PHOTOGRAPHS, Vincent F. Seyfried and William Asadorian. Over 160 rare photographs of Maspeth, Jamaica, Jackson Heights, and other areas. Vintage views of DeWitt Clinton mansion, 1939 World's Fair and more. Captions. 192pp. 8⅞ x 11. 26358-4

CAPTURED BY THE INDIANS: 15 Firsthand Accounts, 1750-1870, Frederick Drimmer. Astounding true historical accounts of grisly torture, bloody conflicts, relentless pursuits, miraculous escapes and more, by people who lived to tell the tale. 384pp. 5⅜ x 8½. 24901-8

THE WORLD'S GREAT SPEECHES (Fourth Enlarged Edition), Lewis Copeland, Lawrence W. Lamm, and Stephen J. McKenna. Nearly 300 speeches provide public speakers with a wealth of updated quotes and inspiration–from Pericles' funeral oration and William Jennings Bryan's "Cross of Gold Speech" to Malcolm X's powerful words on the Black Revolution and Earl of Spenser's tribute to his sister, Diana, Princess of Wales. 944pp. 5⅜ x 8⅜. 40903-1

THE BOOK OF THE SWORD, Sir Richard F. Burton. Great Victorian scholar/adventurer's eloquent, erudite history of the "queen of weapons"–from prehistory to early Roman Empire. Evolution and development of early swords, variations (sabre, broadsword, cutlass, scimitar, etc.), much more. 336pp. 6⅛ x 9¼. 25434-8

CATALOG OF DOVER BOOKS

AUTOBIOGRAPHY: The Story of My Experiments with Truth, Mohandas K. Gandhi. Boyhood, legal studies, purification, the growth of the Satyagraha (nonviolent protest) movement. Critical, inspiring work of the man responsible for the freedom of India. 480pp. 5⅜ x 8½. (Available in U.S. only.)   24593-4

CELTIC MYTHS AND LEGENDS, T. W. Rolleston. Masterful retelling of Irish and Welsh stories and tales. Cuchulain, King Arthur, Deirdre, the Grail, many more. First paperback edition. 58 full-page illustrations. 512pp. 5⅜ x 8½.   26507-2

THE PRINCIPLES OF PSYCHOLOGY, William James. Famous long course complete, unabridged. Stream of thought, time perception, memory, experimental methods; great work decades ahead of its time. 94 figures. 1,391pp. 5⅜ x 8½. 2-vol. set.
Vol. I: 20381-6   Vol. II: 20382-4

THE WORLD AS WILL AND REPRESENTATION, Arthur Schopenhauer. Definitive English translation of Schopenhauer's life work, correcting more than 1,000 errors, omissions in earlier translations. Translated by E. F. J. Payne. Total of 1,269pp. 5⅜ x 8½. 2-vol. set.   Vol. 1: 21761-2   Vol. 2: 21762-0

MAGIC AND MYSTERY IN TIBET, Madame Alexandra David-Neel. Experiences among lamas, magicians, sages, sorcerers, Bonpa wizards. A true psychic discovery. 32 illustrations. 321pp. 5⅜ x 8½. (Available in U.S. only.)   22682-4

THE EGYPTIAN BOOK OF THE DEAD, E. A. Wallis Budge. Complete reproduction of Ani's papyrus, finest ever found. Full hieroglyphic text, interlinear transliteration, word-for-word translation, smooth translation. 533pp. 6½ x 9¼.   21866-X

MATHEMATICS FOR THE NONMATHEMATICIAN, Morris Kline. Detailed, college-level treatment of mathematics in cultural and historical context, with numerous exercises. Recommended Reading Lists. Tables. Numerous figures. 641pp. 5⅜ x 8½.   24823-2

PROBABILISTIC METHODS IN THE THEORY OF STRUCTURES, Isaac Elishakoff. Well-written introduction covers the elements of the theory of probability from two or more random variables, the reliability of such multivariable structures, the theory of random function, Monte Carlo methods of treating problems incapable of exact solution, and more. Examples. 502pp. 5⅜ x 8½.   40691-1

THE RIME OF THE ANCIENT MARINER, Gustave Doré, S. T. Coleridge. Doré's finest work; 34 plates capture moods, subtleties of poem. Flawless full-size reproductions printed on facing pages with authoritative text of poem. "Beautiful. Simply beautiful."—Publisher's Weekly. 77pp. 9¼ x 12.   22305-1

NORTH AMERICAN INDIAN DESIGNS FOR ARTISTS AND CRAFTSPEOPLE, Eva Wilson. Over 360 authentic copyright-free designs adapted from Navajo blankets, Hopi pottery, Sioux buffalo hides, more. Geometrics, symbolic figures, plant and animal motifs, etc. 128pp. 8⅜ x 11. (Not for sale in the United Kingdom.)   25341-4

SCULPTURE: Principles and Practice, Louis Slobodkin. Step-by-step approach to clay, plaster, metals, stone; classical and modern. 253 drawings, photos. 255pp. 8⅛ x 11.   22960-2

THE INFLUENCE OF SEA POWER UPON HISTORY, 1660–1783, A. T. Mahan. Influential classic of naval history and tactics still used as text in war colleges. First paperback edition. 4 maps. 24 battle plans. 640pp. 5⅜ x 8½.   25509-3

CATALOG OF DOVER BOOKS

THE STORY OF THE TITANIC AS TOLD BY ITS SURVIVORS, Jack Winocour (ed.). What it was really like. Panic, despair, shocking inefficiency, and a little heroism. More thrilling than any fictional account. 26 illustrations. 320pp. 5⅜ x 8½.
20610-6

FAIRY AND FOLK TALES OF THE IRISH PEASANTRY, William Butler Yeats (ed.). Treasury of 64 tales from the twilight world of Celtic myth and legend: "The Soul Cages," "The Kildare Pooka," "King O'Toole and his Goose," many more. Introduction and Notes by W. B. Yeats. 352pp. 5⅜ x 8½.
26941-8

BUDDHIST MAHAYANA TEXTS, E. B. Cowell and others (eds.). Superb, accurate translations of basic documents in Mahayana Buddhism, highly important in history of religions. The Buddha-karita of Asvaghosha, Larger Sukhavativyuha, more. 448pp. 5⅜ x 8½.
25552-2

ONE TWO THREE . . . INFINITY: Facts and Speculations of Science, George Gamow. Great physicist's fascinating, readable overview of contemporary science: number theory, relativity, fourth dimension, entropy, genes, atomic structure, much more. 128 illustrations. Index. 352pp. 5⅜ x 8½.
25664-2

EXPERIMENTATION AND MEASUREMENT, W. J. Youden. Introductory manual explains laws of measurement in simple terms and offers tips for achieving accuracy and minimizing errors. Mathematics of measurement, use of instruments, experimenting with machines. 1994 edition. Foreword. Preface. Introduction. Epilogue. Selected Readings. Glossary. Index. Tables and figures. 128pp. 5⅜ x 8½.
40451-X

DALÍ ON MODERN ART: The Cuckolds of Antiquated Modern Art, Salvador Dalí. Influential painter skewers modern art and its practitioners. Outrageous evaluations of Picasso, Cézanne, Turner, more. 15 renderings of paintings discussed. 44 calligraphic decorations by Dalí. 96pp. 5⅜ x 8½. (Available in U.S. only.)
29220-7

ANTIQUE PLAYING CARDS: A Pictorial History, Henry René D'Allemagne. Over 900 elaborate, decorative images from rare playing cards (14th–20th centuries): Bacchus, death, dancing dogs, hunting scenes, royal coats of arms, players cheating, much more. 96pp. 9¼ x 12¼.
29265-7

MAKING FURNITURE MASTERPIECES: 30 Projects with Measured Drawings, Franklin H. Gottshall. Step-by-step instructions, illustrations for constructing handsome, useful pieces, among them a Sheraton desk, Chippendale chair, Spanish desk, Queen Anne table and a William and Mary dressing mirror. 224pp. 8⅛ x 11¼.
29338-6

THE FOSSIL BOOK: A Record of Prehistoric Life, Patricia V. Rich et al. Profusely illustrated definitive guide covers everything from single-celled organisms and dinosaurs to birds and mammals and the interplay between climate and man. Over 1,500 illustrations. 760pp. 7½ x 10⅛.
29371-8

Paperbound unless otherwise indicated. Available at your book dealer, online at **www.doverpublications.com**, or by writing to Dept. GI, Dover Publications, Inc., 31 East 2nd Street, Mineola, NY 11501. For current price information or for free catalogues (please indicate field of interest), write to Dover Publications or log on to **www.doverpublications.com** and see every Dover book in print. Dover publishes more than 500 books each year on science, elementary and advanced mathematics, biology, music, art, literary history, social sciences, and other areas.